MAPQUEST®

Road Atlas

UNITED STATES • CANADA • MEXICO

CONTENTS

How to Use This Atlas

National Parks
Pages 8–17

Top national parks are described in detail. Close-up maps include major trails, mountains, and points of interest, shown with shaded topographic relief. Park profiles include handy information on visitors centers, opening dates, entrance fees, contact numbers and more. Tan tabs list the pages of relevant state or province maps.

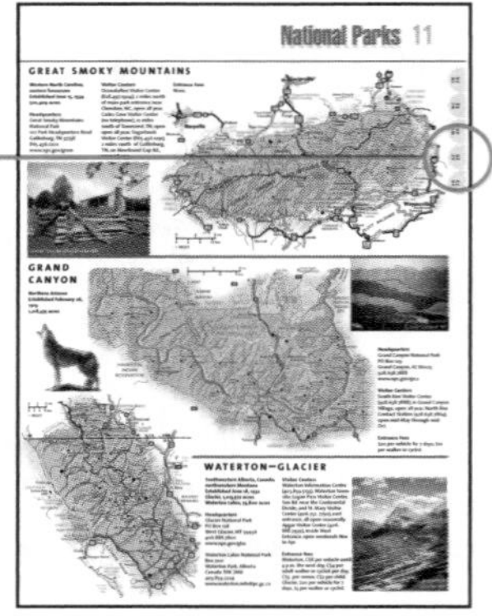

Road Maps Pages 18–82
Road maps for all 50 states, followed by Canadian provinces and Mexico are provided in alphabetical order. Use the Keymap on the inside front cover to locate a specific road map.

Inset Map Boxes
Red tabs at city locations refer you to pages of detailed city maps.

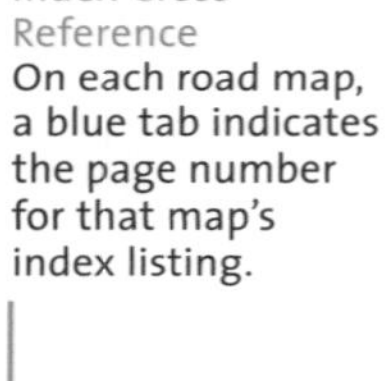

Index Cross-Reference
On each road map, a blue tab indicates the page number for that map's index listing.

City Maps Pages 83–99
Larger-scale city maps show the level of detail you need to navigate in metro areas. Better map detail means more help in finding your destination.

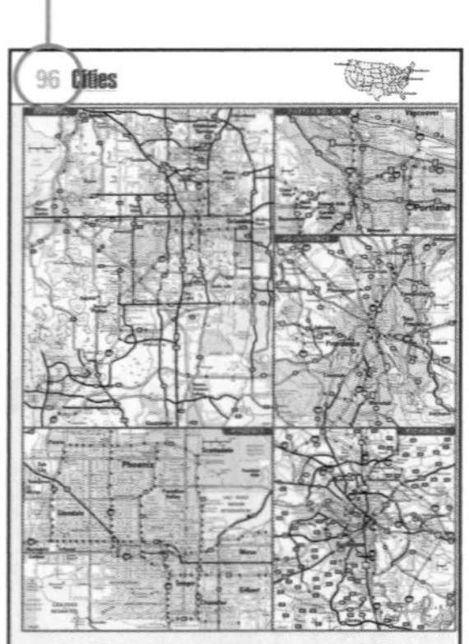

Index Pages 100–107
Use this handy index to look up your destination. The index provides page numbers and map coordinates for cities in each state or province.

Map Coordinates
Coordinates for each city help you easily locate it in the road map section.

Road Map Legend

TRANSPORTATION

CONTROLLED ACCESS HIGHWAYS
- Freeway
- Tollway
- Under Construction
- Interchange and Exit Number

OTHER HIGHWAYS
- Primary Highway
- Secondary Highway
- Divided Highway
- Other Paved Road
- Unpaved Road
  Check conditions locally

HIGHWAY MARKERS
- Interstate Route
- U.S. Route
- State or Provincial Route
- County or Other Route
- Trans-Canada Highway
- Canadian Provincial Autoroute
- Mexican Federal Route

OTHER SYMBOLS
- Distances along Major Highways
  Miles in U.S.; kilometers in Canada and Mexico
- Tunnel; Pass
- Auto Ferry; Passenger Ferry

RECREATION
- National Park
- National Forest; National Grassla
- Other Large Park or Recreation A
- Small State Park with and without Camping
- Military Lands
- Indian Reservation
- Trail
- Ski Area
- Point of Interest

CITIES AND TOWNS
- National Capital
- State or Provincial Capital
- Cities, Towns, and Populated Plac
  Type size indicates relative importance
- Urban Area
  State and province maps only
- Large Incorporated Cities
  City maps only

OTHER MAP FEATURES
- Time Zone Boundary
- Mountain Peak; Elevation
  in Feet
  (Mt. Olympus 7,965)
- Perennial; Intermittent River

Road Map Table of Contents 3

4 United States

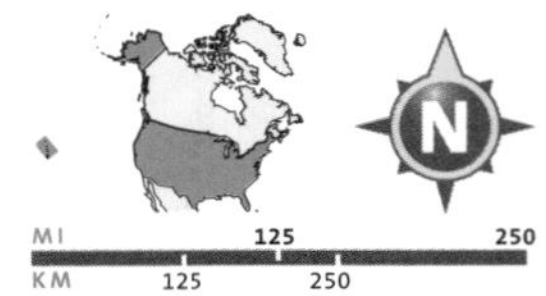

ALASKA

HAWAI'I

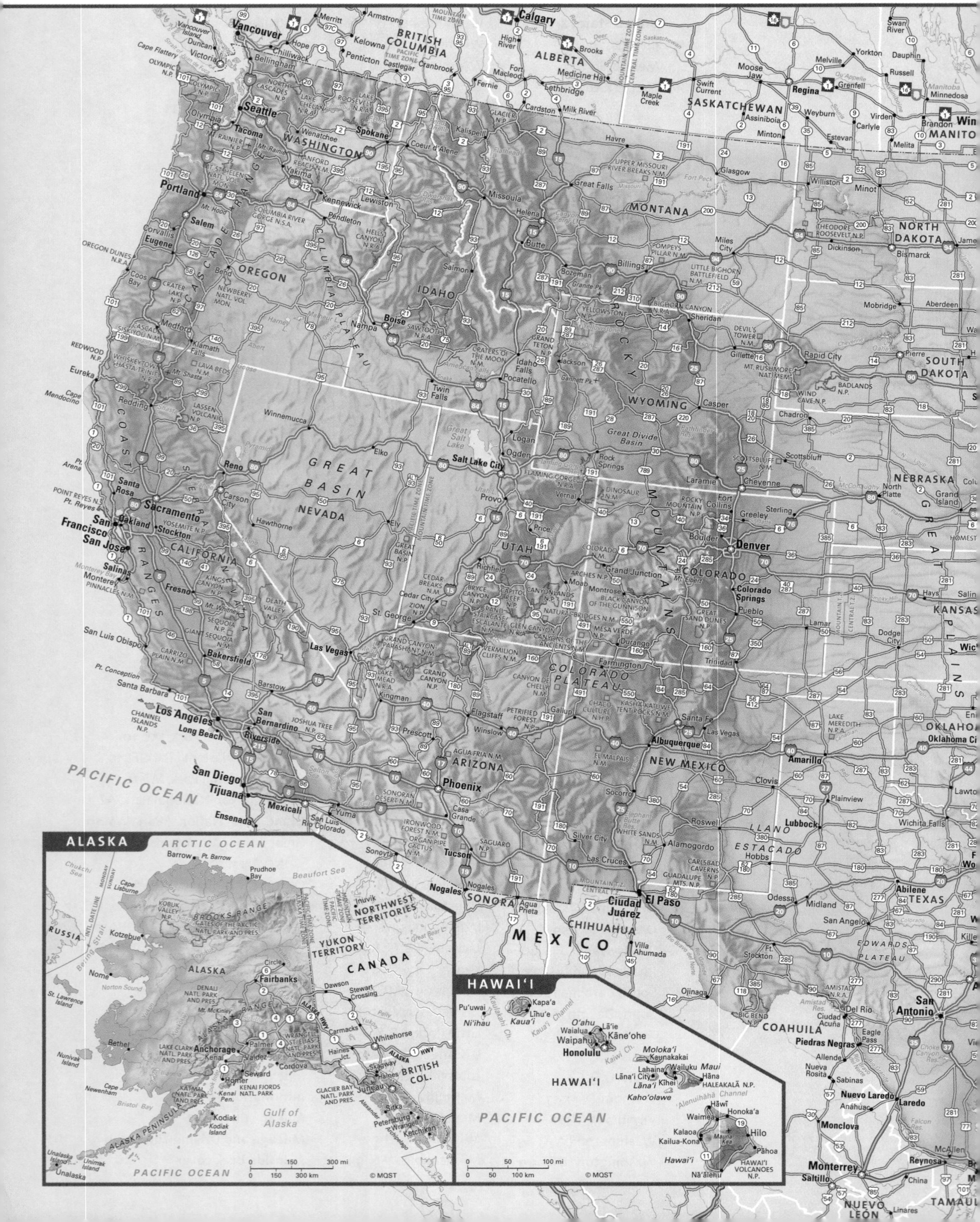

NADA
ONTARIO
QUÉBEC
NEW BRUNSWICK
MAINE
MINNESOTA
WISCONSIN
MICHIGAN
IOWA
ILLINOIS
INDIANA
OHIO
PENNSYLVANIA
NEW YORK
NEW JERSEY
MASS.
VT.
N.H.
CT
R.I.
MD
DE.
WEST VIRGINIA
VIRGINIA
KENTUCKY
MISSOURI
TENNESSEE
NORTH CAROLINA
SOUTH CAROLINA
GEORGIA
ALABAMA
MISSISSIPPI
ARKANSAS
LOUISIANA
FLORIDA
BAHAMAS
APPALACHIAN MOUNTAINS
OZARK PLATEAU
ATLANTIC OCEAN
GULF OF MEXICO
Lake Superior
Lake Michigan
Lake Huron
Lake Erie
Lake Ontario
Chibougamau
Baie-Comeau
Ste-Anne-des-Monts
Percé
Bonaventure
Dalhousie
Bathurst
Miramichi
Edmundston
Fredericton
Saint John
Moncton
Dolbeau-Mistassini
Chicoutimi
Tadoussac
Rivière-du-Loup
Lebel-sur-Quévillon
Hearst
Kapuskasing
Cochrane
Geraldton
Dryden
Ignace
Nipigon
Thunder Bay
Atikokan
Fort Frances
International Falls
Marathon
Wawa
Chapleau
Timmins
Foleyet
Kirkland Lake
Rouyn-Noranda
Val-d'Or
New Liskeard
Ville-Marie
Témiscaming
Maniwaki
Mont-Laurier
Trois-Rivières
Québec
La Tuque
Baie-St-Paul
St-Georges
Thetford Mines
Sherbrooke
Montréal
Ottawa
Pembroke
North Bay
Sudbury
Sault Ste. Marie
Espanola
Parry Sound
Huntsville
Tobermory
Owen Sound
Port Elgin
Barrie
Orillia
Peterborough
Perth
Cornwall
Cobourg
Oshawa
Toronto
Brampton
Kitchener
Hamilton
London
St. Thomas
Sarnia
Windsor
Niagara Falls
Hibbing
Duluth
Superior
Houghton
Marquette
Escanaba
St. Cloud
Minneapolis
St. Paul
Eau Claire
Wausau
Green Bay
Appleton
Sheboygan
Mankato
Rochester
Winona
La Crosse
Mason City
Madison
Milwaukee
Racine
Muskegon
Grand Rapids
Lansing
Flint
Detroit
Ann Arbor
Kalamazoo
Toledo
Alpena
Fort Dodge
Waterloo
Dubuque
Cedar Rapids
Rockford
Chicago
Gary
South Bend
Des Moines
Davenport
Joliet
Fort Wayne
Lima
Ottumwa
Peoria
Bloomington
Lafayette
Muncie
Columbus
Dayton
Cincinnati
Indianapolis
Champaign
Decatur
Springfield
Quincy
Terre Haute
Kansas City
Columbia
Jefferson City
St. Louis
Evansville
Owensboro
Louisville
Frankfort
Lexington
Huntington
Charleston
Parkersburg
Wheeling
Morgantown
Cleveland
Akron
Canton
Pittsburgh
Erie
Buffalo
Jamestown
Rochester
Syracuse
Watertown
Utica
Albany
Binghamton
Scranton
Williamsport
Altoona
Harrisburg
Newark
New York
Trenton
Philadelphia
Wilmington
Atlantic City
Cape May
Dover
Baltimore
Annapolis
Washington, DC
Cumberland
Salisbury
Burlington
Montpelier
Rutland
Concord
Portsmouth
Boston
Worcester
Providence
Hartford
New Haven
Portland
Lewiston
Augusta
Bangor
Bar Harbor
Presque Isle
Houlton
Calais
Cape Cod
Nantucket Island
Martha's Vineyard
Block Island
Charlottesville
Richmond
Newport News
Norfolk
Virginia Beach
Roanoke
Danville
Greensboro
Durham
Raleigh
Winston-Salem
Charlotte
Asheville
Fayetteville
Wilmington
Cape Hatteras
Cape Lookout
Cape Fear
Myrtle Beach
Columbia
Spartanburg
Greenville
Charleston
Augusta
Athens
Atlanta
Macon
Columbus
Savannah
Brunswick
Albany
Valdosta
Tallahassee
Jacksonville
St. Augustine
Daytona Beach
Ocala
Orlando
Cape Canaveral
Melbourne
Tampa
St. Petersburg
Sarasota
Fort Myers
Naples
West Palm Beach
Fort Lauderdale
Miami
Key West
Florida Keys
Panama City
Pensacola
Mobile
Montgomery
Birmingham
Tuscaloosa
Huntsville
Gadsden
Decatur
Chattanooga
Knoxville
Nashville
Clarksville
Bowling Green
Paducah
Cape Girardeau
Carbondale
Cairo
Poplar Bluff
Jonesboro
Memphis
Jackson
Tupelo
Meridian
Hattiesburg
Natchez
Greenville
Little Rock
Pine Bluff
Hot Springs
Ft. Smith
Fayetteville
Joplin
Springfield
Rolla
Muskogee
Texarkana
El Dorado
Monroe
Shreveport
Longview
Tyler
Alexandria
Lafayette
Baton Rouge
New Orleans
Biloxi
Houma
Lake Charles
Beaumont
Houston
Galveston
Freeport
Nassau
New Providence
Grand Bahama
Abaco Island
Bimini Islands
Andros Island
Eleuthera
Cat Island
San Salvador
Great Exuma
Long Island
Rum Cay
Samana Cay
Crooked Island
Great Guana Cay
Straits of Florida
Grand Bahama Bank
Exuma Sound
DRY TORTUGAS N.P.
EVERGLADES N.P.
BISCAYNE N.P.
CANAVERAL N.S.
CUMBERLAND ISLAND N.S.
GULF ISLANDS N.S.
CONGAREE N.P.
GREAT SMOKY MTNS. N.P.
MAMMOTH CAVE N.P.
MOUNT ROGERS N.R.A.
SHENANDOAH N.P.
ASSATEAGUE ISLAND N.S.
CAPE HATTERAS N.S.
CAPE LOOKOUT N.S.
FIRE ISLAND N.S.
GATEWAY N.R.A.
CAPE COD N.S.
ACADIA N.P.
CUYAHOGA VALLEY N.P.
SLEEPING BEAR DUNES N.L.
PICTURED ROCKS N.L.
APOSTLE ISLANDS N.L.
ISLE ROYALE N.P.
VOYAGEURS N.P.
HOT SPRINGS N.P.
EASTERN TIME ZONE
CENTRAL TIME ZONE
MAPQUEST

6 Climate Maps

SUNSHINE

CITY	DAYS OF SUNSHI
Las Vegas, NV	211.1
Phoenix, AZ	211.0
Los Angeles, CA	186.0
San Francisco, CA	160.3
Grand Junction, CO	136.6
Dallas/Fort Worth, TX	135.5
Salt Lake City, UT	125.0
Little Rock, AR	118.7
Denver, CO	115.2
Atlanta, GA	110.4
New York, NY	106.7
San Antonio, TX	106.1
Nashville, TN	102.9
Charleston, SC	102.3
New Orleans, LA	101.4
Portland, ME	101.3
Boston, MA	98.4
Washington, DC	96.7
Sheridan, WY	95.8
Orlando, FL	89.9
Chicago, IL	83.8
International Falls, MN	76.7
Miami, FL	75.1
Seattle, WA	71.0
Cleveland, OH	66.4
Pittsburgh, PA	58.3
Burlington, VT	57.9

RAINFALL

CITY	DAYS OF RAINFA
Cleveland, OH	156.0
Burlington, VT	154.0
Pittsburgh, PA	153.3
Seattle, WA	150.4
International Falls, MN	131.3
Miami, FL	129.5
Portland, ME	128.5
Boston, MA	126.5
Chicago, IL	126.3
New York, NY	120.6
Nashville, TN	118.6
Orlando, FL	115.8
Atlanta, GA	115.1
New Orleans, LA	114.5
Charleston, SC	112.9
Washington, DC	112.3
Sheridan, WY	106.8
Little Rock, AR	104.5
Salt Lake City, UT	90.6
Denver, CO	89.1
San Antonio, TX	82.1
Dallas/Fort Worth, TX	78.9
Grand Junction, CO	72.8
San Francisco, CA	62.0
Phoenix, AZ	36.5
Los Angeles, CA	35.2
Las Vegas, NV	26.5

SNOWFALL

CITY	DAYS OF SNOWFALL
Sheridan, WY	23.6
Burlington, VT	22.0
International Falls, MN	19.5
Cleveland, OH	18.4
Denver, CO	17.9
Salt Lake City, UT	17.8
Portland, ME	17.3
Pittsburgh, PA	12.8
Chicago, IL	11.6
Boston, MA	10.7
Grand Junction, CO	8.7
New York, NY	7.9
Washington, DC	4.6
Nashville, TN	3.5
Seattle, WA	2.4
Little Rock, AR	1.9
Dallas/Fort Worth, TX	1.1
Atlanta, GA	0.6
Las Vegas, NV	0.4
Charleston, SC	0.2
San Antonio, TX	0.2
New Orleans, LA	rare
San Francisco, CA	rare
Los Angeles, CA	0.0
Miami, FL	0.0
Orlando, FL	0.0
Phoenix, AZ	0.0

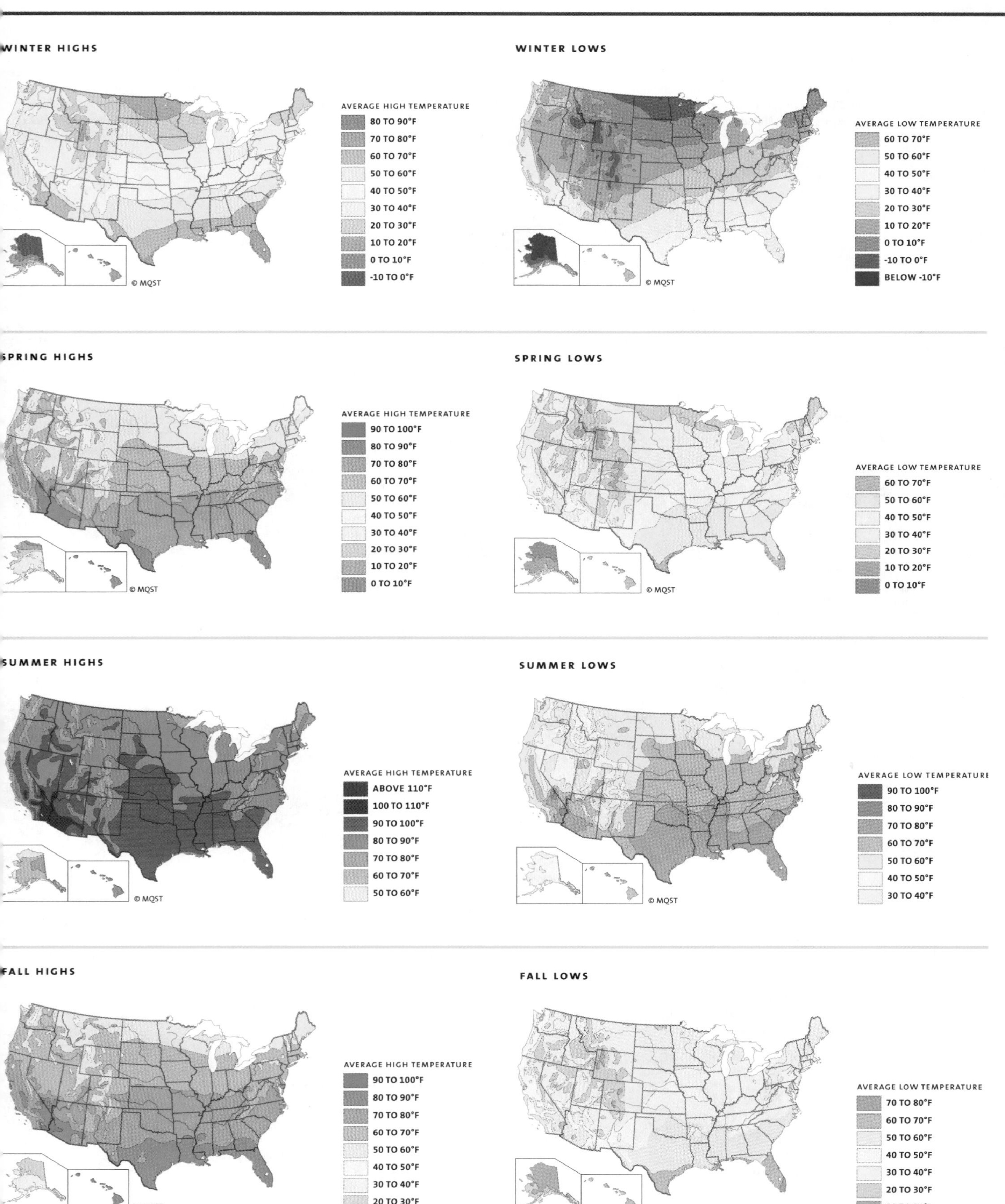
WINTER HIGHS
AVERAGE HIGH TEMPERATURE
80 TO 90°F
70 TO 80°F
60 TO 70°F
50 TO 60°F
40 TO 50°F
30 TO 40°F
20 TO 30°F
10 TO 20°F
0 TO 10°F
-10 TO 0°F
© MQST
WINTER LOWS
AVERAGE LOW TEMPERATURE
60 TO 70°F
50 TO 60°F
40 TO 50°F
30 TO 40°F
20 TO 30°F
10 TO 20°F
0 TO 10°F
-10 TO 0°F
BELOW -10°F
© MQST
SPRING HIGHS
AVERAGE HIGH TEMPERATURE
90 TO 100°F
80 TO 90°F
70 TO 80°F
60 TO 70°F
50 TO 60°F
40 TO 50°F
30 TO 40°F
20 TO 30°F
10 TO 20°F
0 TO 10°F
© MQST
SPRING LOWS
AVERAGE LOW TEMPERATURE
60 TO 70°F
50 TO 60°F
40 TO 50°F
30 TO 40°F
20 TO 30°F
10 TO 20°F
0 TO 10°F
© MQST
SUMMER HIGHS
AVERAGE HIGH TEMPERATURE
ABOVE 110°F
100 TO 110°F
90 TO 100°F
80 TO 90°F
70 TO 80°F
60 TO 70°F
50 TO 60°F
© MQST
SUMMER LOWS
AVERAGE LOW TEMPERATURE
90 TO 100°F
80 TO 90°F
70 TO 80°F
60 TO 70°F
50 TO 60°F
40 TO 50°F
30 TO 40°F
© MQST
FALL HIGHS
AVERAGE HIGH TEMPERATURE
90 TO 100°F
80 TO 90°F
70 TO 80°F
60 TO 70°F
50 TO 60°F
40 TO 50°F
30 TO 40°F
20 TO 30°F
© MQST
FALL LOWS
AVERAGE LOW TEMPERATURE
70 TO 80°F
60 TO 70°F
50 TO 60°F
40 TO 50°F
30 TO 40°F
20 TO 30°F
10 TO 20°F
© MQST

8 National Parks

The National Park System protects areas of natural and historical importance in the U.S., ranging from scenic rivers to historic battlefields. In addition to the 55 National Parks, the park system maintains sites as diverse as a cattle ranch in Montana and Independence Hall in Philadelphia.

Abbreviations

IHS	International Historic Site
NB	National Battlefield
NBP	National Battlefield Park
NBS	National Battlefield Site
NHA	National Historic Area
NHP	National Historical Park
NHP & PRES	National Historical Park & Preserve
NH RES	National Historical Rese
NHS	National Historic Site
NL	National Lakeshore
NM	National Monument
NM & PRES	National Monument & Preserve

MP	National Military Park	N RES	National Reserve
MEM	National Memorial	NS	National Seashore
‣	National Park	NST	National Scenic Trail
‣ & PRES	National Park & Preserve	PKWY	Parkway
PRES	National Preserve		
R	National River		
RA	National Recreation Area		
RRA	National River & Recreation Area		

Boston Area
Adams NHS
Boston African American NHS
Boston Harbor Islands NRA
Boston NHP
Frederick Law Olmstead NHS
John F. Kennedy NHS
Longfellow NHS
Lowell NHP
Minute Man NHP
Salem Maritime NHS
Saugus Iron Works NHS

New York City Area
African Burial Ground NM
Castle Clinton NM
Edison NHS
Federal Hall N MEM
General Grant N MEM
Hamilton Grange N MEM
Sagamore Hill NHS
Saint Paul's Church NHS
Statue of Liberty NM
Theodore Roosevelt Birthplace NHS

Philadelphia Area
Edgar Allan Poe NHS
Independence NHP
Thaddeus Kosciuszko N MEM

Baltimore Area
Ft. McHenry NM and Historic Shrine
Hampton NHS

District of Columbia
Anacostia Park
Carter G. Woodson Home NHS
Constitution Gardens
Ford's Theatre NHS
Franklin Delano Roosevelt Memorial
Frederick Douglass NHS
George Mason Memorial
Korean War Veterans Memorial
Lincoln Memorial
Mary McLeod Bethune Council House NHS
National Mall
National World War II Memorial
Pennsylvania Avenue NHS
Rock Creek Park
Sewall-Belmont House NHS
Thomas Jefferson Memorial
Vietnam Veterans Memorial
Washington Monument
White House

Maryland
Chesapeake and Ohio Canal NHP
Clara Barton NHS
Fort Washington Park
Greenbelt Park
Monocacy NB
Piscataway Park

Virginia
Arlington House
George Washington Memorial PKWY
Wolf Trap NP for the Performing Arts

The National Park of American Samoa and the War in the Pacific NHP are also administered by the National Park Service but are not shown on this map.

ACADIA

Central coastal Maine
Established February 26, 1919
35,000 acres

Headquarters
Acadia National Park
PO Box 177
Eagle Lake Rd
Bar Harbor, ME 04609
207.288.3338
www.nps.gov/acad

Visitor Centers
Hulls Cove Visitor Center (207.288.3338), on Rte. 3 just before entrance to Park Loop Rd., open May to Oct. Mount Desert Information Center, on Rte. 3 just before driving onto Mt. Desert Island, open seasonally.

Entrance Fees
$20 per vehicle for 7 days; $5 per walker or cyclist for 7 days. No fee Nov to Apr.

Seaside cliffs in winter
Acadia NP

GRAND TETON

Northwestern Wyoming
Established February 26, 19
309,590 acres

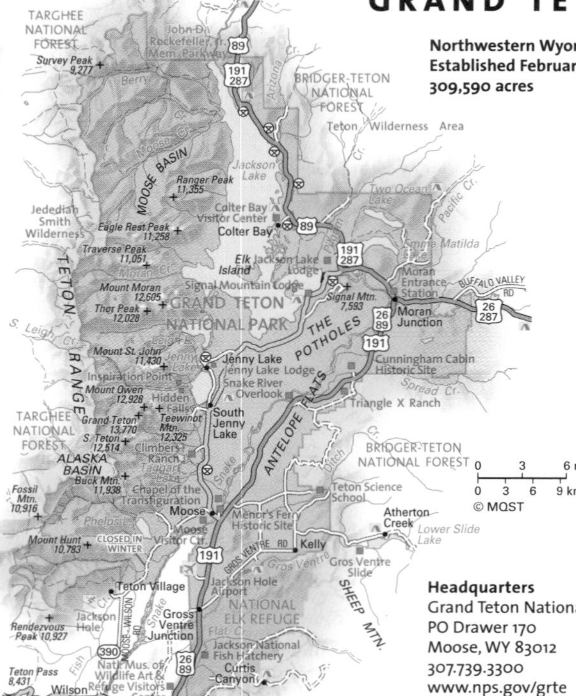

Headquarters
Grand Teton National Park
PO Drawer 170
Moose, WY 83012
307.739.3300
www.nps.gov/grte

Visitor Centers
Moose Visitor Center (307.739.3399), 12 miles nort of Jackson on Rte. 89/191/28 open daily except Christmas Colter Bay Visitor Center (307.739.3594), on Jackson Lake, open mid-May to end Sept. Jenny Lake Visitor Cent (307.739.3392), 8 miles north of Moose Visitor Center, ope June to Sept. Flagg Ranch Information Station, 16 miles north of Colter Bay Junction on Rte. 89/191/287, open Jun to Sept.

Entrance Fees
$20 per vehicle for 7 days (al good for Yellowstone).

Snake River and Grand Tetons
Grand Teton NP

EVERGLADES

Southern Florida
Established December 6, 1947
1,509,000 acres

Tidelands
Everglades NP

Headquarters
Everglades National Park
40001 State Road 9336
Homestead, FL 33034
305.242.7700
www.nps.gov/ever

Visitor Centers
Ernest F. Coe Visitor Center (305.242.7700), 12 miles west of Florida City. Royal Palm Visitor Center (305.242.7700), 4 miles past Coe Visitor Center. Flamingo Visitor Center (239.695.2945), 38 miles past Coe Visitor Center. Shark Valley Visitor Center (305.221.8776), 30 miles west of the Florida Turnpike on U. S. 41. Gulf Coast Visitor Center (239.695.3311), 3 miles south of U. S. 41 on Hwy. 29. All open daily except Flamingo, open Nov to Apr

Entrance Fees
$10 per vehicle for 7 days and $5 per walker or cyclist at the main entrance. $10 per vehicle for 7 days and $5 per walker or cyclist at Shark Valley.

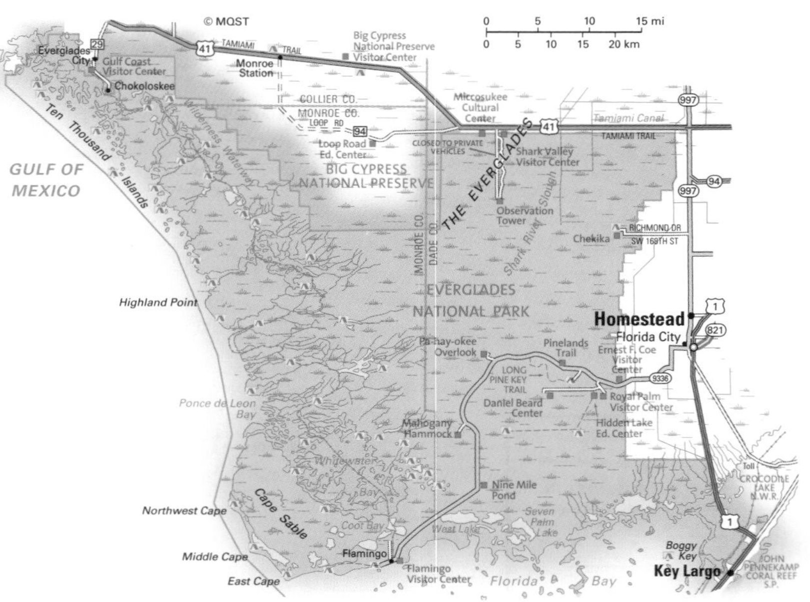

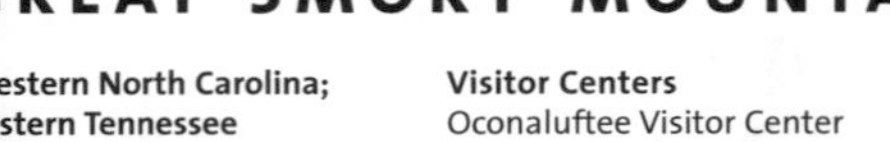

GREAT SMOKY MOUNTAINS

Western North Carolina; eastern Tennessee
Established June 15, 1934
520,409 acres

Headquarters
Great Smoky Mountains National Park
107 Park Headquarters Road
Gatlinburg, TN 37738
865.436.1200
www.nps.gov/grsm

Visitor Centers
Oconaluftee Visitor Center (828.497.1904), 2 miles north of main park entrance near Cherokee, NC, open all year. Cades Cove Visitor Center (no telephone), 12 miles south of Townsend, TN, open all year. Sugarlands Visitor Center (865.436.3255), 2 miles south of Gatlinburg, TN, on Newfound Gap Rd., open all year.

Entrance Fees
None.

Great Smoky Mountains NP

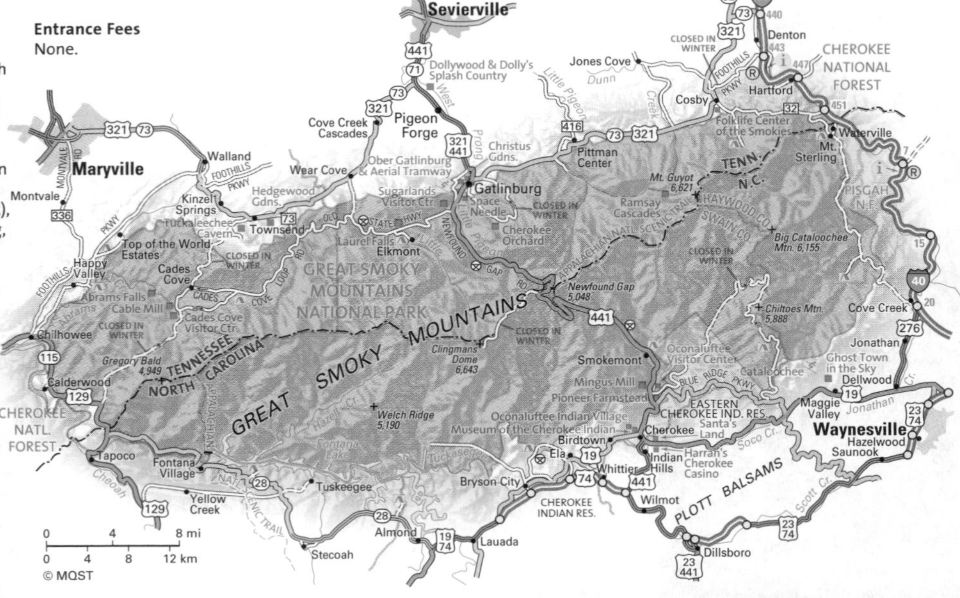

GRAND CANYON

Northern Arizona
Established February 26, 1919
1,218,375 acres

Grand Canyon at sunset
Grand Canyon NP

Headquarters
Grand Canyon National Park
PO Box 129
Grand Canyon, AZ 86023
928.638.7888
www.nps.gov/grca

Visitor Centers
South Rim Visitor Center (928.638.7888), in Grand Canyon Village, open all year. North Rim Contact Station (928.643.7298), open mid-May through mid-Oct.

Entrance Fees
$20 per vehicle for 7 days; $10 per walker or cyclist.

WATERTON–GLACIER

Southwestern Alberta, Canada; northwestern Montana
Established June 18, 1932
Glacier, 1,013,572 acres
Waterton Lakes, 73,800 acres

Headquarters
Glacier National Park
PO Box 128
West Glacier, MT 59936
406.888.7800
www.nps.gov/glac

Waterton Lakes National Park
Box 200
Waterton Park, Alberta
Canada T0K 2M0
403.859.2224
www.pc.gc.ca/index_e.asp

Visitor Centers
Waterton Information Centre (403.859.5133), Waterton townsite; Logan Pass Visitor Center, Sun Rd. near the Continental Divide; and St. Mary Visitor Center (406.732. 7750), east entrance, all open seasonally. Apgar Visitor Center (406. 888.7939), inside West Entrance, open weekends Nov to Apr.

Entrance fees
Waterton, C$8 per vehicle until 4 p.m. the next day. C$4 per adult walker or cyclist per day, C$3 per senior, C$2 per child. Glacier, $20 per vehicle for 7 days, $5 per walker or cyclist.

Going-to-the-Sun Mountain
Glacier NP

WA 65
VA 66
CO 24

OLYMPIC

Western Washington
Established June 29, 1938
922,000 acres

Headquarters
Olympic National Park
600 East Park Avenue
Port Angeles, WA 98362
360.565.3132
www.nps.gov/olym

Trail through Hoh Rain Forest
Olympic NP

Visitor Centers
Olympic National Park Visitor Center (360.565.3132) in Port Angeles, take Race St. off U. S. 101, open and staffed all year. Hurricane Ridge Visitor Center, 17 miles south of Port Angeles visitor center, and Hoh Rain Forest Visitor Center (360.374.6925), 19 miles east of U. S. 101 on the west side of park, open all year (road and weather conditions permitting), but may be self-service fall through spring, dependent on staffing.

Entrance Fees
$10 per vehicle for 7 days; $5 per cyclist, walker, or bus passenger.

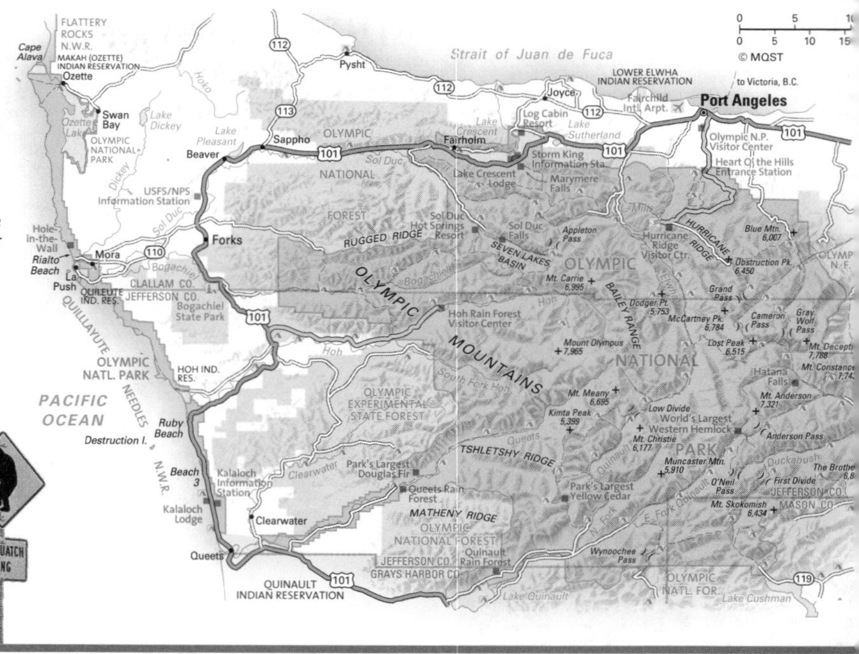

SHENANDOAH

Northern Virginia
Established December 26, 1935
196,000 acres

Headquarters
Shenandoah National Park
3655 U. S. Highway 211E
Luray, VA 22835
540.999.3500
www.nps.gov/shen

Visitor Centers
Dickey Ridge Visitor Center (540.635.3566), at Mile 4.6, and Harry F. Byrd, Sr., Visitor Center (540.999.3283), at Mile 51, open spring to late fall. Mileposts, numbered from north to south on Skyline Drive, help visitors locate park facilities, services, and areas of interest.

Entrance Fees
$10 per vehicle for 7 days; $5 per walker or cyclist.

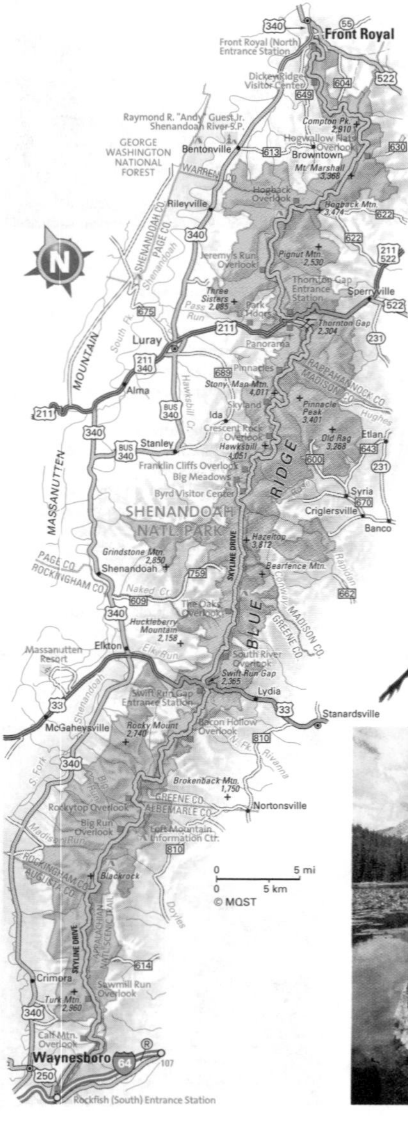

Shenandoah NP

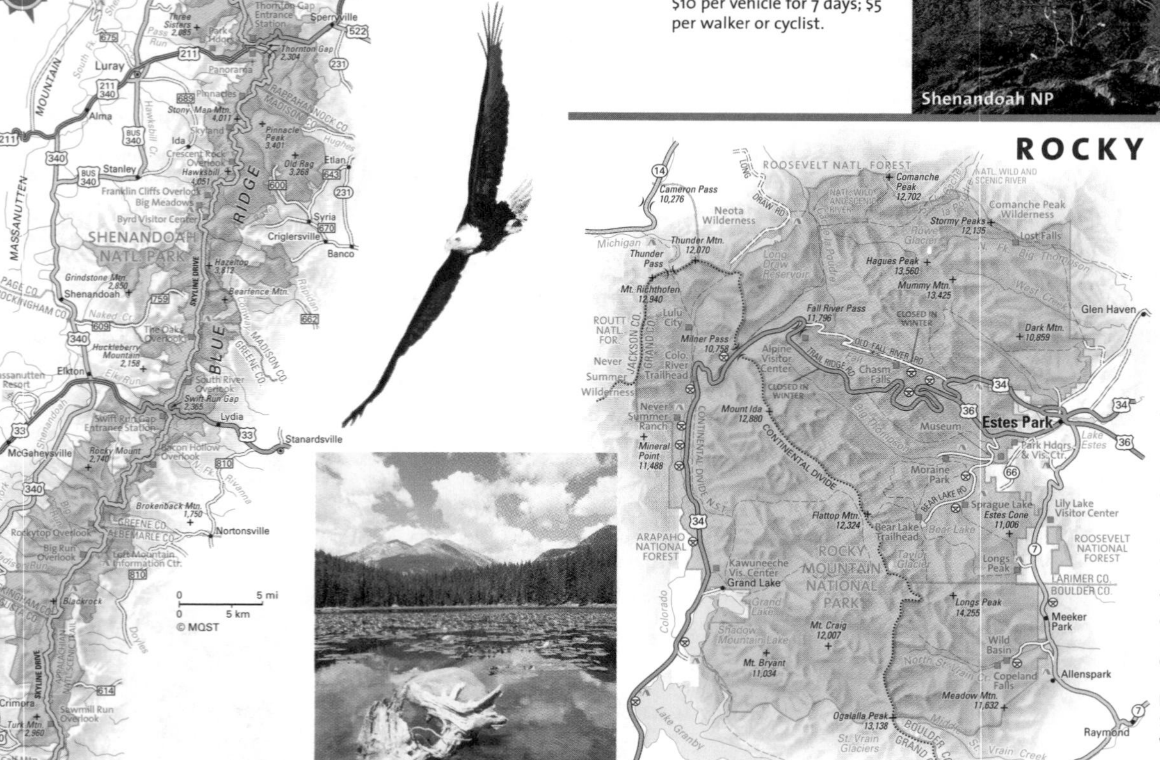

Rocky Mountain NP

ROCKY MOUNTAIN

Northern Colorado
Established January 26, 1915
265,727 acres

Headquarters
Rocky Mountain National Pa
1000 Highway 36
Estes Park, CO 80517
970.586.1206
www.nps.gov/romo

Visitor Centers
Headquarters Visitor Center (970.586.1206), U.S. 36 at eas entrance, and Kawuneeche Visitor Center (970.586.1513), U.S. 34 north of Grand Lake, open all year. Alpine Visitor Center, on U.S. 34, and Moraine Park Museum and Visitor Center (970.586.1206) on Bear Lake Rd., south of Beaver Meadows entrance, open May to mid-Oct.

Entrance Fees
$15 per private vehicle; $5 per walker or cyclist.

WY 69
UT 64
MT 44
ID 30
CA 22

YELLOWSTONE

Northwestern Wyoming, with portions extending into southwestern Montana and eastern Idaho
Established March 1, 1872
2,221,766 acres

Lower Falls of the Yellowstone River
Yellowstone NP

Headquarters
Yellowstone National Park
PO Box 168
Yellowstone National Park, WY 82190
307.344.7381
www.nps.gov/yell

Visitor Centers
Albright Visitor Center (307.344.2263), in Mammoth Hot Springs, open all year. Old Faithful Visitor Center (307.545.2750), open mid-Apr to late Oct and mid-Dec to mid-Mar. Canyon Visitor Center (307.242.2550), Fishing Bridge Visitor Center (307.242.2450), and Grant Village Visitor Center (307.242.2650), all open mid-May through Sept. West Thumb Information Station, open early June to Sept.

Entrance Fees
$20 per vehicle for 7 days (also good for Grand Teton); $15 per snowmobile or motorcycle; $10 per walker, cyclist, or skier.

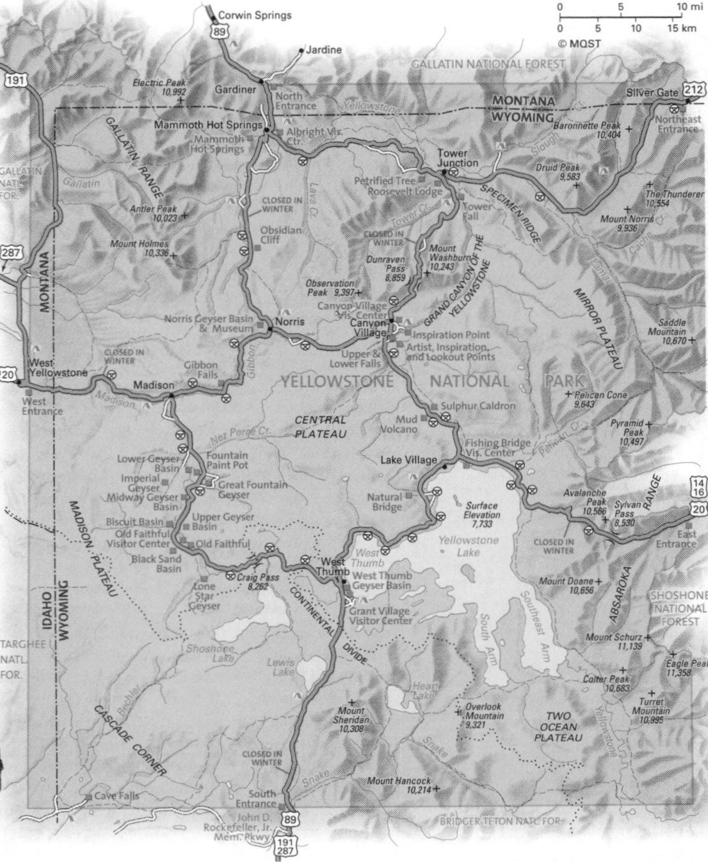

El Capitan and Merced River
Yosemite NP

YOSEMITE

East-central California
Established October 1, 1890
747,956 acres

Headquarters
Yosemite National Park
PO Box 577
Yosemite, CA 95389
209.372.0200
www.nps.gov/yose

Visitor Centers
Yosemite Valley Visitor Center and Yosemite Valley, open all year. Wawona Information Station (209.375.9531), open May to Sept. Big Oak Flat Information Station (209.379.1899), near park entrance at Hwy. 120, open June to Aug. Tuolumne Meadows Visitor Center (209.372.0263), on Tioga Rd., open in summer with opening of Tioga Pass.

Entrance Fees
$20 per vehicle for 7 days; $10 per walker, cyclist, or bus passenger.

ZION

Southwestern Utah
Established November 19, 1919
146,559 acres

The peaceful Virgin River
Zion NP

Headquarters
Zion National Park
State Route 9
Springdale, UT 84767
435.772.3256
www.nps.gov/zion

Visitor Centers
Zion Canyon Visitor Center (435.772.3256), near southern entrance on Utah Rte. 9, and Kolob Canyons Visitor Center (435.586.9548), northwest corner of park via Exit 40 off I-15, open all year except major holidays. The visitor center at Watchman Campground(800.365.CAMP) is open from April to October.

Entrance Fees
$20 per vehicle for 7 days; $10 per walker or cyclist.

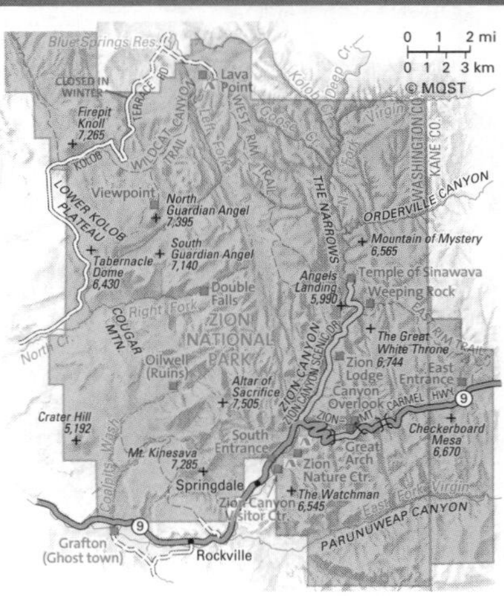

14 National Parks

ABBREVIATIONS

NB	National Battlefield	NMP	National Military Park	NS	National Seashore
NBP	National Battlefield Park	NP	National Park	NSR	National Scenic River/ Riverway
NHP	National Historical Park	N PRES	National Preserve	PKWY	Parkway
NHS	National Historic Site	NRA	National Recreation Area	WSR	Wild and Scenic River
NL	National Lakeshore	NRRA	National River and Recreation Area		
N MEM	National Memorial	N RES	National Reserve		
NM	National Monument				

	Park	Address / Phone	Fees	(Disabled Access) Visitor Center	Programs and Tours	Picnic area	(Disabled Access) Campground	Hiking	Horse Trail	Swimming	Boating	Fishing	Hunting	Bicycle Trail	Cabin Rental	Hotel, Motel, Lodge	Restaurant, Snacks
A	Abraham Lincoln Birthplace NHS	2995 Lincoln Farm Road, Hodgenville, KY 42748 270-358-3137		●		■		■									
	Acadia NP	PO Box 177, Eagle Lake Rd, Bar Harbor, ME 04609 207-288-3338	■	●	■	■	●	■	■	■	■	■		■			■
	Adams NHP	135 Adams St, Quincy, MA 02169 617-770-1175	■	●	■												
	Agate Fossil Beds NM	301 River Road, Harrison, NE 69346 308-668-2211	■	●	■	■		■				■					
	Allegheny Portage Railroad NHS	110 Federal Park, Gallitzin, PA 16641 814-886-6150	■	●	■	■		■									
	Amistad NRA	4121 Hwy 90 West, Del Rio, TX 78840 830-775-7491	■		■	■	●	■		■	■	■	■				
	Andersonville NHS	496 Cemetery Road, Andersonville, GA 31711 229-924-0343		●	■	■											
	Andrew Johnson NHS	121 Monument Avenue, Greeneville, TN 37743 423-638-3551	■	●	■												
	Antietam NB	PO Box 158, Sharpsburg, MD 21782 301-432-5124	■	●	■			■				■					
	Apostle Islands NL	415 Washington Ave, Bayfield, WI 54814 715-779-3397	■	●	■	■	■	■		■	■	■	■				
	Appomattox Court House NHP	PO Box 218 Route 24, Appomattox, VA 24522 434-352-8987, ext 26	■	●		■		■									
	Arches NP	PO Box 907, Moab, UT 84532 435-719-2299	■	●	■	■	●	■									
	Arkansas Post N MEM	1741 Old Post Road, Gillett, AR 72055 870-548-2207		●	■	■		■				■					
	Assateague Island NS	7206 National Seashore Lane, Berlin, MD 21811 410-641-1441	■	●	■	■	●	■		■	■	■	■	■			
	Aztec Ruins NM	84 County Road, Aztec, NM 87410 505-334-6174, ext 30	■	●		■											
B	Badlands NP	PO Box 6, Interior, SD 57750 605-433-5361	■	●	■	■	●	■							■	■	■
	Bandelier NM	15 Entrance Rd, Los Alamos, NM 87544 505-672-0343	■	●	■	■	●	■									■
	Bent's Old Fort NHS	35110 Hwy 194 East, La Junta, CO 81050 719-383-5010	■		■	■											
	Big Bend NP	PO Box 129, Big Bend National Park, TX 79834 432-477-2251	■	●	■	■	■	■	■		■	■				■	■
	Big Cypress N PRES	33100 Tamiami Trail, Ochopee, FL 34141 239-695-1201	■	●	■	■	■	■	■		■	■	■	■			
	Big Hole NB	PO Box 237, Wisdom, MT 59761 406-689-3155	■	●	■	■						■					
	Big South Fork NRRA	4564 Leatherwood Road, Oneida, TN 37841 423-286-7275		●		■	●	■	■	■	■	■	■	■		■	
	Big Thicket N PRES	6044 FM420, Kountze, TX 77625 409-951-6725		●	■	■		■	■		■	■	■	■			
	Biscayne NP	9709 SW 328 Street, Homestead, FL 33033 305-230-7275	■	●	■	■	■				■	■					
	Black Canyon of the Gunnison NP	102 Elk Creek, Gunnison, CO 81230 970-641-2337 ext 205	■	●	■	■	●	■				■				■	■
	Blue Ridge PKWY	199 Hemphill Knob Road, Asheville, NC 28803 828-298-0398		●	■	■	●	■	■		■	■		■	■	■	■
	Bluestone NSR	PO Box 246, Glen Jean, WV 25846 304-465-0508			■			■			■	■	■				
	Booker T. Washington NM	12130 Booker T. Washington Hwy, Hardy, VA 24101 540-721-2094		●	■	■		■									
	Boston African American NHS	14 Beacon Street, Suite 503, Boston, MA 02108 617-742-5415			■												
	Boston NHP	Charlestown Navy Yard, Boston, MA 02129 617-242-5601	■	●	■	■											■
	Bryce Canyon NP	PO Box 640201, Bryce Canyon, UT 84764 435-834-5322	■	●	■	■	●	■	■						■	■	■
	Buffalo NR	402 N. Walnut, Suite 136, Harrison, AR 72601 870-741-5443	■	●	■	■	●	■	■	■	■	■	■		■		■
C	Cabrillo NM	1800 Cabrillo Memorial Drive, San Diego, CA 92106 619-557-5450	■	●	■	■		■				■					
	Canaveral NS	308 Julia Street, Titusville, FL 32796 321-267-1110	■	●	■	■		■	■	■	■	■	■				
	Canyon de Chelly NM	PO Box 588, Chinle, AZ 86503 928-674-5500		●	■	■	●	■	■							■	■
	Canyonlands NP	2282 S West Resource Blvd, Moab, UT 84532 435-719-2313	■	●	■	■	■	■			■						
	Cape Cod NS	99 Marconi Site Road, Wellfleet, MA 02667 508-255-3421	■	●	■	■		■		■	■	■	■	■		■	■
	Cape Hatteras NS	1401 National Park Drive, Manteo, NC 27954 252-995-4474	■	●	■	■	●	■	■	■	■	■	■		■	■	■
	Cape Lookout NS	131 Charles Street, Harkers Island, NC 28531 252-728-2250		●		■		■			■	■	■		■		
	Capitol Reef NP	HC 70 Box 15, Torrey, UT 84775 435-425-3791	■	●	■	■	●	■	■								
	Capulin Volcano NM	PO Box 40, Capulin, NM 88414 505-278-2201	■	●	■	■		■									
	Carl Sandburg Home NHS	81 Carl Sandburg Lane, Flat Rock, NC 28731 828-693-4178	■	●	■	■		■									
	Carlsbad Caverns NP	3225 National Parks Hwy, Carlsbad, NM 88220 505-785-2232	■	●	■	■		■									■
	Casa Grande Ruins NM	1100 Ruins Drive, Coolidge, AZ 85228 520-723-3172	■	●	■	■											
	Castillo de San Marcos NM	1 South Castillo Drive, St. Augustine, FL 32084 904-829-6506	■		■												
	Castle Clinton NM	1 Bowling Green, New York, NY 10005 212-344-7220		●	■												
	Cedar Breaks NM	2390 W Hwy 56, Suite 11, Cedar City, UT 84720 435-586-9451	■	●	■	■	●	■									
	Chaco Culture NHP	PO Box 220, Nageezi, NM 87037 505-786-7014	■	■	■	■	●	■						■			
	Chamizal N MEM	800 S San Marcial Street, El Paso, TX 79905 915-532-7273		●	■	■											
	Channel Islands NP	1901 Spinnaker Drive, Ventura, CA 93001 805-658-5700		●	■	■	■	■		■	■	■					
	Charles Pinckney NHS	1214 Middle Street, Sullivans Island, SC 29482 843-881-5516		●	■												
	Chattahoochee River NRA	1978 Island Ford Pkwy, Atlanta, GA 30350 678-538-1200	■		■	■		■	■		■	■		■			■
	Chesapeake and Ohio Canal NHP	1850 Dual Hwy, Suite 100, Hagerstown, MD 21740 301-739-4200	■	●	■	■	●	■	■		■	■		■			■
	Chickamauga and Chattanooga NMP	PO Box 2128, Fort Oglethorpe, GA 30742 706-866-9241	■	●	■	■		■	■								
	Chickasaw NRA	1008 W Second Street, Sulphur, OK 73086 580-622-3165		●	■	■	●	■		■	■	■	■				
	Chiricahua NM	13063 E Bonita Canyon Road, Willcox, AZ 85643 520-824-3560	■	●	■	■	●	■	■								
	City of Rocks N RES	PO Box 169, Almo, ID 83312 208-824-5519	■	●	■	■	●	■	■				■	■			
	Colonial NHP	PO Box 210, Yorktown, VA 23690 757-898-2410	■	●	■	■		■				■		■			
	Colorado NM	Fruita, CO 81521 970-858-3617	■	●	■	■	●	■	■								
	Congaree NP	100 National Park Road, Hopkins, SC 29061 803-776-4396		●	■	■		■			■	■					
	Coronado N MEM	4101 E Montezuma Canyon Road, Hereford, AZ 85615 520-366-5515		●		■		■									
	Cowpens NB	PO Box 308, Chesnee, SC 29323 864-461-2828		●		■											
	Crater Lake NP	PO Box 7, Crater Lake, OR 97604 541-594-3100	■	●	■	■	●	■	■			■				■	■
	Craters of the Moon NM	PO Box 29, Arco, ID 83213 208-527-3257	■	●	■	■	■	■									
	Cumberland Gap NHP	PO Box 1848, Middlesboro, KY 40965 606-248-2817	■	●	■	■	●	■	■		■			■			
	Cumberland Island NS	PO Box 806, St. Marys, GA 31558 888-817-3421	■	●	■	■	●	■		■		■	■				
	Curecanti NRA	102 Elk Creek, Gunnison, CO 81230 970-641-2337, ext 205	■	●	■	■	●	■	■	■	■	■	■				■
	Cuyahoga Valley NP	15610 Vaughn Road, Brecksville, OH 44141 216-524-1497		●	■	■		■	■	■		■		■		■	■
D	Dayton Aviation Heritage NHP	PO Box 9280, Wright Brothers Station, Dayton, OH 45409 937-225-7705	■		■									■			
	Death Valley NP	PO Box 579, Death Valley, CA 92328 760-786-3200	■	●	■	■	●	■	■	■				■	■	■	■
	Delaware Water Gap NRA	River Rd, Bushkill, PA 18324 570-588-2451	■	●	■	■	■	■	■	■	■	■	■	■			
	Denali NP & PRES	PO Box 9, Denali Park, AK 99755 907-683-2294	■	●	■	■	●	■				■	■			■	■

REVIATIONS

	National Battlefield	NMP	National Military Park	NS	National Seashore
	National Battlefield Park	NP	National Park	NSR	National Scenic River/ Riverway
	National Historical Park	N PRES	National Preserve		
	National Historic Site	NRA	National Recreation Area	PKWY	Parkway
	National Lakeshore	NRRA	National River and Recreation Area	WSR	Wild and Scenic River
EM	National Memorial				
	National Monument	N RES	National Reserve		

Park	Address	Phone	Fees	(Disabled Access) Visitor Center	Programs and Tours	Picnic area	(Disabled Access) Campground	Hiking	Horse Trail	Swimming	Boating	Fishing	Hunting	Bicycle Trail	Cabin Rental	Hotel, Motel, Lodge	Restaurant, Snacks
De Soto N MEM	PO Box 15390, Bradenton, FL 34280	941-792-0458		X	X							X					
Devils Postpile NM	PO Box 3999, Mammoth Lakes, CA 93546	760-934-2289	X	X	X	X	X	X	X			X					
Devils Tower NM	PO Box 10, Devils Tower, WY 82714	307-467-5283	X	X	X	X	X	X				X					
Dinosaur NM	4545 E Hwy 40, Dinosaur, CO 81610	970-374-3000	X	X	X	X	X	X			X	X					
Dry Tortugas NP	P.O. Box 6208, Key West, FL 33031	305-242-7700	X	X	X	X	X			X	X	X					
Edison NHS	Main Street and Lakeside Avenue, West Orange, NJ 07052	973-736-0551	X	X	X												
Effigy Mounds NM	151 Hwy 76, Harpers Ferry, IA 52146	563-873-3491	X	X	X			X				X					
Eisenhower NHS	97 Taneytown Road, Gettysburg, PA 17325	717-338-9114	X	X	X												
Eleanor Roosevelt NHS	4097 Albany Post Road, Hyde Park, NY 12538	845-229-9115	X		X	X		X									
Everglades NP	40001 State Road 9336, Homestead, FL 33034	305-242-7700	X	X	X	X	X	X	X		X	X		X	X	X	X
Federal Hall N MEM	26 Wall Street, New York, NY 10005	212-825-6888		X	X												
Fire Island NS	120 Laurel Street, Patchogue, NY 11772	631-289-4810	X	X	X	X	X	X		X	X	X	X				X
Florissant Fossil Beds NM	PO Box 185, Florissant, CO 80816	719-748-3253	X	X	X	X		X									
Ford's Theatre NHS	900 Ohio Drive SW, Washington, DC 20024	202-426-6924		X	X												
Fort Caroline N MEM	12713 Fort Caroline Road, Jacksonville, FL 32225	904-641-7155		X	X	X		X									
Fort Davis NHS	PO Box 1379, Fort Davis, TX 79734	432-426-3224	X	X													
Fort Donelson NB	PO Box 434, Dover, TN 37058	931-232-5706		X		X		X									
Fort Frederica NM	6515 Frederica Road, St. Simons Island, GA 31522	912-638-3639	X	X	X			X				X					
Fort Laramie NHS	965 Gray Rocks Road, Fort Laramie, WY 82212	307-837-2221	X	X	X	X						X					
Fort Larned NHS	RR 3 Box 69, Larned, KS 67550	620-285-6911	X	X	X	X											
Fort Matanzas NM	8635 A1A South, St. Augustine, FL 32080	904-471-0116		X	X					X	X	X					
Fort McHenry NM and Historic Shrine	2400 East Fort Avenue, Baltimore, MD 21230	410-962-4290	X	X	X	X											
Fort Necessity NB	1 Washington Pkwy, Farmington, PA 15437	724-329-5512	X	X	X	X		X									
Fort Point NHS	Long Ave & Marine Dr, Presidio of San Francisco, CA 94129	415-556-1693		X	X							X		X			
Fort Pulaski NM	PO Box 30757,Hwy 80 East, Savannah, GA 31410	912-786-5787	X	X	X	X		X			X	X		X			
Fort Raleigh NHS	1401 National Park Drive, Manteo, NC 27954	252-473-5772		X	X	X		X								X	X
Fort Scott NHS	PO Box 918, Fort Scott, KS 66701	620-223-0310	X	X	X	X											
Fort Smith NHS	301 Parker Avenue, Fort Smith, AR 72901	479-783-3961	X	X	X												
Fort Stanwix NM	112 E Park Street, Rome, NY 13440	315-336-2090	X	X	X												
Fort Sumter NM	1214 Middle Street, Sullivans Island, SC 29482	843-883-3123	X	X	X	X						X					
Fort Union NM	PO Box 127, Watrous, NM 87753	505-425-8025	X	X	X	X											
Fort Union Trading Post NHS	15550 Hwy 1804, Williston, ND 58801	701-572-9083		X	X	X						X					
Fort Vancouver NHS	612 E Reserve Street, Vancouver, WA 98661	360-816-6230	X	X	X	X											
Fossil Butte NM	PO Box 592, Kemmerer, WY 83101	307-877-4455		X	X	X		X									
Franklin Delano Roosevelt Memorial	NCP Central, 900 Ohio Drive SW, Washington, DC 20024	202-426-6841			X												
Frederick Douglass NHS	1411 W St SE, Washington, DC 20020	202-426-5961	X	X	X												
Fredericksburg and Spotsylvania NMP	120 Chatham Lane, Fredericksburg, VA 22405	540-371-6122	X	X	X	X		X									
Friendship Hill NHS	1 Washington Pkwy, Farmington, PA 15437	724-725-9190		X	X	X		X				X					
Gates of the Arctic NP & PRES	PO Box 26030, Bettles Field, AK 99726	907-692-5494		X	X			X			X	X	X				
Gateway NRA	210 New York Avenue, Staten Island, NY 10305	718-354-4500		X	X	X	X	X	X	X	X	X		X			X
Gauley River NRA	PO Box 246, Glen Jean, WV 25846	304-465-0508					X	X			X	X	X				
General Grant N MEM	122nd Street and Riverside Drive, New York, NY 10027	212-666-1640		X	X												
George Rogers Clark NHP	401 S 2nd Street, Vincennes, IN 47591	812-882-1776, ext 110	X	X	X	X											
George Washington Birthplace NM	1732 Popes Creek Road, Colonial Beach, VA 22443	804-224-1732	X	X	X	X		X				X					
George Washington Carver NM	5646 Carver Road, Diamond, MO 64840	417-325-4151	X	X	X	X											
George Washington MEM PKWY	Turkey Run Park, McLean, VA 22101	703-289-2500	X	X	X	X		X	X		X	X		X			X
Gettysburg NMP	97 Taneytown Road, Gettysburg, PA 17325	717-334-1124		X	X	X		X									
Gila Cliff Dwellings NM	HC 68 Box 100, Silver City, NM 88061	505-536-9461		X	X	X	X	X	X			X					
Glacier Bay NP & PRES	PO Box 140, Gustavus, AK 99826	907-697-2230		X	X		X	X			X	X	X			X	X
Glacier NP	PO Box 128, West Glacier, MT 59936	406-888-7800	X	X	X	X	X	X	X	X	X	X		X	X	X	X
Glen Canyon NRA	PO Box 1507, Page, AZ 86040	928-608-6404	X	X	X	X	X	X	X	X	X	X	X	X		X	X
Golden Gate NRA	Fort Mason, Building 201, San Francisco, CA 94123	415-561-4700	X	X	X	X	X	X	X	X	X	X		X		X	X
Golden Spike NHS	PO Box 897, Brigham City, UT 84302	435-471-2209, ext 29	X	X	X	X		X						X			
Grand Canyon NP	PO Box 129, Grand Canyon, AZ 86023	928-638-7888	X	X	X	X	X	X	X			X			X	X	X
Grand Portage NM	PO Box 668, Grand Marais, MN 55604	218-387-2788	X		X	X		X				X					
Grand Teton NP	PO Drawer 170, Moose, WY 83012	307-739-3300	X	X	X	X	X	X	X	X	X	X			X	X	X
Grant-Kohrs Ranch NHS	266 Warren Lane, Deer Lodge, MT 59722	406-846-2070	X	X	X												
Great Basin NP	100 Great Basin National Park, Baker, NV 89311	775-234-7331	X	X	X	X	X	X	X			X					X
Great Sand Dunes NP & N PRES	11500 Hwy 150, Mosca, CO 81146	719-378-6399	X	X	X	X	X	X									X
Great Smoky Mountains NP	107 Park Headquarters Road, Gatlinburg, TN 37738	865-436-1200	X	X	X	X	X	X	X			X		X		X	
Guadalupe Mountains NP	HC 60 Box 400, Salt Flat, TX 79847	915-828-3251		X	X	X	X	X	X								
Guilford Courthouse NMP	2332 New Garden Road, Greensboro, NC 27410	336-288-1776		X	X			X						X			
Gulf Islands NS (Florida District)	1801 Gulf Breeze PKWY, Gulf Breeze, FL 32563	850-934-2600	X	X	X	X	X	X		X	X	X	X	X			X
Gulf Islands NS (Mississippi District)	3500 Park Road, Ocean Springs, MS 39564	228-875-9057		X	X	X	X	X		X	X	X		X			X
Haleakala NP	PO Box 369, Makawao, HI 96768	808-572-4400	X	X	X	X	X	X	X	X					X		
Hampton NHS	535 Hampton Lane, Towson, MD 21286	410-823-1309	X	X	X												X
Harpers Ferry NHP	PO Box 65, Harpers Ferry, WV 25425	304-535-6029	X	X	X	X		X				X					
Harry S Truman NHS	223 N Main Street, Independence, MO 64050	816-254-9929	X	X	X												
Hawaii Volcanoes NP	PO Box 52, Hawaii National Park, HI 96718	808-985-6000	X	X	X	X	X	X	X					X	X	X	X
Herbert Hoover NHS	PO Box 607, West Branch, IA 52358	319-643-2541	X	X	X	X		X									
Home of Franklin D. Roosevelt NHS	4097 Albany Post Road, Hyde Park, NY 12538	845-229-9115	X	X		X		X									
Homestead NM of America	8523 W State Hwy 4, Beatrice, NE 68310	402-223-3514		X	X	X											

16 National Parks

ABBREVIATIONS

NB	National Battlefield	NMP	National Military Park	NS	National Seashore
NBP	National Battlefield Park	NP	National Park	NSR	National Scenic River/ Riverway
NHP	National Historical Park	N PRES	National Preserve	PKWY	Parkway
NHS	National Historic Site	NRA	National Recreation Area	WSR	Wild and Scenic River
NL	National Lakeshore	NRRA	National River and Recreation Area		
N MEM	National Memorial	N RES	National Reserve		
NM	National Monument				

	Park	Address	Phone	Fees	(Disabled Access) Visitor Center	Programs and Tours	Picnic area	(Disabled Access) Campground	Hiking	Horse Trail	Swimming	Boating	Fishing	Hunting	Bicycle Trail	Cabin Rental	Hotel, Motel, Lodge	Restaurant, Snacks
H	Hopewell Culture NHP	16062 State Route 104, Chillicothe, OH 45601	740-774-1125	■	■	■	■		■									
	Hopewell Furnace NHS	2 Mark Bird Lane, Elverson, PA 19520	610-582-8773	■	■	■	■		■	■								
	Horseshoe Bend NMP	11288 Horseshoe Bend Road, Daviston, AL 36256	265-234-7111		■	■	■		■	■	■	■	■		■			
	Hot Springs NP	101 Reserve Street, Hot Springs, AR 71902	501-624-2701		■	■	■	■	■								■	■
	Hovenweep NM	McElmo Route, Cortez, CO 81321	970-562-4282	■	■	■	■	■	■									
	Hubbell Trading Post NHS	PO Box 150, Ganado, AZ 86505	928-755-3475		■	■	■											
I	Independence NHP	143 South Third Street, Philadelphia, PA 19106	215-965-2305		■	■												
	Indiana Dunes NL	1100 N Mineral Springs Road, Porter, IN 46304	219-926-7561, ext 225		■	■	■	■	■	■	■	■	■		■			■
	Isle Royale NP	800 E Lakeshore Drive, Houghton, MI 49931	906-482-0984	■	■	■	■	■	■			■	■			■	■	■
J	Jean Lafitte NHP & PRES	419 Decatur Street, New Orleans, LA 70130	504-589-3882		■	■	■		■			■	■	■				
	Jefferson National Expansion Memorial	11 N 4th Street, St. Louis, MO 63102	314-655-1700	■	■	■												
	Jewel Cave NM	11149 Bldg B12, US Hwy 16, Custer, SD 57730	605-673-2288	■	■	■	■		■									
	Jimmy Carter NHS	300 N Bond Street, Plains, GA 31780	229-824-4104		■	■	■											
	John Day Fossil Beds NM	32651 Highway 19, Kimberly, OR 97848	541-987-2333		■	■	■						■					
	John Muir NHS	4202 Alhambra Avenue, Martinez, CA 94553	925-228-8860	■	■	■	■		■									
	Johnstown Flood N MEM	733 Lake Road, South Fork, PA 15956	814-495-4643	■	■	■	■		■									
	Joshua Tree NP	74485 National Park Drive, Twentynine Palms, CA 92277	760-367-5500	■	■	■	■	■	■	■								
K	Kalaupapa NHP	PO Box 2222, Kalaupapa, HI 96742	808-567-6802		■		■		■									
	Kaloko-Honokohau NHP	73-4786 Kanalani, Street #14, Kailua-Kona, HI 96740	808-329-6881		■		■		■		■	■	■					
	Katmai NP & PRES	PO Box 7, King Salmon, AK 99613	907-246-3305	■	■	■	■	■	■			■	■	■		■	■	■
	Kenai Fjords NP	PO Box 1727, Seward, AK 99664	907-224-7500	■	■	■	■	■	■			■	■			■		
	Kennesaw Mountain NBP	900 Kennesaw Mountain Drive, Kennesaw, GA 30152	770-427-4686		■		■		■	■								
	Kings Canyon NP	47050 Generals Hwy, Three Rivers, CA 93271	559-565-3341	■	■	■	■	■	■	■			■			■	■	■
	Kings Mountain NMP	2625 Park Road, Blacksburg, SC 29702	864-936-7921		■	■			■	■								
	Klondike Gold Rush NHP-Alaska	PO Box 517, Skagway, AK 99840	907-983-2921	■	■	■	■	■	■								■	■
	Klondike Gold Rush NHP-Seattle	319 Second Avenue, Seattle, WA 98104	206-220-4240		■	■												
	Knife River Indian Villages NHS	PO Box 9, Stanton, ND 58571	701-745-3300		■	■	■		■				■					
	Kobuk Valley NP	PO Box 1029, Kotzebue, AK 99752	907-442-3890		■	■			■			■	■					
	Korean War Veterans Memorial	NCP Central, 900 Ohio Drive SW, Washington, DC 20024	202-426-6841			■												
L	Lake Chelan NRA	810 State Route 20, Sedro-Woolley, WA 98284	360-856-5700		■	■	■	■	■	■	■	■	■	■		■	■	■
	Lake Clark NP & PRES	4230 University Drive, Suite 311, Anchorage, AK 99508	907-781-2218		■	■			■		■	■	■	■		■	■	■
	Lake Mead NRA	601 Nevada Hwy, Boulder City, NV 89005	702-293-8990		■	■	■	■	■	■	■	■	■	■	■		■	■
	Lake Meredith NRA	PO Box 1460, Fritch, TX 79036	806-857-3151	■	■		■	■	■	■	■	■	■	■				
	Lake Roosevelt NRA	1008 Crest Drive, Coulee Dam, WA 99116	509-633-9441		■	■	■	■			■	■	■	■			■	■
	Lassen Volcanic NP	PO Box 100, Mineral, CA 96063	530-595-4444	■	■	■	■	■	■	■	■	■	■			■		■
	Lava Beds NM	1 Indian Well Headquarters, Tulelake, CA 96134	530-667-8100	■	■	■	■	■	■	■								
	Lewis & Clark NHP	92343 Fort Clatsop Road, Astoria, OR 97103	503-861-2471	■	■	■	■											
	Lincoln Boyhood N MEM	PO Box 1816, Lincoln City, IN 47552	812-937-4541	■	■	■	■											
	Lincoln Home NHS	413 S 8th Street, Springfield, IL 62701	217-492-4241, ext 221		■	■												
	Lincoln Memorial	900 Ohio Drive SW, Washington, DC 20024	202-426-6841			■												■
	Little Bighorn Battlefield NM	PO Box 39, Crow Agency, MT 59022	406-638-3204	■	■	■												
	Lowell NHP	67 Kirk Street, Lowell, MA 01852	978-970-5000	■	■	■	■					■	■				■	■
	Lyndon B. Johnson NHP	PO Box 329, Johnson City, TX 78636	830-868-7128, ext 244	■	■	■												
M	Mammoth Cave NP	PO Box 7, Mammoth Cave, KY 42259	270-758-2180	■	■	■	■	■	■	■		■	■		■	■	■	■
	Manassas NBP	12521 Lee Highway, Manassas, VA 20109	703-361-1339	■	■	■	■		■	■			■					
	Martin Luther King, Jr., NHS	450 Auburn Avenue NE, Atlanta, GA 30312	404-331-5190	■	■	■											■	
	Martin Van Buren NHS	1013 Old Post Road, Kinderhook, NY 12106	518-758-9689	■	■	■	■		■									
	Mesa Verde NP	PO Box 8, Mesa Verde, CO 81330	970-529-4465	■	■	■	■	■	■								■	■
	Minute Man NHP	174 Liberty Street, Concord, MA 01742	978-369-6993		■	■			■						■			
	Mojave N PRES	2701 Barstow Road, Barstow, CA 92311	760-252-6100	■	■	■	■	■	■	■				■	■		■	■
	Montezuma Castle NM	PO Box 219, Camp Verde, AZ 86322	928-567-3322	■	■		■											
	Moores Creek NB	40 Patriots Hall Drive, Currie, NC 28435	910-283-5591		■	■	■						■					
	Morristown NHP	30 Washington Place, Morristown, NJ 07960	908-766-8215	■	■	■			■	■								
	Mount Rainier NP	Tahoma Woods, Star Route, Ashford, WA 98304	360-569-2211	■	■	■	■	■	■	■			■				■	■
	Mount Rushmore N MEM	13000 Highway 244, Building 31, Suite 1, Keystone, SD 57751	605-574-2523	■	■	■												■
	Muir Woods NM	Mill Valley, CA 94941	415-388-2596	■	■	■			■									■
N	Natchez NHP	640 S Canal Street, Box E, Natchez, MS 39120	601-442-7047	■	■	■	■						■				■	■
	Natchez Trace PKWY	2680 Natchez Trace Pkwy, Tupelo, MS 38804	800-305-7417		■	■	■	■	■	■	■	■	■		■			■
	Natural Bridges NM	HC 60, Box 1, Lake Powell, UT 84533	435-692-1234	■	■	■	■	■	■									
	Navajo NM	HC 71, Box 3, Tonalea, AZ 86044	928-672-2700		■	■	■	■	■	■								
	New River Gorge NR	PO Box 246, Glen Jean, WV 25846	304-465-0508		■	■	■	■	■	■		■	■	■	■			
	Nez Perce NHP	39063 US Hwy, Spalding, ID 83540	208-843-7001		■	■	■											
	Ninety Six NHS	PO Box 496, Ninety Six, SC 29666	864-543-4068		■	■	■		■	■			■					
	North Cascades NP	810 State Route 20, Sedro-Woolley, WA 98284	360-856-5700		■			■	■	■			■					
O	Obed WSR	PO Box 429, Wartburg, TN 37887	423-346-6294		■		■	■	■		■	■	■	■				
	Ocmulgee NM	1207 Emery Hwy, Macon, GA 31217	478-752-8257		■		■		■				■					
	Olympic NP	600 E Park Avenue, Port Angeles, WA 98362	360-565-3130	■	■	■	■	■	■	■	■	■	■		■	■	■	■
	Oregon Caves NM	19000 Caves Hwy, Cave Junction, OR 97523	541-592-2100	■		■	■		■								■	■
	Organ Pipe Cactus NM	10 Organ Pipe Drive, Ajo, AZ 85321	520-387-6849	■	■	■	■	■	■									
	Ozark NSR	PO Box 490, Van Buren, MO 63965	573-323-4236			■	■	■	■		■	■	■	■		■		■
P	Padre Island NS	PO Box 181300, Corpus Christi, TX 78480	361-949-8068	■	■	■	■	■	■		■	■	■					■
	Pea Ridge NMP	15930 Highway 62, Pea Ridge, AR 72751	479-451-8122	■	■	■	■		■	■								

BBREVIATIONS

IB	National Battlefield	NMP	National Military Park	NS	National Seashore
IBP	National Battlefield Park	NP	National Park	NSR	National Scenic River/ Riverway
IHP	National Historical Park	N PRES	National Preserve		
IHS	National Historic Site	NRA	National Recreation Area	PKWY	Parkway
IL	National Lakeshore	NRRA	National River and Recreation Area	WSR	Wild and Scenic River
I MEM	National Memorial				
IM	National Monument	N RES	National Reserve		

Park	Address	Phone	Fees	(Disabled Access) Visitor Center	Programs and Tours	Picnic area	(Disabled Access) Campground	Hiking	Horse Trail	Swimming	Boating	Fishing	Hunting	Bicycle Trail	Cabin Rental	Hotel, Motel, Lodge	Restaurant, Snacks
Pecos NHP	PO Box 418, Pecos, NM 87552	505-757-6414, ext 1	■	■	■	■											
Perry's Victory & International Peace Memorial	PO Box 549, Put-in-Bay, OH 43456	419-285-2184	■	■	■							■					
Petersburg NB	1539 Hickory Hill Road, Petersburg, VA 23803	804-732-3531	■	■	■	■		■	■			■		■			
Petrified Forest NP	PO Box 2217, Petrified Forest, AZ 86028	928-524-6228	■	■	■	■		■									■
Petroglyph NM	6001 Unser Blvd NW, Albuquerque, NM 87120	505-899-0205	■	■	■	■		■	■								
Pictured Rocks NL	PO Box 40, Munising, MI 49862	906-387-3700	■	■		■	■	■		■	■	■	■				
Pinnacles NM	5000 Hwy 146, Paicines, CA 95043	831-389-4485	■	■	■	■	■	■									
Pipe Spring NM	HC 65 Box 5, Fredonia, AZ 86022	928-643-7105	■	■	■			■									■
Pipestone NM	36 Reservation Avenue, Pipestone, MN 56164	507-825-5464	■	■		■		■									
Point Reyes NS	1 Bear Valley Rd, Point Reyes Station, CA 94956	415-464-5100	■	■	■	■	■	■	■	■		■		■			■
Pu'uhonua o Honaunau NHP	PO Box 129, Honaunau, HI 96726	808-328-2288	■	■	■	■		■		■		■					
Puukohola Heiau NHS	62-3601 Kawaihae Road, Kawaihae, HI 96743	808-882-7218		■	■												
Rainbow Bridge NM	PO Box 1507, Page, AZ 86040	928-608-6404			■						■						
Redwood NP	1111 2nd Street, Crescent City, CA 95531	707-464-6101		■	■	■	■	■	■	■	■	■		■			
Richmond NBP	3215 E Broad Street, Richmond, VA 23223	804-226-1981		■	■	■											
Rocky Mountain NP	1000 Highway 36, Estes Park, CO 80517	970-586-1206	■	■	■	■	■	■	■			■					■
Roger Williams N MEM	282 N Main Street, Providence, RI 02903	401-521-7266		■		■											
Ross Lake NRA	810 State Route 20, Sedro-Woolley, WA 98284	360-856-5700	■	■	■	■	■	■	■		■	■	■		■		
Russell Cave NM	3729 County Road 98, Bridgeport, AL 35740	256-495-2672		■	■	■		■									
Sagamore Hill NHS	20 Sagamore Hill Road, Oyster Bay, NY 11771	516-922-4788	■	■	■	■											
Saguaro NP	3693 S Old Spanish Trail, Tucson, AZ 85730	520-733-5153	■	■	■	■		■	■					■			
Saint Croix NSR	PO Box 708, St. Croix Falls, WI 54024	715-483-3284		■	■	■	■	■			■	■	■				
Saint-Gaudens NHS	139 Saint Gaudens Road, Cornish, NH 03745	603-675-2175	■		■	■		■									
Salem Maritime NHS	174 Derby Street, Salem, MA 01970	978-740-1650	■	■	■	■											
Salinas Pueblo Missions NM	PO Box 517, Mountainair, NM 87036	505-847-2585, ext 20		■	■	■											
San Antonio Missions NHP	2202 Roosevelt Avenue, San Antonio, TX 78210	210-932-1001		■	■	■		■						■			
San Francisco Maritime NHP	Building E, Fort Mason Center, San Francisco, CA 94123	415-447-5000	■		■	■				■				■			
San Juan Island NHP	PO Box 429, Friday Harbor, WA 98250-0429	360-378-2240		■	■	■		■									
San Juan NHS	501 Norzagaray Street, San Juan, PR 00901	787-729-6777	■	■	■												
Santa Monica Mountains NRA	401 W Hillcrest Drive, Thousand Oaks, CA 91360	805-370-2301		■	■	■	■	■	■	■				■		■	■
Saratoga NHP	648 Route 32, Stillwater, NY 12170	518-664-9821, ext 224	■	■		■		■	■								
Scotts Bluff NM	PO Box 27, 190276 Hwy 92, Gering, NE 69341	308-436-4340	■	■	■	■		■						■			
Sequoia NP	47050 Generals Hwy, Three Rivers, CA 93271	559-565-3341	■	■	■	■	■	■	■			■			■	■	■
Shenandoah NP	3655 US Hwy 211 E, Luray, VA 22835	540-999-3500	■	■	■	■	■	■	■			■			■	■	■
Shiloh NMP	1055 Pittsburg Landing Road, Shiloh, TN 38376	731-689-5696	■	■		■		■									
Sitka NHP	103 Monastery Street, Sitka, AK 99835	907-747-0110	■	■	■	■		■				■					
Sleeping Bear Dunes NL	9922 Front Street, Empire, MI 49630	231-326-5134	■	■	■	■	■	■	■	■	■	■	■				
Statue of Liberty NM and Ellis Island	Liberty Island, New York, NY 10004	212-363-3200		■	■	■											■
Steamtown NHS	150 S Washington Avenue, Scranton, PA 18503	888-693-9391	■	■	■	■											
Sunset Crater Volcano NM	6400 N. Highway 89, Flagstaff, AZ 86004	928-526-0502	■	■	■	■	■	■									
Theodore Roosevelt Birthplace NHS	28 E 20th Street, New York, NY 10003	212-260-1616	■	■	■												
Theodore Roosevelt Island	G.W. Mem Pkwy, Turkey Run Park, McLean, VA 22101	703-289-2500			■			■				■					
Theodore Roosevelt NP	PO Box 7, Medora, ND 58645	701-623-4466	■	■	■	■	■	■	■		■	■					
Thomas Jefferson Memorial	900 Ohio Drive SW, Washington, DC 20024	202-426-6841			■	■						■					■
Timpanogos Cave NM	RR 3 Box 200, American Fork, UT 84003	801-756-5238	■	■	■	■		■				■					■
Tonto NM	HC 02 Box 4602, Roosevelt, AZ 85545	928-467-2241	■	■	■	■											
Tumacacori NHP	PO Box 67, Tumacacori, AZ 85640	520-398-2341	■	■	■	■		■									
Tuskegee Institute NHS	1212 West Montgomery Rd, Tuskegee Institute, Tuskegee, AL 36088	334-727-3200		■	■											■	■
Tuzigoot NM	PO Box 219, Camp Verde, AZ 86322	928-634-5564	■	■													
USS Arizona Memorial	1 Arizona Memorial Place, Honolulu, HI 96818	808-422-0561		■	■												
Valley Forge NHP	1400 North Outerline Dr, King of Prussia, PA 19406	610-783-1000	■	■		■		■	■		■	■		■			■
Vanderbilt Mansion NHS	4097 Albany Post Road, Hyde Park, NY 12538	845-229-9115	■	■		■		■									
Vicksburg NMP	3201 Clay Street, Vicksburg, MS 39183	601-636-0583	■	■		■		■									
Vietnam Veterans Memorial	900 Ohio Drive SW, Washington, DC 20024	202-426-6841			■												■
Virgin Islands NP	1300 Cruz Bay Creek, St. John, VI 00830	340-776-6201		■	■	■	■	■		■	■	■				■	■
Voyageurs NP	3131 Hwy 53, South International Falls, MN 56649	218-283-9821		■	■	■	■	■		■	■	■			■	■	■
Walnut Canyon NM	6400 N. Hwy 89, Flagstaff, AZ 86004	928-526-3367	■	■	■	■											
Washington Monument	900 Ohio Drive SW, Washington, DC 20024	202-426-6841			■												■
Whiskeytown-Shasta-Trinity NRA	PO Box 188, Whiskeytown, CA 96095	530-242-3400	■	■	■	■	■	■	■	■	■	■	■	■			
White House	1450 Pennsylvania Avenue NW, Room 1894, Washington, DC 20230	202-208-1631		■	■												■
White Sands NM	PO Box 1086, Holloman AFB, NM 88330	505-479-6124	■	■	■	■		■	■								■
Whitman Mission NHS	328 Whitman Mission Road, Walla Walla, WA 99362	509-529-6357	■	■	■	■											
Wilson's Creek NB	6424 W Farm Road 182, Republic, MO 65738	417-732-2662	■	■		■		■	■								
Wind Cave NP	RR 1 Box 190, Hot Springs, SD 57747	605-745-4600	■	■	■	■	■	■	■								
Wolf Trap NP for the Performing Arts	1551 Trap Road, Vienna, VA 22182	703-255-1800			■	■											■
Women's Rights NHP	136 Fall Street, Seneca Falls, NY 13148	315-568-2991	■	■	■												
Wrangell-St. Elias NP & PRES	PO Box 439, Copper Center, AK 99573	907-822-5234		■		■		■	■		■	■	■	■	■	■	■
Wright Brothers N MEM	1401 National Park Drive, Manteo, NC 27954	252-441-7430	■	■	■											■	■
Wupatki NM	6400 N Hwy 89, Flagstaff, AZ 86004	928-679-2365	■	■	■	■		■									
Yellowstone NP	PO Box 168, Yellowstone National Park, WY 82190	307-344-7381	■	■	■	■	■	■	■	■	■	■		■	■	■	■
Yosemite NP	PO Box 577, Yosemite National Park, CA 95389	209-372-0200	■	■	■	■	■	■	■	■	■	■		■	■	■	■
Zion NP	SR 9, Springdale, UT 84767	435-772-3256	■	■	■	■	■	■	■					■	■	■	■

Alabama

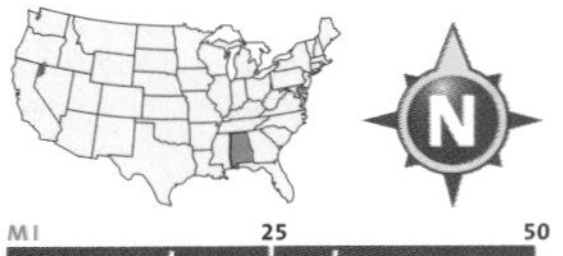

N
MI
25
50
KM
25
50

TENN.
FLORIDA
GEORGIA
MISSISSIPPI
GULF OF MEXICO
mississippi
42
florida
28
AL
100
Huntsville
Madison
Decatur
Florence
Sheffield
Muscle Shoals
Tuscumbia
Athens
Hartselle
Cullman
Arab
Albertville
Guntersville
Boaz
Scottsboro
Fort Payne
Gadsden
Attalla
Rainbow City
Jacksonville
Anniston
Oxford
Talladega
Birmingham
Fairfield
Homewood
Hoover
Bessemer
Hueytown
Center Point
Leeds
Pell City
Pelham
Alabaster
Tuscaloosa
Northport
Jasper
Sylacauga
Alexander City
Clanton
Prattville
Millbrook
Montgomery
Wetumpka
Tallassee
Auburn
Opelika
Phenix City
Tuskegee
Selma
Demopolis
Greenville
Troy
Eufaula
Enterprise
Ozark
Dothan
Andalusia
Opp
Brewton
Atmore
Monroeville
Jackson
Bay Minette
Saraland
Prichard
Mobile
Tillmans Corner
Daphne
Fairhope
Foley
Gulf Shores
Spanish Fort
Theodore
Grand Bay
Bayou La Batre
Chattanooga
Fort Oglethorpe
Ringgold
Dalton
La Fayette
Rome
Cartersville
Cedartown
Kennesaw
Marietta
Powder Springs
Douglasville
Atlanta
Carrollton
Newnan
La Grange
Columbus
Fort Benning Mil. Res.
Cusseta
Corinth
Iuka
Ripley
Booneville
New Albany
Pontotoc
Tupelo
Verona
Okolona
Amory
Aberdeen
West Point
Starkville
Columbus
Louisville
Macon
Meridian
Quitman
Waynesboro
Richton
Beaumont
Lucedale
Pascagoula
Biloxi
Pensacola
Gulf Breeze
Milton
Pace
Gonzalez
Crestview
Niceville
Valparaiso
Fort Walton Beach
Destin
DeFuniak Springs
Bonifay
Chipley
Marianna
Blountstown
Bristol
Lynn Haven
Panama City
Panama City Beach
Florala
Geneva
Samson
Hartford
Slocomb
Headland
Abbeville
Clayton
Union Springs
Lafayette
Lanett
Valley
Roanoke
Wedowee
Ashland
Lineville
Heflin
Piedmont
Anniston Army Depot
Cheaha Mtn. 2,407
Talladega Natl. For.
William B. Bankhead Natl. For.
Conecuh Natl. For.
Tuskegee Natl. For.
Redstone Arsenal
U.S. Space & Rocket Ctr.
Wheeler N.W.R.
Eglin A.F.B.
Maxwell A.F.B.
Fort Rucker Mil. Res.
Horseshoe Bend Natl. Mil. Park
Russell Cave Natl. Mon.
Natchez Trace Pkwy.
Appalachian Mts.
Chattahoochee Natl. For.
Gulf Islands Natl. Seashore
Mobile Bay
Bon Secour N.W.R.
Dauphin Island
Ft. Morgan H.S.
Ft. Gaines H.S.
Ft. Mims
Chickasaw S.P.
Lake Lurleen S.P.
Moundville Arch. Park
Old Cahawba Arch. Park
Tuskegee Institute N.H.S.
Tuskegee Airmen N.H.S.
MAPQUEST
1
2
3
4
5
6
7
B
C
D
E
F
G
H
J
K

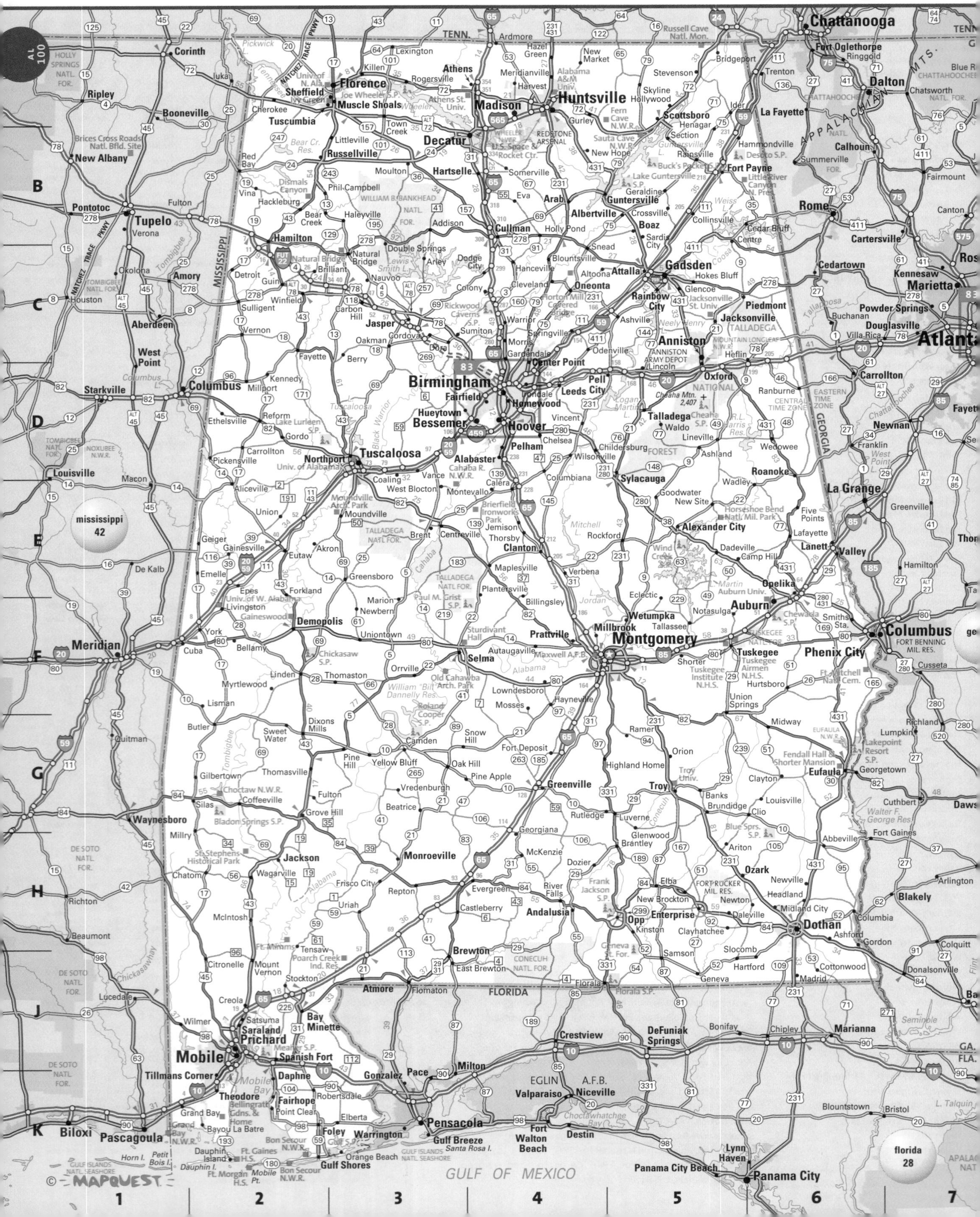

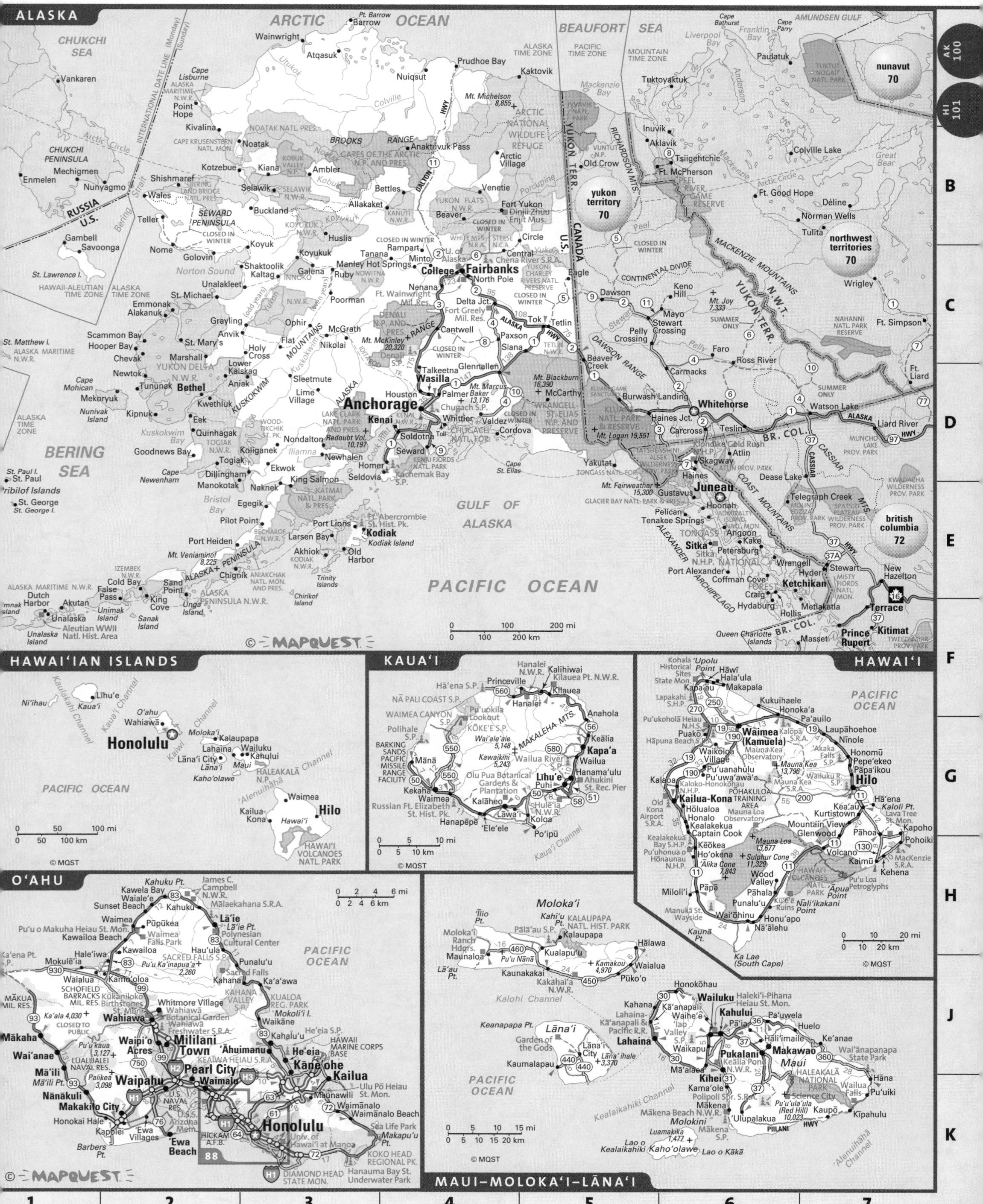

ALASKA

ARCTIC OCEAN
BEAUFORT SEA
CHUKCHI SEA
BERING SEA
GULF OF ALASKA
PACIFIC OCEAN
AMUNDSEN GULF

Pt. Barrow, Barrow, Wainwright, Atqasuk, Nuiqsut, Prudhoe Bay, Kaktovik, Cape Lisburne, Point Hope, Kivalina, Noatak, Kotzebue, Kiana, Ambler, Anaktuvuk Pass, Arctic Village, Shishmaref, Wales, Selawik, Buckland, Bettles, Allakaket, Venetie, Fort Yukon, Beaver, Teller, Nome, Golovin, Koyuk, Huslia, Koyukuk, Galena, Ruby, Tanana, Rampart, Manley Hot Springs, Minto, College, Fairbanks, North Pole, Central, Circle, Eagle, Shaktoolik, Kaltag, Unalakleet, St. Michael, Emmonak, Alakanuk, Grayling, Anvik, Holy Cross, Ophir, Flat, McGrath, Nikolai, Poorman, Nenana, Delta Jct., Fort Greely Mil. Res., Cantwell, Tok, Tetlin, Paxson, Slana, Glennallen, Talkeetna, Wasilla, Palmer, Anchorage, Houston, Kenai, Whittier, Valdez, Cordova, McCarthy, Soldotna, Seward, Homer, Seldovia, Nondalton, Newhalen, Iliamna, Koliganek, Ekwok, Togiak, Dillingham, Manokotak, Naknek, King Salmon, Egegik, Pilot Point, Port Heiden, Chignik, Port Lions, Larsen Bay, Kodiak, Akhiok, Old Harbor, Sand Point, King Cove, Cold Bay, False Pass, Akutan, Unalaska, Dutch Harbor, Bethel, Kwethluk, Eek, Quinhagak, Goodnews Bay, Tununak, Mekoryuk, Kipnuk, Newtok, Chevak, Hooper Bay, Scammon Bay, Marshall, St. Mary's, Lower Kalskag, Aniak, Sleetmute, Lime Village, Gambell, Savoonga, St. Paul, St. George, Yakutat, Haines, Haines Jct., Skagway, Juneau, Hoonah, Gustavus, Pelican, Tenakee Springs, Sitka, Angoon, Kake, Petersburg, Wrangell, Port Alexander, Coffman Cove, Craig, Hydaburg, Hollis, Ketchikan, Metlakatla, Hyder, Stewart

Mt. McKinley 20,320; Mt. Michelson 8,855; Mt. Blackburn 16,390; Mt. Marcus Baker 13,176; Redoubt Vol. 10,197; Mt. Veniaminof 8,225; Mt. Logan 19,551; Mt. Fairweather 15,300; Mt. Joy 7,333

BROOKS RANGE, ALASKA RANGE, KUSKOKWIM MOUNTAINS, COAST MOUNTAINS, MACKENZIE MOUNTAINS, RICHARDSON MTS., DAWSON RANGE, CONTINENTAL DIVIDE, ALEXANDER ARCHIPELAGO

Vankaren, Enmelen, Mechigmen, Nunyagmo, CHUKCHI PENINSULA, RUSSIA, U.S., CANADA

yukon territory 70; northwest territories 70; nunavut 70; british columbia 72

Tuktoyaktuk, Paulatuk, Inuvik, Aklavik, Tsiigehtchic, Ft. McPherson, Old Crow, Colville Lake, Ft. Good Hope, Déline, Norman Wells, Tulita, Wrigley, Ft. Simpson, Ft. Liard, Dawson, Keno Hill, Mayo, Stewart Crossing, Pelly Crossing, Faro, Ross River, Carmacks, Beaver Creek, Burwash Landing, Whitehorse, Carcross, Teslin, Watson Lake, Liard River, Atlin, Dease Lake, Telegraph Creek, New Hazelton, Terrace, Kitimat, Prince Rupert, Masset

0 100 200 mi / 0 100 200 km

© MAPQUEST

HAWAI'IAN ISLANDS

Ni'ihau, Kaua'i, Līhu'e, O'ahu, Wahiawā, Honolulu, Moloka'i, Kalaupapa, Lāna'i City, Lāna'i, Lahaina, Wailuku, Kahului, Maui, Kaho'olawe, Waimea, Hilo, Kailua-Kona, Hawai'i, HALEAKALĀ N.P., HAWAI'I VOLCANOES NATL. PARK, PACIFIC OCEAN

0 50 100 mi / 0 50 100 km

© MQST

KAUA'I

Hanalei, Princeville, Kīlauea, Anahola, Kapa'a, Wailua, Hanamā'ulu, Līhu'e, Puhi, Kōloa, Po'ipū, Kalāheo, Lāwa'i, 'Ele'ele, Hanapēpē, Waimea, Kekaha, Mānā, Hā'ena S.P., NĀ PALI COAST S.P., WAIMEA CANYON S.P., KŌKE'E S.P., Wai'ale'ale 5,148, Kawaikini 5,243, MAKALEHA MTS.

0 5 10 mi / 0 5 10 km

© MQST

HAWAI'I

'Upolu Point, Hāwī, Hala'ula, Kapa'au, Makapala, Kukuihaele, Honoka'a, Pa'auilo, Laupāhoehoe, Nīnole, Waimea (Kamuela), Puakō, Waikoloa Village, Pu'uanahulu, Kailua-Kona, Hōlualoa, Honalo, Kealakekua, Captain Cook, Kēōkea, Ho'okena, Miloli'i, Pāpā, Wai'ōhinu, Nā'ālehu, Pāhala, Wood Valley, Volcano, Hilo, Kea'au, Kurtistown, Mountain View, Glenwood, Pāhoa, Kapoho, Kaimū, Kalapana, Kehena, Mauna Kea 13,796, Mauna Loa 13,677, Ka Lae (South Cape), PACIFIC OCEAN

0 10 20 mi / 0 10 20 km

© MQST

O'AHU

Kahuku Pt., Kawela Bay, Kahuku, Sunset Beach, Waimea, Pūpūkea, Lā'ie, Hau'ula, Punalu'u, Hale'iwa, Waialua, Kahana, Ka'a'awa, Wahiawā, Whitmore Village, Waikāne, Kahalu'u, Mililani Town, Waipi'o Acres, 'Āhuimanu, He'eia, Kāne'ohe, Kailua, Waimānalo, Waimānalo Beach, Pearl City, Waipahu, Waimalu, Mākaha, Wai'anae, Mā'ili, Nānākuli, Makakilo City, Honokai Hale, Kapolei, 'Ewa Villages, 'Ewa Beach, Barbers Pt., Honolulu, Makapu'u Pt., PACIFIC OCEAN

0 2 4 6 mi / 0 2 4 6 km

© MAPQUEST

MAUI-MOLOKA'I-LĀNA'I

Moloka'i, Kalaupapa, Kualapu'u, Maunaloa, Kaunakakai, Hālawa, Waialua, Pūko'o, Kamakou 4,970, Lāna'i, Lāna'i City, Kaumalapau, Lāna'ihale 3,370, Honokōhau, Kahana, Kā'anapali, Lahaina, Wailuku, Kahului, Pā'ia, Ha'ikū, Huelo, Ke'anae, Pukalani, Makawao, Kīhei, Kama'ole, Mākena, Hāna, Kīpahulu, Kaupō, 'Ulupalakua, Molokini, Kaho'olawe, Pu'u'ula'ula (Red Hill) 10,023, PACIFIC OCEAN

0 5 10 15 mi / 0 5 10 15 20 km

© MQST

Arizona

nevada 46
utah 64
california 22
mexico 82
AZ 100

PAHRANAGAT N.W.R.
DIXIE NATL. FOR.
ZION NATL. PARK
13
GRAND STAIRCASE-ESCALANTE NATL. MON.
GLEN CANYON NATL. REC. AREA
Hovenweep Natl. Mon.
PAIUTE IND. RES.
St. George
Hurricane
Kanab
L. Powell
Rainbow Bridge Natl. Mon.
Navajo Mtn. 10,388
NAVAJO NATION IND. RES.
Mexican Hat
Four Corners Mon.
MONUMENT VALLEY
PACIFIC TIME ZONE
MOUNTAIN TIME ZONE
+ Mormon Pk. 7,411
UTAH
Colorado City
Fredonia
KAIBAB IND. RES.
Pipe Spring Natl. Mon.
VERMILION CLIFFS NATL. MON.
Glen Canyon Dam
Navajo Bridge
Page
MONUMENT VALLEY NAVAJO TRIBAL PARK
Teec Nos Pos
Mexican Water
Dennehotso
Pastora Pk. 9,412
Rock Point
Littlefield
Mesquite
Mt. Bangs 8,012
SHIVWITS PLATEAU
NEVADA
MOAPA RIVER IND. RES.
Glendale
Marble Canyon
Jacob Lake
Bitter Springs
Kaibito
Navajo Natl. Mon.
Shonto
Kayenta
Round Rock
Lukachukai
KAIBAB NATL. FOR.
White Mesa Natural Bridge
Mt. Trumbull
Mt. Trumbull 8,029
Nellis A.F.B.
B
LAKE MEAD NATL. REC. AREA
90
Las Vegas
Henderson
11
GRAND CANYON NATL. PARK
House Rock Buffalo Ranch
Pt. Imperial 8,803
North Rim
GRAND CANYON-PARASHANT NATL. MON.
Supai
HAVASUPAI IND. RES.
Grand Canyon
Tusayan Ruin and Mus.
Tusayan
Tonalea
Cow Springs
NAVAJO NATION IND. RES.
Rough Rock
Many Farms
Tsaile
Chinle
CANYON DE CHELLY NATL. MON.
White House Ruins
Tuba City
Moenkopi
HOPI
Pinon
Hoover Dam
LAKE MEAD NATL. REC. AREA
Boulder City
Meadview
GRAND CANYON NATL. PARK
Joshua Tree Forest
Red L.
Natural Bridge
HUALAPAI IND. RES.
KAIBAB NATL. FOR.
Cameron
PAINTED DESERT
Hotevilla
Kykotsmovi
IND. RES.
Hopi Cultural Center
Polacca
Second Mesa
Keams Canyon
Hubbell Trading Post Natl. Hist. Site
Ganado
Fort Defiance
St. Michaels
C
Dolan Springs
Mt. Tipton 7,148
Truxton
Grand Canyon Caverns
Peach Springs
Gray Mountain
WUPATKI NATL. MON.
Grand Falls
Mohave
LAKE MEAD N.R.A.
Hackberry
Valentine
Seligman
Ash Fork
Williams
Parks
KAIBAB NATL. FOR.
Humphreys Pk. 12,633
Sunset Crater Volcano Natl. Mon.
Flagstaff
Leupp
Bidahochi
Lupton
Chambers
Sanders
Laughlin
Bullhead City
Kingman
Bellemont
CAMP NAVAJO
Mountainaire
Walnut Canyon Natl. Mon.
Leupp Corner
Homolovi Ruins S.P.
Painted Desert Visitor Ctr.
D
FORT MOJAVE IND. RES.
Mohave Valley
Hualapai Pk. 8,417
Pine Springs
Bill Williams Mtn. 9,256
COCONINO
Oak Creek Canyon
Slide Rock S.P.
Munds Park
Meteor Crater Natural Landmark
Winslow
Joseph City
Holbrook
Sun Valley
PETRIFIED FOREST NATL. PARK
ZUNI
Needles
HAVASU
Yucca
Hide Creek Mtn. 7,272
Paulden
PRESCOTT
Tuzigoot Natl. Mon.
Sedona
Red Rock S.P.
Mormon L.
Mormon Lake
Chino Valley
Clarkdale
Jerome
Jerome S.H.P.
Cottonwood
NATL.
Happy Jack
ZUNI IND. RES.
Topock
Wikieup
Prescott Valley
Lake Montezuma
Montezuma Castle Natl. Mon.
Fort Verde S.H.P.
FOR.
St. Johns
Lyman Lake
Lake Havasu City
CHEMEHUEVI IND. RES.
London Bridge
Bagdad
Prescott
Skull Valley
Kirkland
Kirkland Junction
Dewey
Camp Verde
Strawberry
SITGREAVES
Heber
Snowflake
Taylor
Clay Springs
Fool Hollow Lake Rec. Area
Concho
E
Lake Havasu S.P.
Cattail Cove S.P.
Parker Dam
Bill Williams
Alamo L.
Wilhoit
Mayer
Towers Mtn. 7,528
Arcosanti
FOR.
Pine
Tonto Natural Bridge S.P.
Payson
Star Valley
NATL. FOR.
Show Low
Pinetop-Lakeside
Springerville
Eagar
Vidal Junction
Parker
Buckskin Mountain S.P.
Alamo Lake S.P.
Yarnell
Congress
Wagoner
AGUA FRIA NATL. MON.
Rye
FORT APACHE
Cibecue
Young
Greer
COLORADO RIVER IND. RES.
Poston
Bouse
Aguila
Forepaugh
Wickenburg
Black Canyon City
Mazatzal Pk. 7,888
TONTO
Carrizo
McNary
Mt. Baldy 11,403
Nutrioso
Alpine
CALIF.
F
Salome
Wenden
Morristown
Wittmann
Pleasant
New River
Cave Creek
Carefree
Aztec Pk. 7,694
Theodore Roosevelt L.
IND. RES.
Whiteriver
Fort Apache
APACHE
Blythe
Quartzsite
Brenda
Hope
Pioneer Ariz. Living Hist. Mus.
Sun City
96
FORT MCDOWELL I.R.
Fountain Hills
NATL.
Roosevelt
Salt River Canyon
Ehrenberg
Tonopah
Glendale
SALT RIVER I.R.
Scottsdale
Mesa
Tonto Natl. Mon.
Lost Dutchman S.P.
Apache Jct.
Miami
Globe
SAN CARLOS IND. RES.
NATL. FOR.
PACIFIC TIME ZONE
MOUNTAIN TIME ZONE
CIBOLA N.W.R.
Palm Canyon
KOFA N.W.R.
Palo Verde
Buckeye
Phoenix
Tempe
Chandler
Superior
Boyce Thompson Arboretum S.P.
San Carlos
Peridot
Maple Pk. 8,29
G
YUMA
Imperial N.W.R.
+ Castle Dome Pk. 3,788
Komatke
GILA RIVER IND. RES.
Sun Lakes
Florence Junction
Bylas
Clifton
Painted Rocks Petroglyph Site
SONORAN
Maricopa
MARICOPA (AK-CHIN) I.R.
Ak-Chin
Casa Grande
Sacaton
Florence
McFarland S.H.P.
Casa Grande Ruins Natl. Mon.
Kearny
Hayden
Winkelman
San Carlos L.
Fort Thomas
GILA BOX RIPARIAN NATL. CONS. AREA
Morenci
Guthrie
Martinez Lake
PROVING GROUND
Hyder
Sentinel
Gila Bend
Paloma
DESERT
Coolidge
Dudleyville
CORONADO
Pima
Safford
Thatcher
Fort Yuma Ind. Res.
Dome
Wellton
Tacna
Mohawk
Dateland
NATL. MON.
Table Top Mtn. 4,373
Arizona City
Eloy
Picacho
Table Mtn. 6,158
Mt. Graham 10,713
Roper Lake S.P.
Swift Trail Junction
Duncan
H
Somerton
Yuma
Cocopah Ind. Res.
San Luis
BARRY M. GOLDWATER AIR FORCE RANGE
Picacho Peak S.P.
Biosphere 2
Mammoth
Oracle
Oracle S.P.
San Manuel
CORONADO NATL. FOR.
Bonita
YUMA DESERT
Kaka
North Komelik
Red Rock
Catalina
Catalina S.P.
CORONADO
Mt. Lemmon 9,157
Cochise Visitor Ctr. & Chiricahua Regional Mus.
San Luis Río Colorado
Ajo
Hickiwan
Santa Rosa
IRONWOOD FOREST NATL. MON.
Marana
Cortaro
SAGUARO NATL. PARK
Oro Valley
Cascabel
Willcox
Bowie
CABEZA PRIETA NATL. WILDLIFE REFUGE
Why
TOHONO O'ODHAM NATION
Tucson
South Tucson
Mission San Xavier del Bac
SAGUARO NATL. PARK
Dos Cabezas
Fort Bowie Natl. Hist. Site
U.S. MEXICO
ORGAN PIPE CACTUS NATL. MON.
Quijotoa
Schuchk
Three Points
TOHONO O'ODHAM (SAN XAVIER) IND. RES.
Vail
Colossal Cave
Cochise
CHIRICAHUA NATL. MON.
CORONADO
Cochise Stronghold 8,109
DESIERTO DE ALTAR
Pisinimo
IND. RES.
Haivana Nakya
Sahuarita
Green Valley
Dragoon
CORONADO N.F.
J
Sonoyta
Lukeville
Ali Chuk
Sells
Kitt Peak Natl. Observatory
Continental
Kartchner Caverns S.P.
Benson
St. David
Sunizona
Chiricahua Pk. 9,796
NATL.
Golfo de Santa Clara
Baboquivari Pk. 7,730
BUENOS AIRES N.W.R.
Amado
Mt. Wrightson 9,453
LAS CIENEGAS N.C.A.
SAN PEDRO RIPARIAN N.C.A.
Tombstone
Tombstone Courthouse S.H.P.
Elfrida
Apache FOR.
SONORA
San Miguel
Tubac Presidio
FORT HUACHUCA MIL. RES.
Huachuca City
McNeal
Quitovac
Sasabe
Tumacacori
Tumacácori Natl. Hist. Park
Rio Rico
Patagonia
Patagonia Lake S.P.
Sierra Vista
Bisbee
Pirtleville
Douglas
San Bernardino N.W.R.
K
CORONADO
Nogales
NATL. FOR.
Lavender Pit
Queen Mine
Naco
CORONADO NATL. MEM.
Puerto Peñasco
Nogales
Agua Prieta
GULF OF CALIFORNIA
San Felipe
© MAPQUEST

1 2 3 4 5 6 7

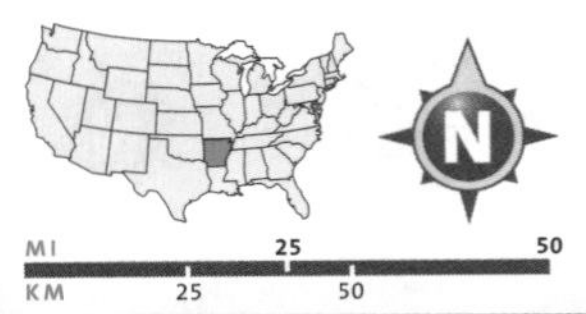

MISSOURI

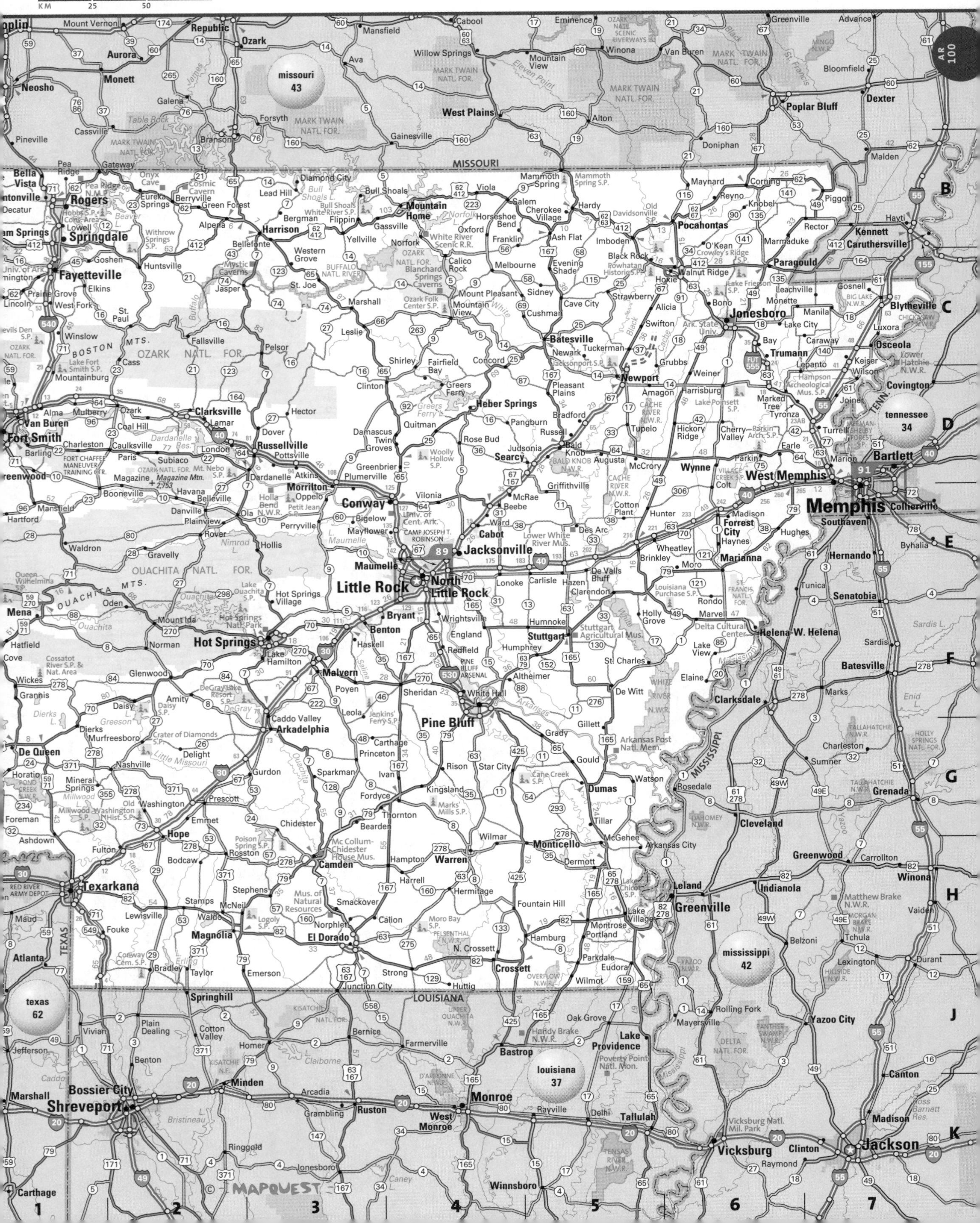

missouri 43

tennessee 34

mississippi 42

louisiana 37

texas 62

LOUISIANA

TEXAS

MISSISSIPPI

Little Rock

North Little Rock

Memphis

Fort Smith

Fayetteville

Springdale

Rogers

Jonesboro

Pine Bluff

Hot Springs

Texarkana

El Dorado

Conway

Jacksonville

Russellville

Searcy

Shreveport

Monroe

Jackson

Vicksburg

Greenville

West Memphis

Blytheville

Harrison

Mountain Home

Batesville

Arkadelphia

Camden

Magnolia

Hope

Helena-W. Helena

Stuttgart

Clarksville

MARK TWAIN NATL. FOR.

OZARK NATL. FOR.

OUACHITA NATL. FOR.

BOSTON MTS.

OUACHITA MTS.

AR 100

© MAPQUEST

B C D E F G H J K

1 2 3 4 5 6 7

MI 30 60
KM 30 60

CA 100
idaho 30
oregon 59
nevada 46
IDAHO
NEVADA
OREGON
GREAT BASIN
PACIFIC OCEAN
COAST RANGES
SIERRA NEVADA
Sacramento
San Francisco
Oakland
San Jose
Reno
Sparks
Carson City
Redding
Chico
Eureka
Santa Rosa
Stockton
Modesto
Klamath Falls
Winnemucca
Elko
Susanville
Yreka
Ukiah
Fort Bragg
Fallon
South Lake Tahoe
Yosemite Natl. Park

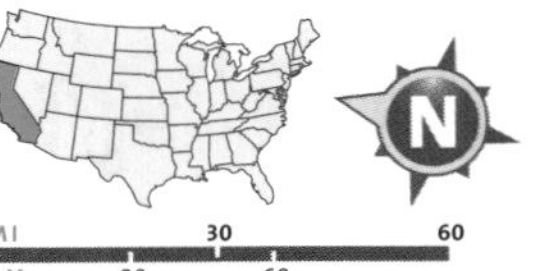

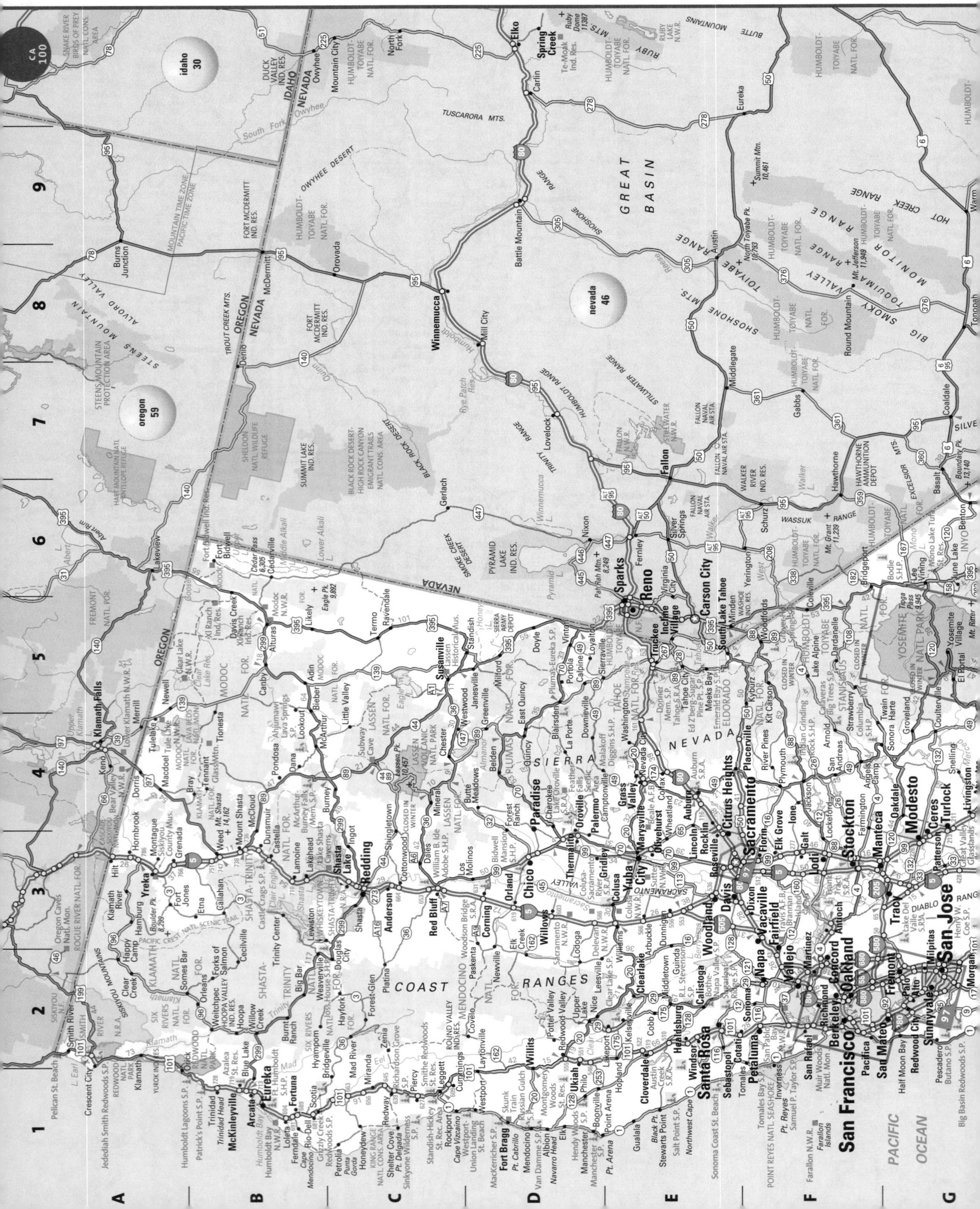

TRAVEL NOTE: California has started numbering freeway exits using a mileage-based numbering system (shown here). Full implementation is expected to take several years.
PACIFIC OCEAN
MOJAVE DESERT
NEVADA
arizona 20
mexico 82
CA 100
BAJA CALIF.
Gulf of Santa Catalina
Los Angeles
San Diego
Las Vegas
Henderson
Bakersfield
Fresno
Salinas
Monterey
Santa Barbara
Ventura
Oxnard
Long Beach
Anaheim
Riverside
San Bernardino
Palm Springs
Indio
Tijuana
Mexicali
Calexico
El Centro
Yuma
Blythe
Barstow
Victorville
Lancaster
Palmdale
Visalia
Tulare
San Luis Obispo
Santa Maria
Lompoc
Oceanside
Escondido
Needles
Bullhead City
Lake Havasu City
DEATH VALLEY NATL. PARK
DESERT NATIONAL WILDLIFE RANGE
NELLIS AIR FORCE RANGE COMPLEX
CHINA LAKE NAVAL AIR WEAPONS STATION
FORT IRWIN NATL. TRAINING CENTER
EDWARDS A.F.B.
VANDENBERG A.F.B.
CHANNEL ISLANDS NATL. PARK
Santa Catalina Island
San Clemente I.
San Nicolas Island
© MAPQUEST

Colorado

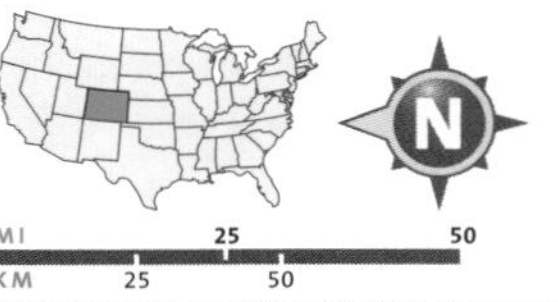

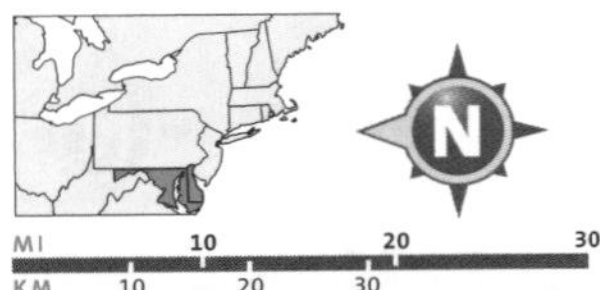

ATLANTIC OCEAN

© MAPQUEST

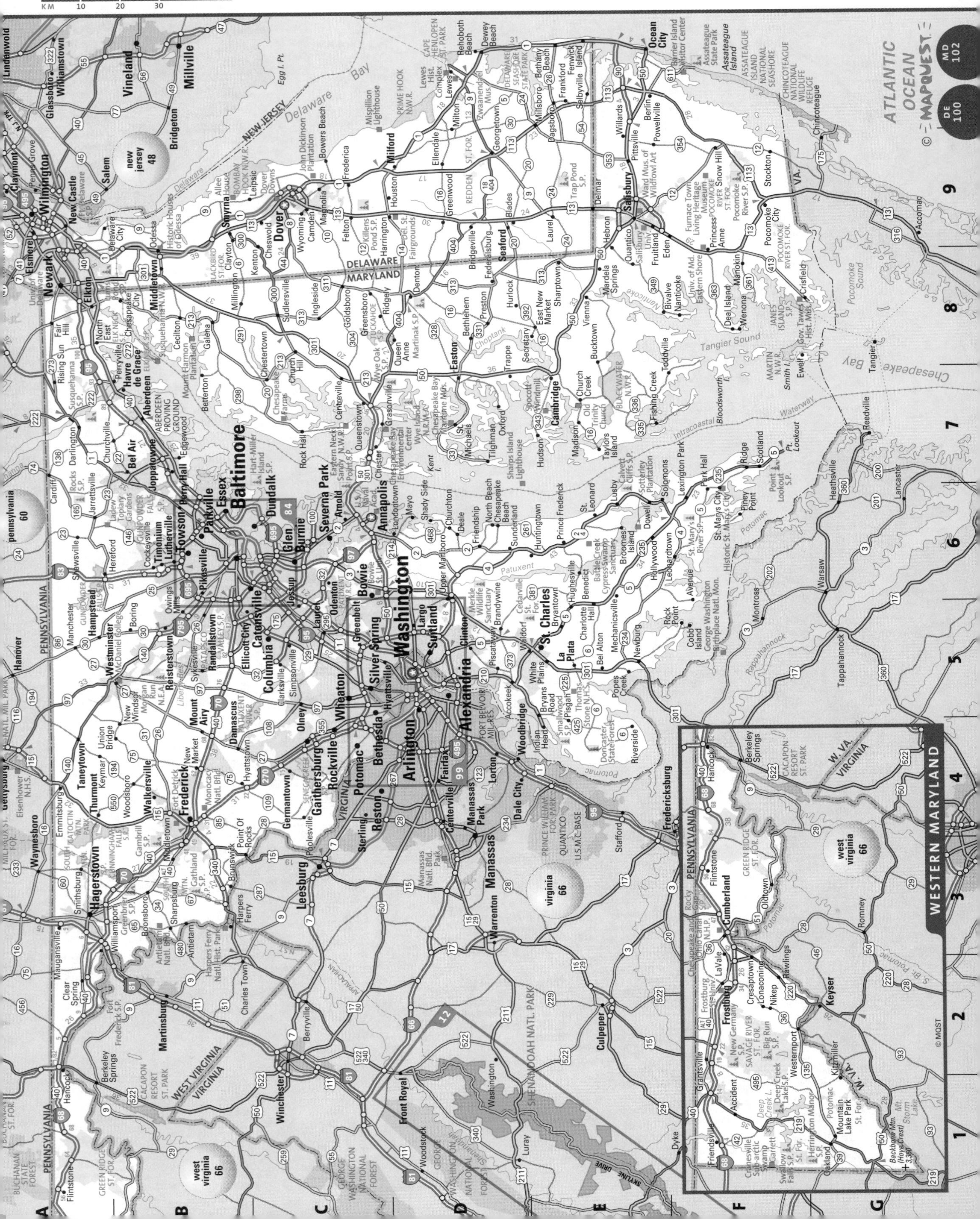

DE 100

MD 102

Delaware Bay

Chesapeake Bay

DELAWARE

MARYLAND

NEW JERSEY

PENNSYLVANIA

VIRGINIA

WEST VIRGINIA

new jersey 48

pennsylvania 60

west virginia 66

virginia 66

Baltimore

Washington

Annapolis

Dover

Wilmington

Salisbury

Ocean City

Frederick

Hagerstown

Cumberland

WESTERN MARYLAND

© MOST

Conn., Mass. & Rhode Island

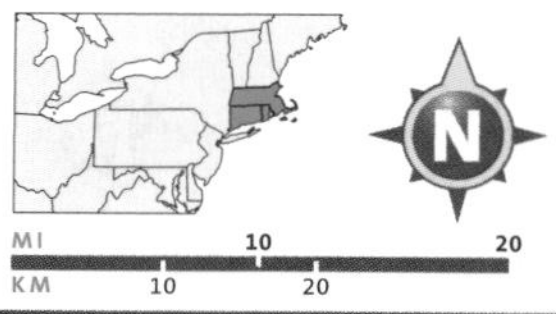

MI 10 20
KM 10 20

RI 105
MA 102
CT 100
vermont 47
new hampshire 47
new york 50

Long Island Sound

Block Island Sound

RI 105
MA 102
CT 100

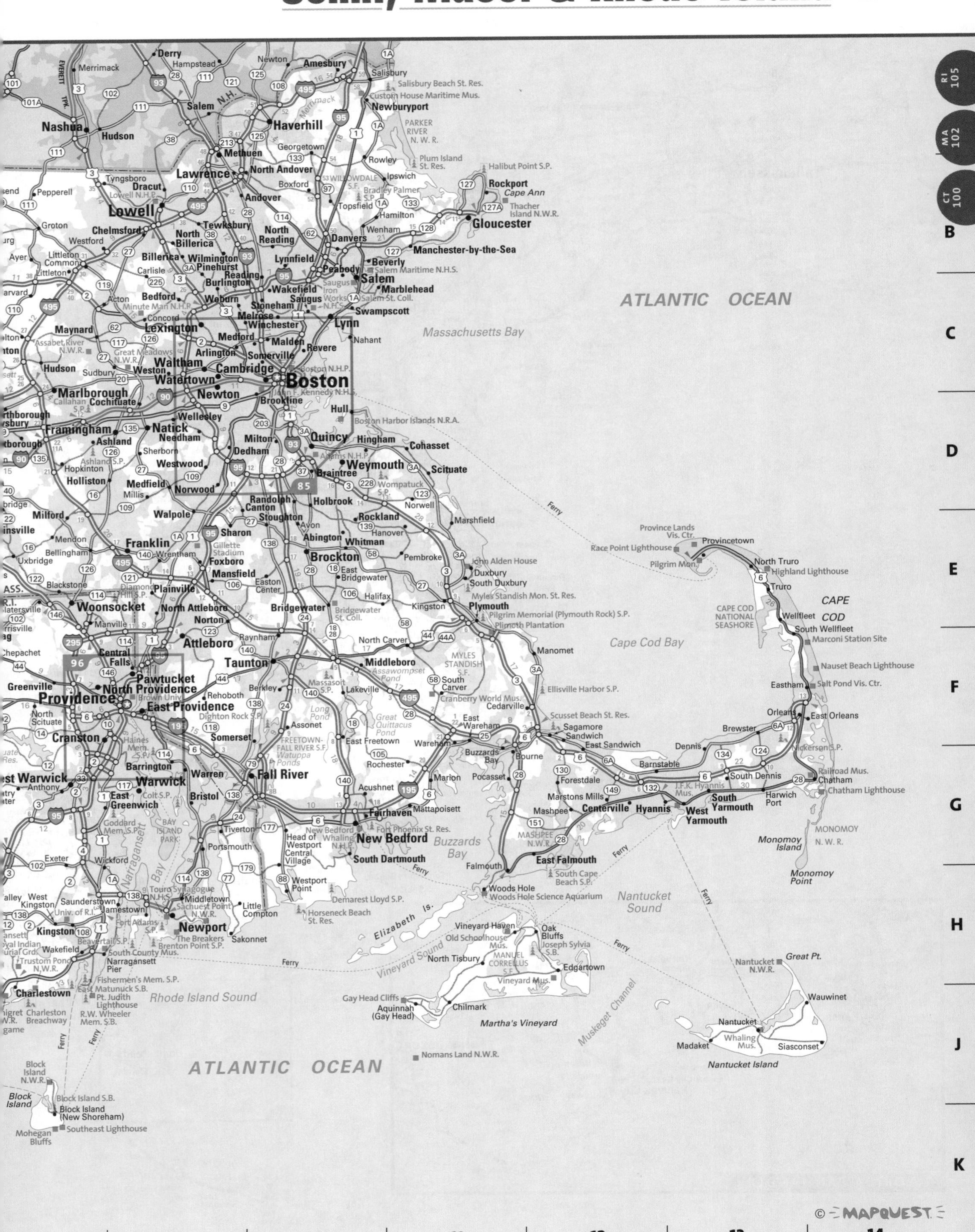

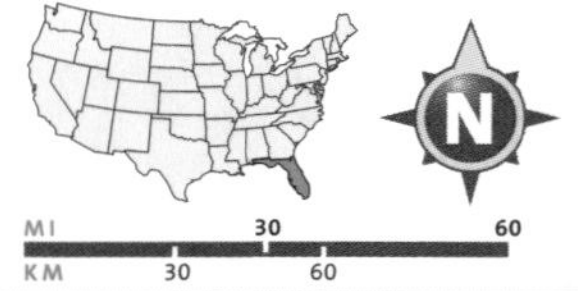

FL 101

georgia 29

ALA. GEORGIA

ATLANTIC OCEAN

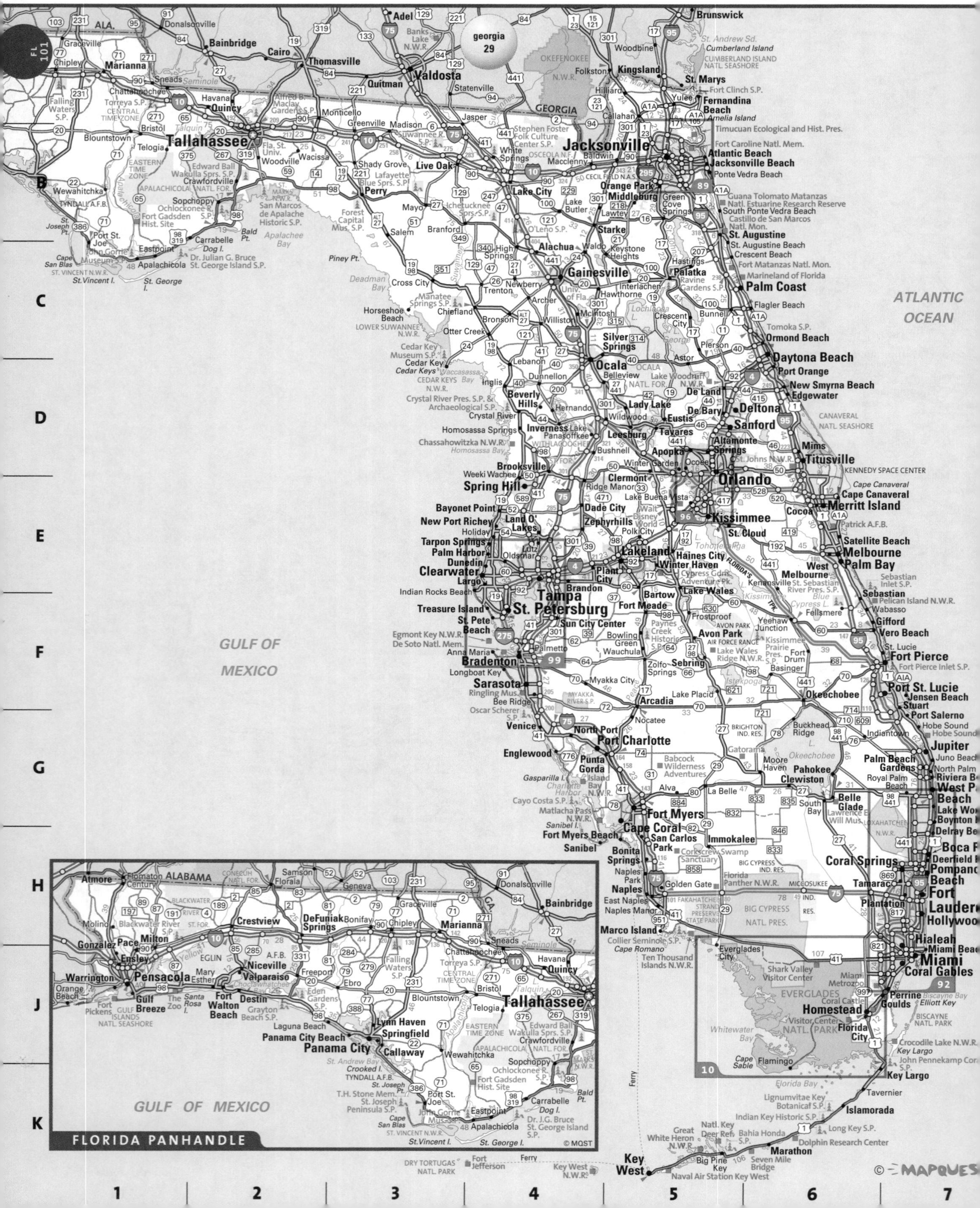

GULF OF MEXICO

Adel, Valdosta, Thomasville, Bainbridge, Cairo, Donalsonville, Quitman, Statenville, Folkston, Kingsland, St. Marys, Brunswick, Woodbine, Cumberland Island, Cumberland Island Natl. Seashore, Okefenokee N.W.R., Banks Lake N.W.R.

Graceville, Chipley, Marianna, Sneads, Chattahoochee, Falling Waters S.P., Torreya S.P., Central Time Zone, Eastern Time Zone, Havana, Quincy, Bristol, Blountstown, Telogia, Tallahassee, Monticello, Greenville, Madison, Jasper, Wewahitchka, Tyndall A.F.B., Port St. Joe, Cape San Blas, St. Vincent I., Apalachicola, Eastpoint, Carrabelle, Sopchoppy, Crawfordville, Wakulla Sprs. S.P., Woodville, Wacissa, Perry, Shady Grove, Live Oak, Mayo, Salem, Branford, Apalachee Bay, Dog I., St. George I., Piney Pt.

Fernandina Beach, Amelia Island, Yulee, Hilliard, Callahan, Jacksonville, Atlantic Beach, Jacksonville Beach, Ponte Vedra Beach, Baldwin, Macclenny, Lake City, White Springs, Orange Park, Middleburg, Green Cove Springs, Lake Butler, Starke, Keystone Heights, St. Augustine, St. Augustine Beach, Crescent Beach, Hastings, Palatka, Marineland of Florida, Palm Coast, Flagler Beach, Bunnell, Ormond Beach, Daytona Beach, Port Orange, New Smyrna Beach, Edgewater

Gainesville, Alachua, High Springs, Newberry, Trenton, Archer, Williston, Cross City, Horseshoe Beach, Chiefland, Bronson, Otter Creek, Cedar Key, Inglis, Crystal River, Homosassa Springs, Beverly Hills, Inverness, Dunnellon, Ocala, Belleview, Silver Springs, Interlachen, Crescent City, Pierson, Astor, De Land, Deltona, Sanford, Lady Lake, Wildwood, Leesburg, Eustis, Tavares, Apopka, Altamonte Springs, Winter Garden, Orlando, Titusville, Kennedy Space Center, Canaveral Natl. Seashore, Cape Canaveral, Merritt Island, Cocoa, Kissimmee, St. Cloud, Clermont, Brooksville, Weeki Wachee, Spring Hill, Dade City, Zephyrhills, Lakeland, Haines City, Winter Haven, Plant City, Brandon

Bayonet Point, New Port Richey, Holiday, Tarpon Springs, Palm Harbor, Dunedin, Clearwater, Largo, Indian Rocks Beach, Treasure Island, St. Pete Beach, Tampa, St. Petersburg, Sun City Center, Bradenton, Anna Maria, Longboat Key, Sarasota, Bee Ridge, Oscar Scherer S.P., Venice, Englewood, North Port, Port Charlotte, Punta Gorda, Arcadia, Nocatee, Myakka City, Bartow, Fort Meade, Wauchula, Bowling Green, Zolfo Springs, Sebring, Avon Park, Frostproof, Lake Wales, Lake Placid, Melbourne, West Melbourne, Palm Bay, Satellite Beach, Patrick A.F.B., Sebastian, Fellsmere, Gifford, Vero Beach, Fort Pierce, Port St. Lucie, Jensen Beach, Stuart, Port Salerno, Hobe Sound, Okeechobee, Lake Okeechobee, Buckhead Ridge

Jupiter, Juno Beach, Palm Beach Gardens, North Palm Beach, Riviera Beach, Royal Palm Beach, West Palm Beach, Lake Worth, Boynton Beach, Delray Beach, Boca Raton, Deerfield Beach, Pompano Beach, Coral Springs, Tamarac, Fort Lauderdale, Plantation, Hollywood, Hialeah, Miami, Miami Beach, Coral Gables, Perrine, Goulds, Homestead, Florida City, Key Largo, Tavernier, Islamorada, Marathon, Big Pine Key, Key West, Dry Tortugas Natl. Park, Everglades Natl. Park, Big Cypress Natl. Pres., Flamingo, Cape Sable, Florida Bay

Belle Glade, South Bay, Pahokee, Clewiston, Moore Haven, La Belle, Alva, Immokalee, Fort Myers, Cape Coral, Fort Myers Beach, Sanibel, San Carlos Park, Bonita Springs, Naples Park, Naples, East Naples, Naples Manor, Golden Gate, Marco Island, Everglades City, Ten Thousand Islands N.W.R., Cape Romano

FLORIDA PANHANDLE

Atmore, Flomaton, Century, Samson, Geneva, Florala, Crestview, Milton, DeFuniak Springs, Bonifay, Pace, Gonzalez, Ensley, Warrington, Pensacola, Gulf Breeze, Orange Beach, Navarre, Mary Esther, Fort Walton Beach, Destin, Niceville, Valparaiso, Eglin A.F.B., Freeport, Ebro, Laguna Beach, Panama City Beach, Panama City, Lynn Haven, Springfield, Callaway, Gulf Islands Natl. Seashore

GULF OF MEXICO

© MQST

1 2 3 4 5 6 7

B C D E F G H J K

N
MI
25
50
KM
25
50

Chattanooga
Dalton
Rome
Cartersville
Marietta
Roswell
Gainesville
Athens
Atlanta
Conyers
Newnan
Peachtree City
Griffin
LaGrange
Columbus
Phenix City
Macon
Warner Robins
Milledgeville
Dublin
Americus
Cordele
Albany
Tifton
Valdosta
Thomasville
Bainbridge
Moultrie
Waycross
Brunswick
Jesup
Hinesville
Savannah
Statesboro
Augusta
Aiken
Columbia
Greenville
Spartanburg
Anderson
Tallahassee
Jacksonville
Dothan
Eufaula
alabama 18
south carolina 52
florida 28
OKEFENOKEE N.W.R.
FORT BENNING MIL. RES.
FORT STEWART MIL. RES.
CHATTAHOOCHEE NATL. FOR.
OCONEE NATL. FOR.
SUMTER NATL. FOR.
U.S. DEPT. OF ENERGY SAVANNAH RIVER SITE
ATLANTIC OCEAN
ALABAMA
FLORIDA
© MAPQUEST
B
C
D
E
F
G
H
J
K
1
2
3
4
5
6
7

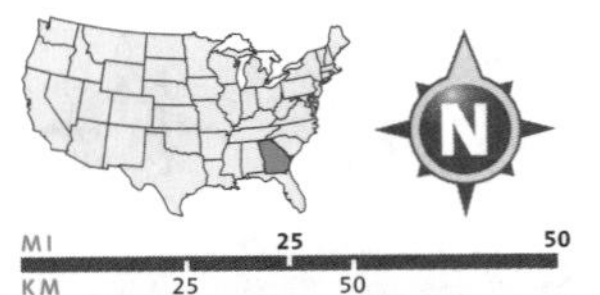

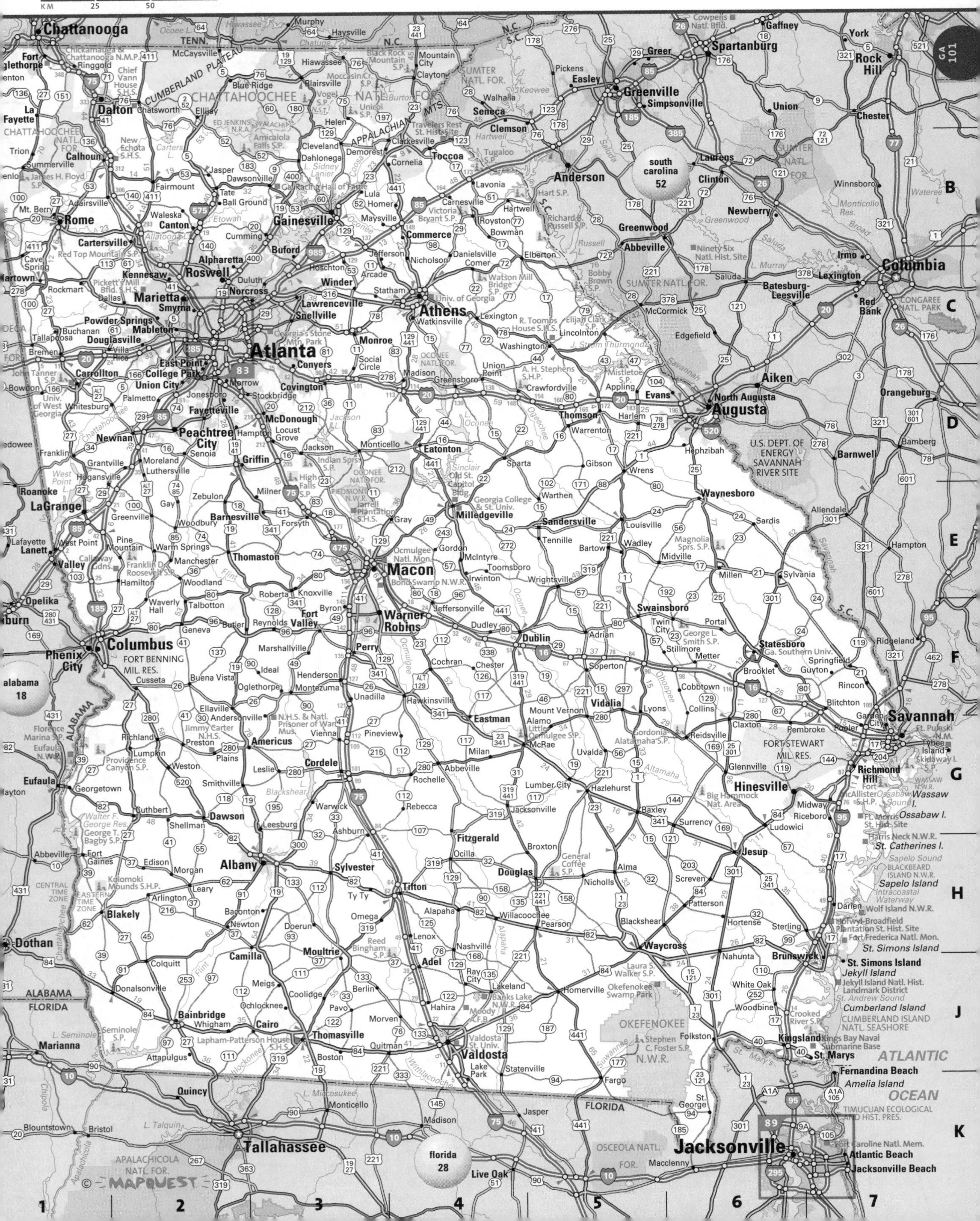

Idaho

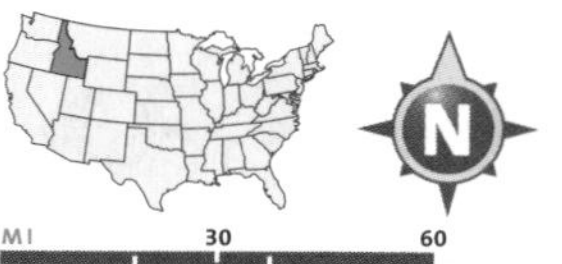

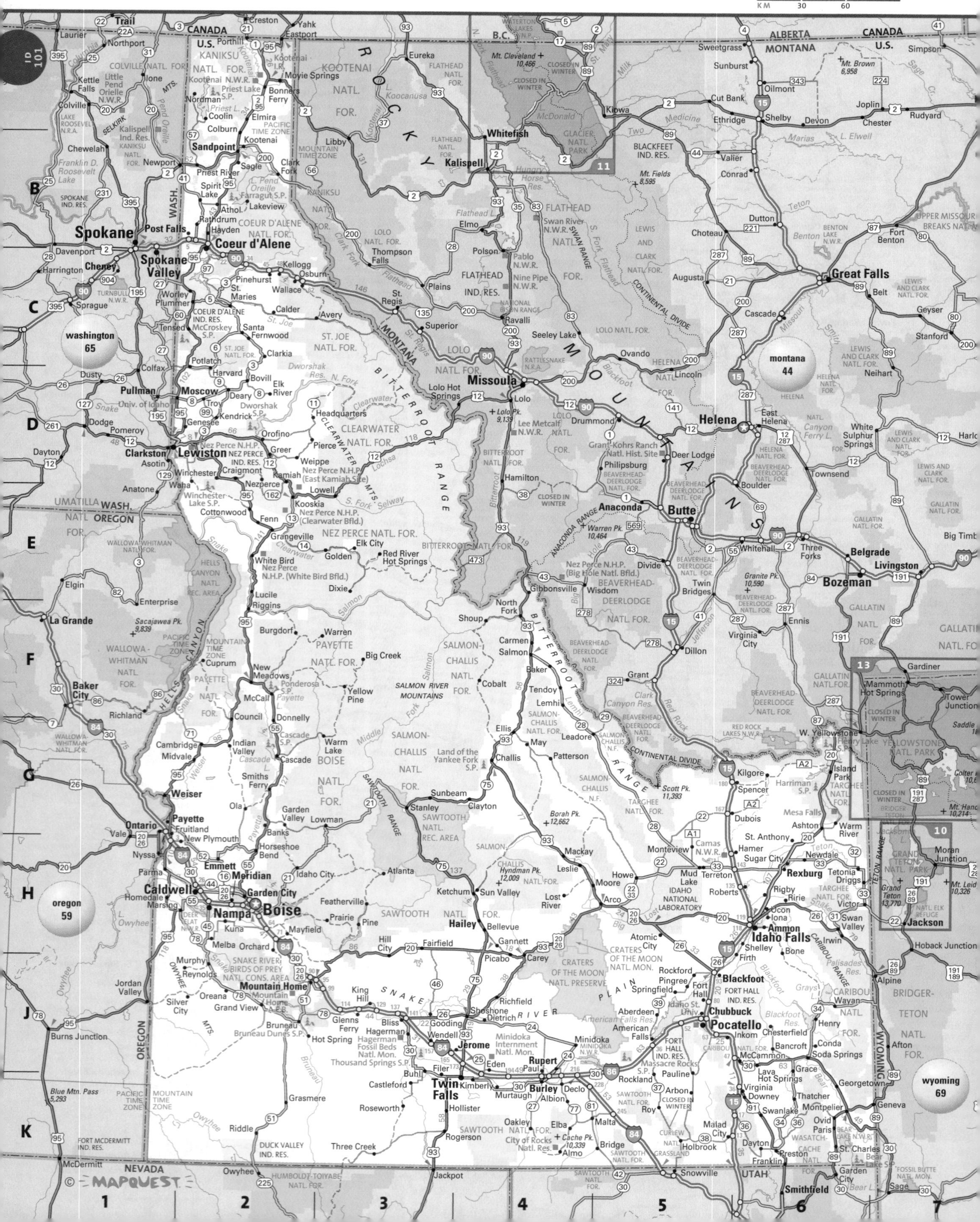

ID 101

washington 65

montana 44

oregon 59

wyoming 69

11

13

10

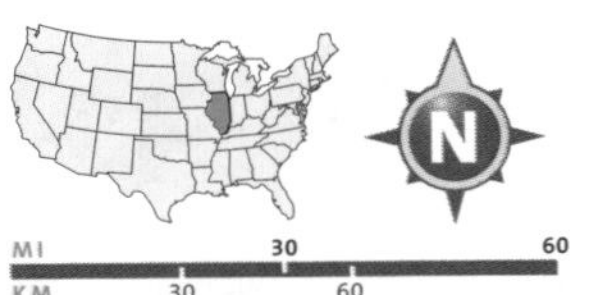

Janesville
Beloit
Kenosha
LAKE MICHIGAN
Waukegan
North Chicago
Highland Park
Rockford
Freeport
Dubuque
Waterloo
Cedar Rapids
Iowa City
Davenport
Rock Island
Moline
Elgin
DeKalb
Aurora
Naperville
Joliet
Chicago
Evanston
Gary
Michigan City
Valparaiso
Benton Harbor
St. Joseph
Kankakee
Peoria
Bloomington
Normal
Champaign
Urbana
Danville
Galesburg
Quincy
Hannibal
Springfield
Decatur
Jacksonville
Mattoon
Charleston
Terre Haute
Lafayette
Effingham
Vandalia
Alton
St. Louis
Belleville
East St. Louis
Granite City
Columbia
Jefferson City
Centralia
Mount Vernon
Carbondale
Marion
Cape Girardeau
Paducah
Evansville
Owensboro
Henderson
Vincennes
iowa 33
missouri 43
indiana 32
kentucky 34
MAPQUEST
1 2 3 4 5 6 7
B C D E F G H J K

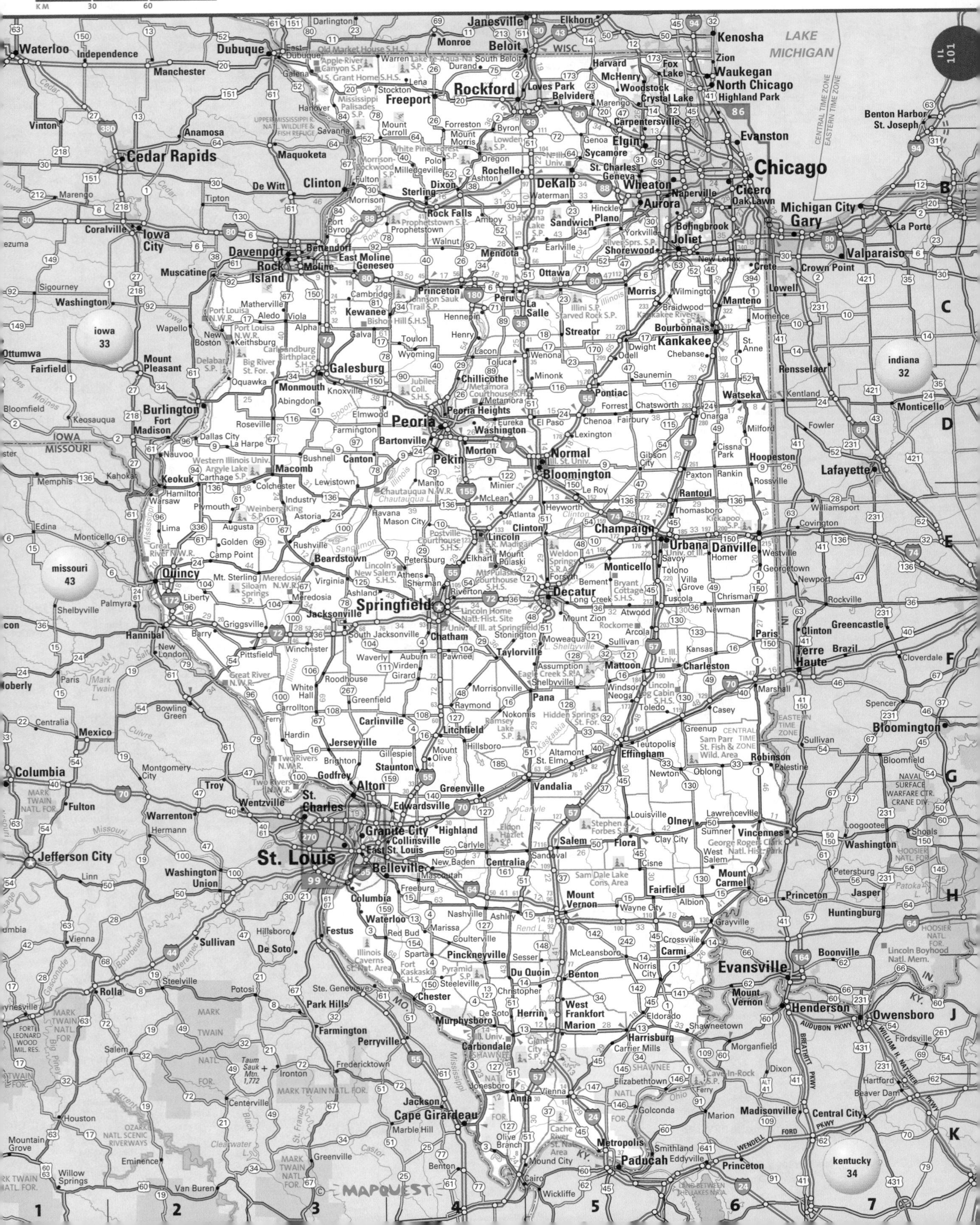

Indiana

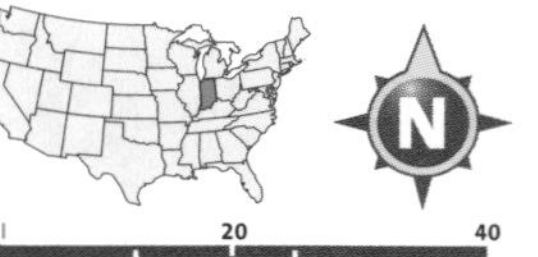

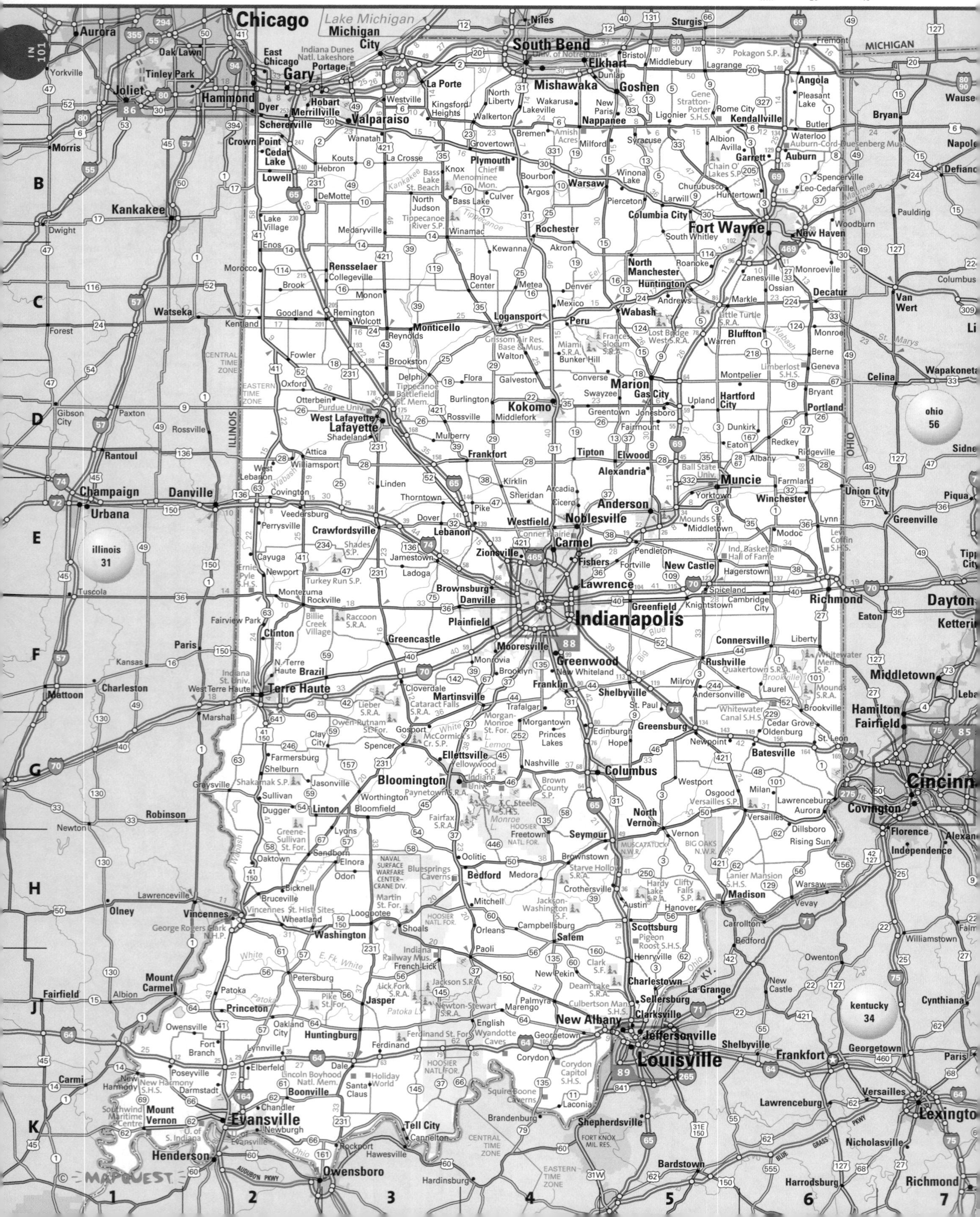

MI 25 50
KM 25 50
N
Des Moines
W. Des Moines
Cedar Rapids
Iowa City
Davenport
Bettendorf
Rock Island
Moline
Dubuque
Waterloo
Cedar Falls
Sioux City
Council Bluffs
Omaha
Lincoln
Ames
Ankeny
Mason City
Fort Dodge
Marshalltown
Ottumwa
Burlington
Clinton
Muscatine
Keokuk
Fort Madison
Sioux Falls
La Crosse
Albert Lea
Austin
Worthington
Spencer
Storm Lake
Le Mars
Carroll
Denison
Atlantic
Creston
Red Oak
Shenandoah
Clarinda
Centerville
Oskaloosa
Pella
Newton
Grinnell
Knoxville
Indianola
Waverly
Charles City
Decorah
Independence
Manchester
Maquoketa
Anamosa
Marion
Hiawatha
Coralville
Washington
Mount Pleasant
Fairfield
Kirksville
Galesburg
Macomb
Maryville
Nebraska City
Fremont
MINNESOTA
MISSOURI
S. DAK.
NEBR.
WIS.
ILL.
illinois 31
missouri 43
nebraska 45
minnesota 39
south dakota 55
68
IA 101
© MAPQUEST
A B C D E F G
1 2 3 4 5 6 7 8 9

Kentucky & Tennessee

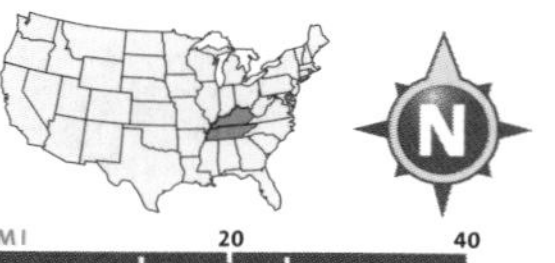

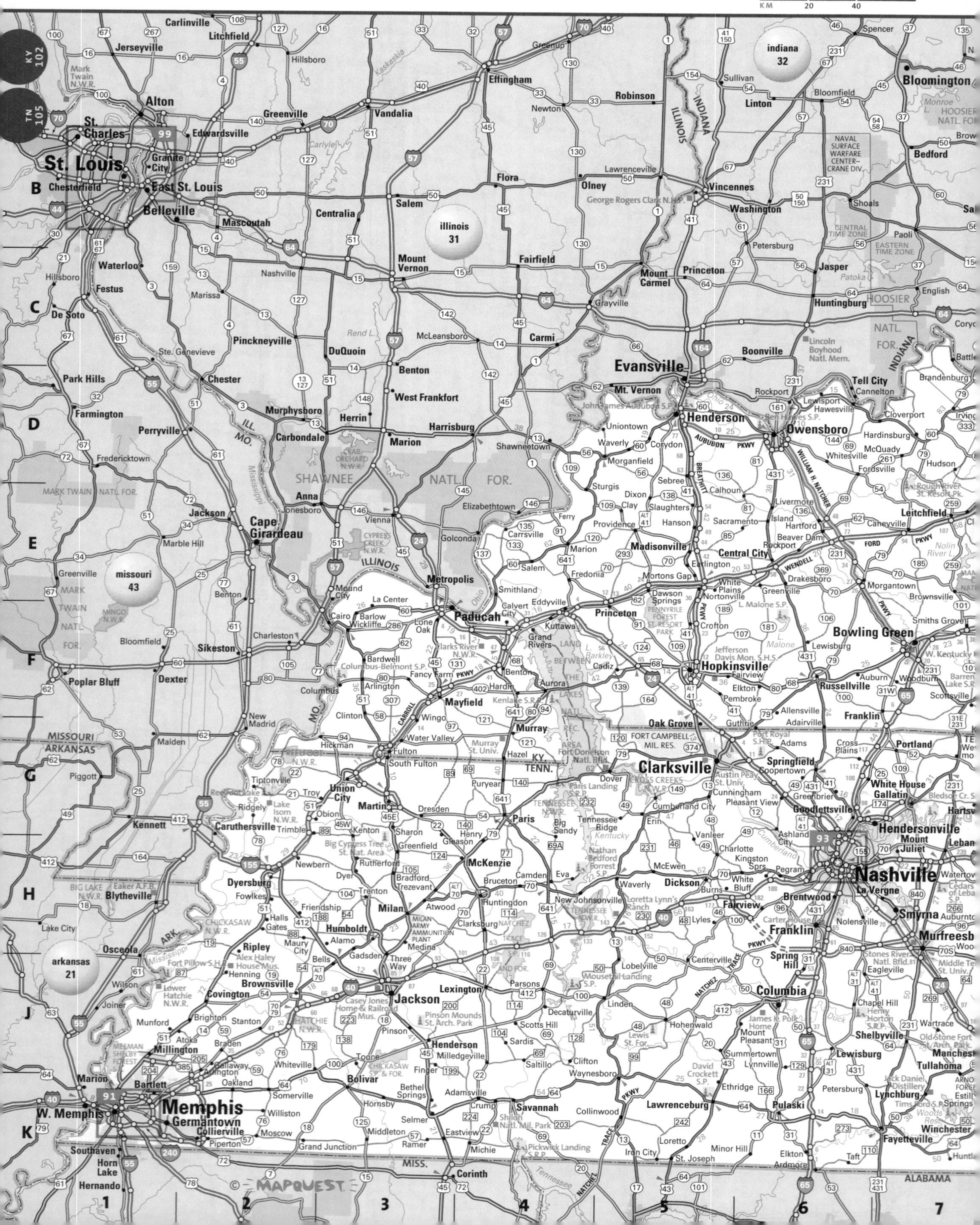

KY 102
TN 105
illinois 31
indiana 32
missouri 43
arkansas 21

St. Louis
East St. Louis
Alton
Belleville
Effingham
Vandalia
Centralia
Salem
Mount Vernon
Carbondale
Marion
Cape Girardeau
Paducah
Evansville
Henderson
Owensboro
Vincennes
Bloomington
Bowling Green
Hopkinsville
Clarksville
Nashville
Murfreesboro
Franklin
Columbia
Jackson
Memphis
Germantown
Collierville
Dyersburg
Union City
Martin
Paris
Blytheville
Poplar Bluff
Sikeston
Mayfield
Murray
Madisonville
Russellville
Gallatin
Hendersonville
Lawrenceburg
Pulaski
Fayetteville
Corinth

SHAWNEE NATL. FOR.
MARK TWAIN NATL. FOR.
HOOSIER NATL. FOR.
LAND BETWEEN THE LAKES NATL. REC. AREA
FORT CAMPBELL MIL. RES.

MISSOURI
ARKANSAS
ILLINOIS
INDIANA
KY.
TENN.
MISS.
ALABAMA

© MAPQUEST

1 2 3 4 5 6 7

Cincinnati
Covington
Florence
Independence
Hillsboro
Georgetown
Maysville
Portsmouth
Wellston
Jackson
Gallipolis
Point Pleasant
Ravenswood
Ripley
Ironton
Ashland
Huntington
Charleston
St. Albans
Nitro
Madison
Carrollton
Scottsburg
La Grange
Louisville
Shelbyville
Frankfort
Georgetown
Lexington
Paris
Cynthiana
Mt. Sterling
Winchester
Morehead
Grayson
Flemingsburg
Versailles
Lawrenceburg
Shepherdsville
Bardstown
Elizabethtown
Nicholasville
Harrodsburg
Richmond
Berea
Danville
Lebanon
Campbellsville
Paintsville
Prestonsburg
Pikeville
Hazard
Jackson
Whitesburg
Harlan
Glasgow
Somerset
London
Corbin
Williamsburg
Middlesboro
Monticello
Cookeville
Crossville
Oak Ridge
Knoxville
Maryville
Sevierville
Pigeon Forge
Gatlinburg
Morristown
Greeneville
Johnson City
Kingsport
Bristol
Abingdon
Elizabethton
Erwin
Asheville
Waynesville
Hendersonville
Brevard
Spartanburg
Chattanooga
Cleveland
Athens
Dayton
McMinnville
Harriman
Kingston
Rockwood
Sweetwater
Lenoir City
Clinton
Jacksboro
La Follette
Murphy
Franklin
Sylva
Bryson City
Morganton
Marion
Burnsville
Boone
Wise
Grundy
Welch
Williamson
Logan
Clingmans Dome 6,643
Mt. Mitchell 6,684
ohio 56
west virginia 66
virginia 66
north carolina 52
south carolina 52
KY 102
TN 105
DANIEL BOONE NATL. FOR.
WAYNE NATL. FOR.
JEFFERSON NATL. FOR.
CHEROKEE NATL. FOR.
PISGAH NATL. FOR.
NANTAHALA NATL. FOR.
GREAT SMOKY MOUNTAINS NATL. PARK
APPALACHIAN MTS.
N. CAROLINA
S. CAROLINA
GEORGIA
VIRGINIA
W. VIRGINIA
OHIO

MI 20 40 60
KM 20 40 60
N

KS 102
missouri 43
nebraska 45
oklahoma 58
texas 62
NEBRASKA
MISSOURI
OKLAHOMA
TEXAS
COLORADO
IOWA
ARK.
Kansas City
Overland Park
Olathe
Lawrence
Topeka
Manhattan
Junction City
Emporia
Salina
Abilene
McPherson
Newton
Wichita
Hutchinson
El Dorado
Augusta
Derby
Haysville
Wellington
Winfield
Arkansas City
Independence
Coffeyville
Parsons
Pittsburg
Fort Scott
Chanute
Iola
Ottawa
Leavenworth
Lansing
Atchison
St. Joseph
Concordia
Great Bend
Hays
Russell
Pratt
Dodge City
Garden City
Liberal
Colby
Goodland
Ulysses
Lincoln
Beatrice
Hastings
Kearney
Holdrege
McCook
Enid
Ponca City
Blackwell
Bartlesville
Guymon
Woodward
Miami
Joplin
KANSAS TPK
FLINT HILLS
CENTRAL TIME ZONE
MOUNTAIN TIME ZONE
Mt. Sunflower 4,039
CIMARRON NATL. GRASSLAND
OSAGE IND. RES.

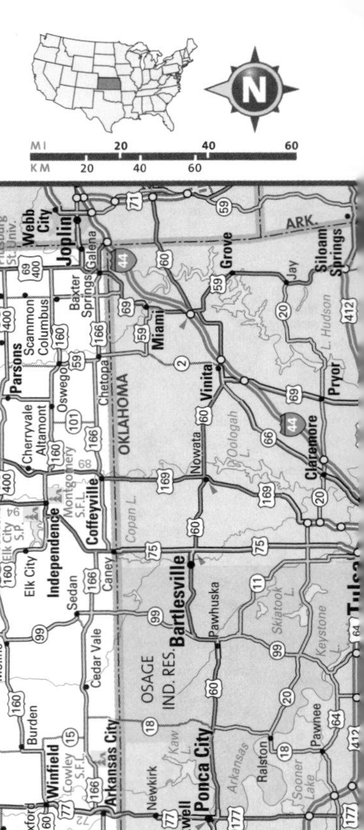

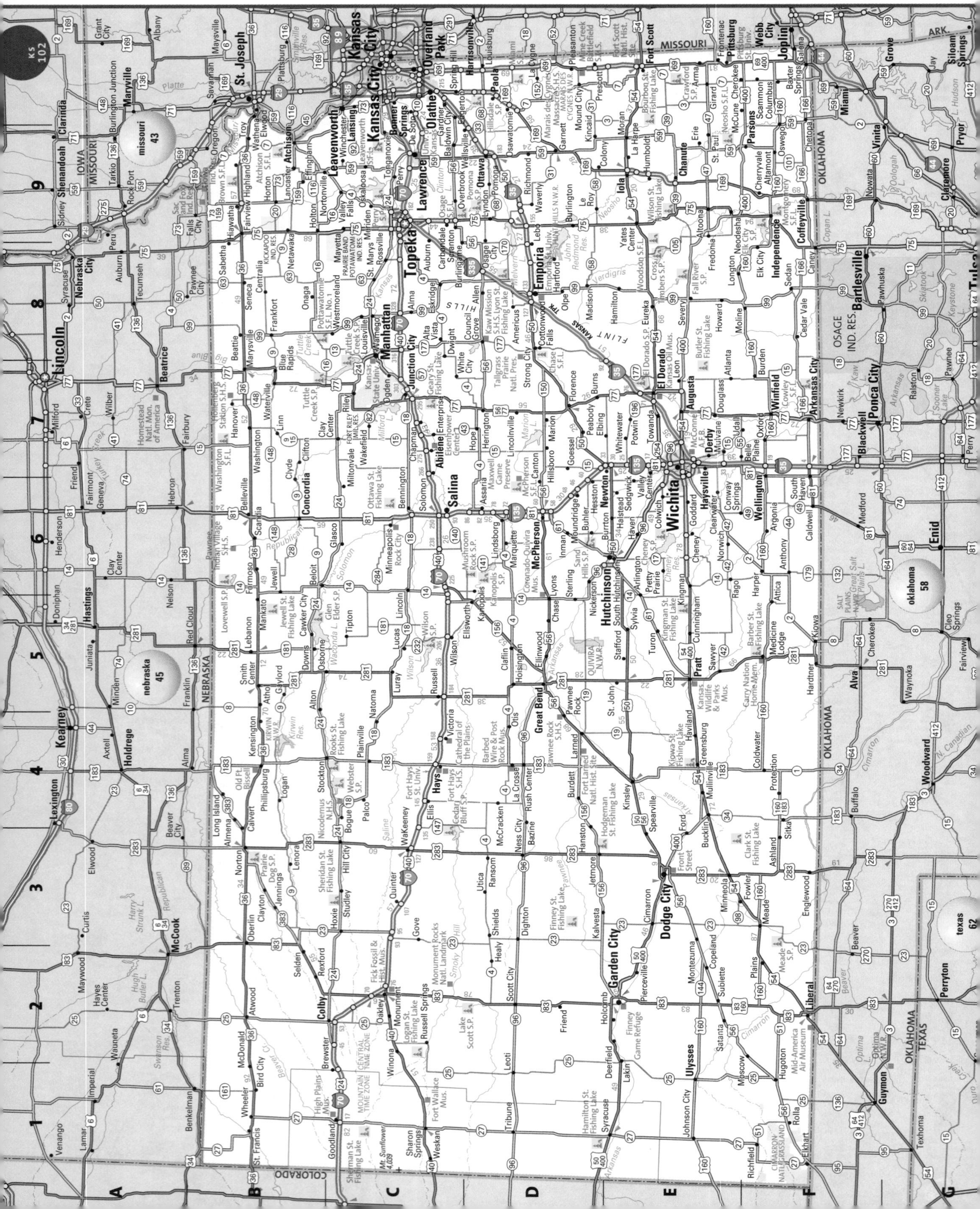

N
MI 25 50
KM 25 50

Shreveport
Bossier City
Monroe
Alexandria
Lafayette
Lake Charles
Baton Rouge
New Orleans
Metairie
Houma
Jackson
Vicksburg
Natchez
Hattiesburg
Gulfport
Biloxi
Beaumont
Port Arthur
Nacogdoches
Lufkin
mississippi 42
texas 62
GULF OF MEXICO
TEXAS
MISSISSIPPI
ARK.
LA 102
© MAPQUEST

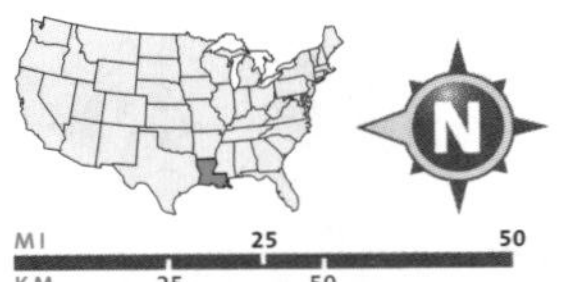

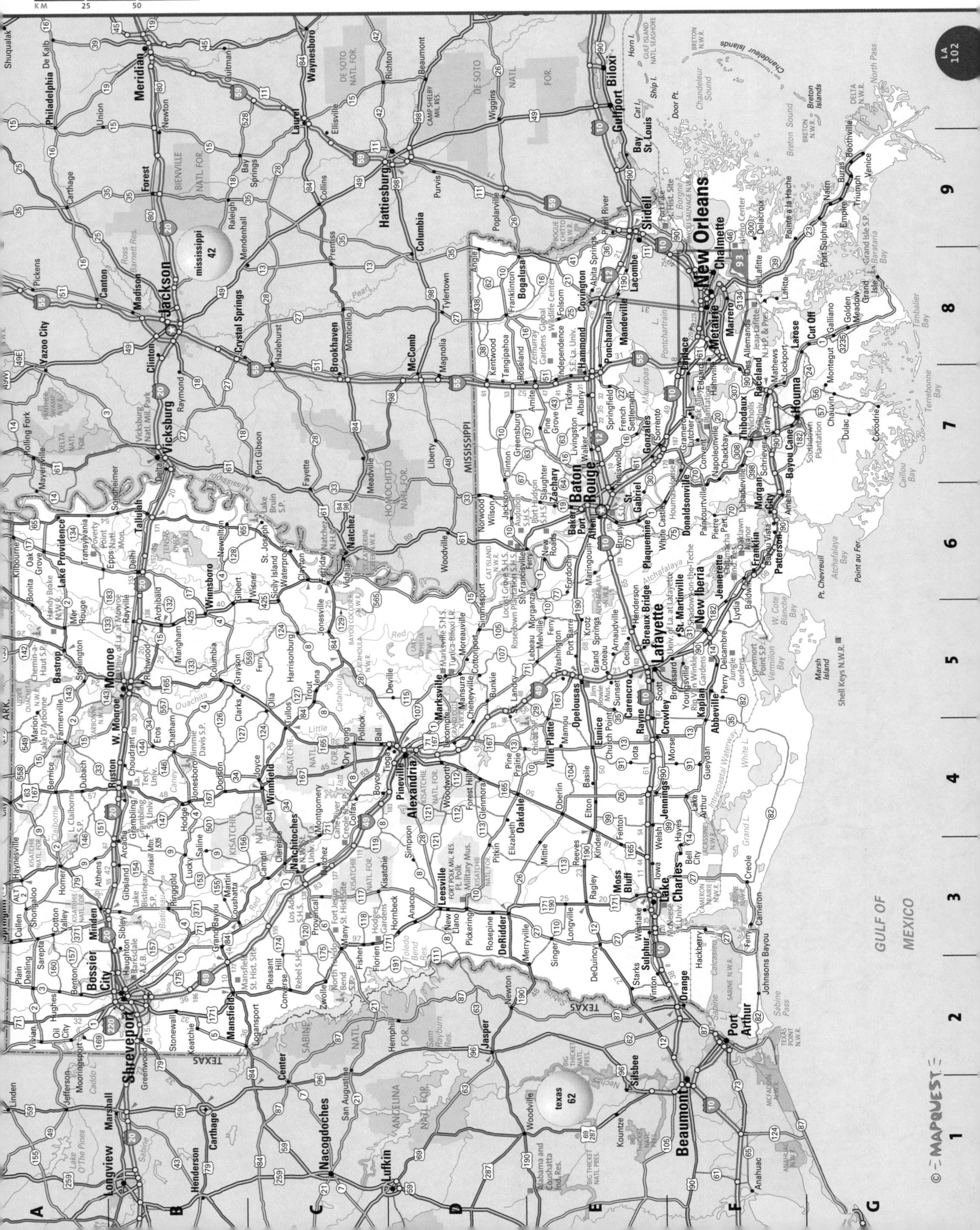

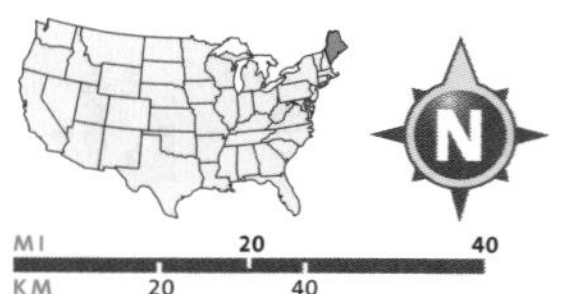
N
MI 20 40
KM 20 40

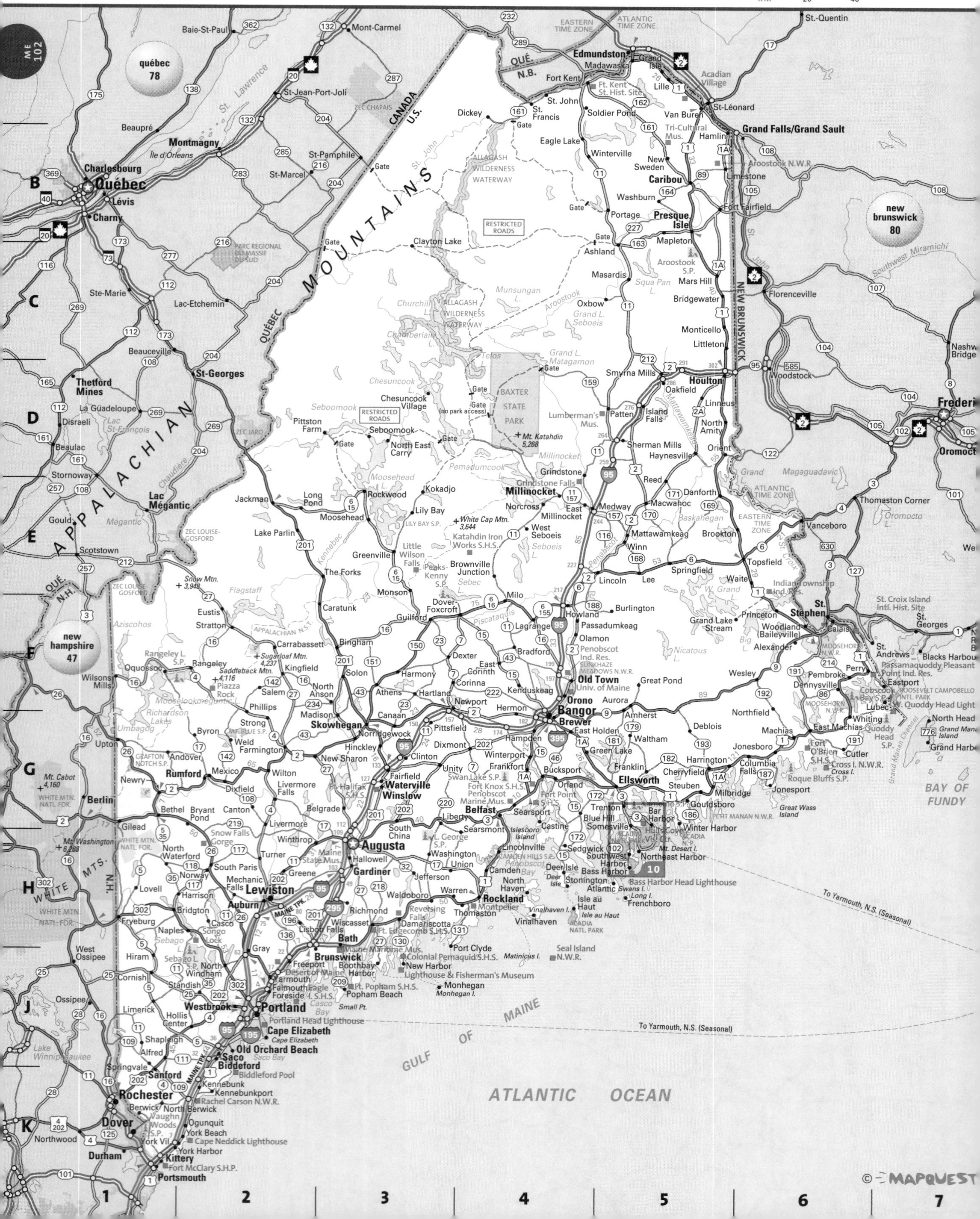

ME 102
québec 78
new brunswick 80
new hampshire 47
APPALACHIAN
MOUNTAINS
ATLANTIC OCEAN
GULF OF MAINE
BAY OF FUNDY
Augusta
Portland
Bangor
Lewiston
Québec
To Yarmouth, N.S. (Seasonal)
© MAPQUEST
1 2 3 4 5 6 7
B C D E F G H J K

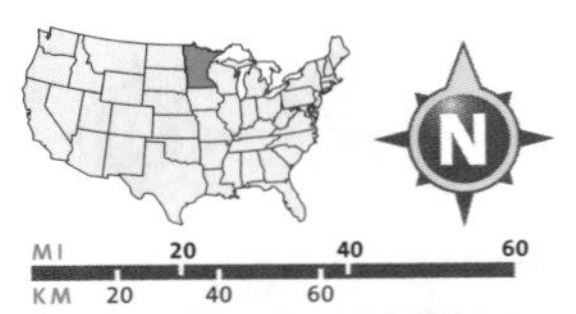

manitoba 75

ontario 76

MN 103

MANITOBA

ONTARIO

CANADA
U.S.

LAKE SUPERIOR

wisconsin 68

south dakota 55

iowa 33

Grand Forks

Fargo

Moorhead

Crookston

Thief River Falls

Bemidji

International Falls

Fort Frances

Hibbing

Virginia

Grand Rapids

Duluth

Superior

Brainerd

St. Cloud

Alexandria

Fergus Falls

Willmar

Minneapolis

St. Paul

Bloomington

Rochester

Mankato

Winona

La Crosse

Eau Claire

Sioux Falls

Worthington

Austin

Albert Lea

Mason City

Red Wing

Marshall

New Ulm

Faribault

Owatonna

Northfield

BOUNDARY WATERS CANOE AREA WILDERNESS

SUPERIOR NATL. FOR.

CHIPPEWA NATL. FOR.

CHEQUAMEGON NATL. FOR.

VOYAGEURS NATL. PARK

QUETICO PROV. PARK

MESABI RANGE

VERMILION RANGE

CENTRAL TIME ZONE

EASTERN TIME ZONE

WISCONSIN

IOWA

S. DAK.

B C D E F G H J K

1 2 3 4 5 6 7

© MAPQUEST

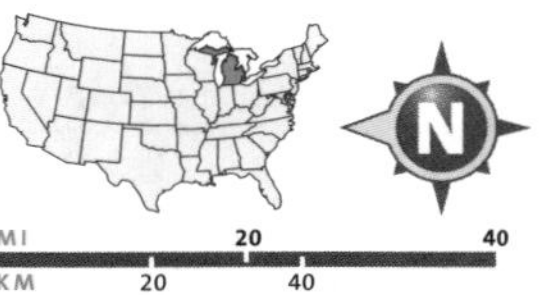

Isle Royale National Park

© MOST

Northwestern Michigan

© MOST

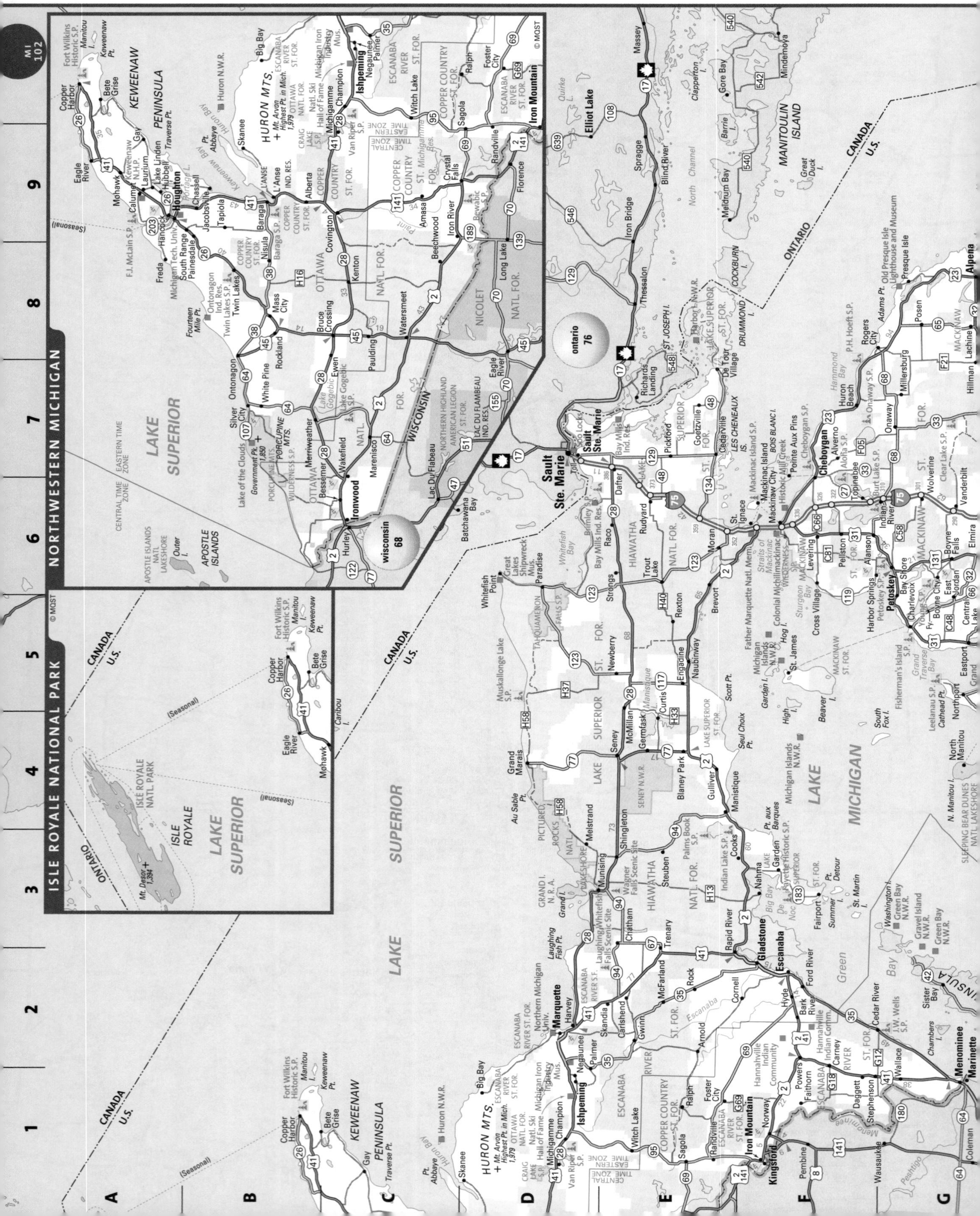

LAKE HURON
LAKE MICHIGAN
LAKE ERIE
Detroit
Windsor
Lansing
Grand Rapids
Flint
Saginaw
Ann Arbor
Kalamazoo
Battle Creek
Jackson
Toledo
Chicago
Milwaukee
Green Bay
South Bend
Traverse City
Muskegon
Port Huron
Sarnia
ontario 76
ohio 56
indiana 32
wisconsin 68
MAPQUEST
MI 102

Mississippi

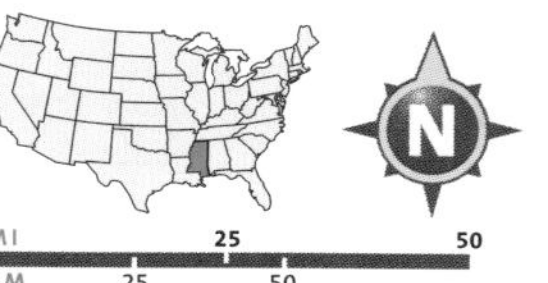

MI 25 50
KM 25 50

Memphis · West Memphis · Collierville · Southaven · Horn Lake · Hernando · Olive Branch · Forrest City · Cabot · Jacksonville · Little Rock · Lonoke · Marianna · Helena · West Helena · Stuttgart · Pine Bluff · White Hall · De Witt · Clarksdale · Sherard · Lambert · Tunica · Coldwater · Senatobia · Holly Springs · Byhalia · Ashland · Ripley · Corinth · Booneville · Iuka · Florence · Tuscumbia · Tishomingo · Russellville · New Albany · Oxford · Batesville · Tupelo · Pontotoc · Fulton · Hamilton · Amory · Aberdeen · Okolona · Houston · Calhoun City · Grenada · Winona · West Point · Starkville · Columbus · Cleveland · Greenwood · Indianola · Greenville · Leland · Ruleville · Drew · Belzoni · Yazoo City · Kosciusko · Louisville · Macon · Philadelphia · Meridian · Canton · Madison · Ridgeland · Jackson · Clinton · Pearl · Brandon · Vicksburg · Tallulah · Monroe · Bastrop · Lake Providence · Forest · Newton · Quitman · Laurel · Waynesboro · Hattiesburg · Petal · Columbia · McComb · Brookhaven · Natchez · Vidalia · Crystal Springs · Hazlehurst · Magee · Picayune · Bogalusa · Slidell · Covington · Hammond · Baton Rouge · Lafayette · Gulfport · Biloxi · Pascagoula · Moss Point · Ocean Springs · Bay St. Louis · Long Beach · Pass Christian · Gautier · Mobile · Prichard · Bay Minette · Daphne · Fairhope · Gulf Shores · Lucedale · Wiggins · Demopolis · Tuscaloosa · Livingston · Butler · Chatom · Jackson · Eutaw · Aliceville · Winfield · Vernon · Fayette · Marksville · Opelousas · Plaquemine · Gonzales · Zachary · Baker · Denham Springs · Mandeville

TENNESSEE · ARKANSAS · LOUISIANA · ALABAMA · MISSISSIPPI

arkansas 21 · louisiana 37 · alabama 18 · MS 103

1 2 3 4 5 6 7 · B C D E F G H J K

© MAPQUEST

MI 20 40 60
KM 20 40 60

illinois 31
kentucky 34
tennessee 34
MO 103
arkansas 21
kansas 36
oklahoma 58
nebraska 45
Kansas City
St. Louis
Jefferson City
Springfield
Columbia
Joplin
St. Joseph
Cape Girardeau
MAPQUEST

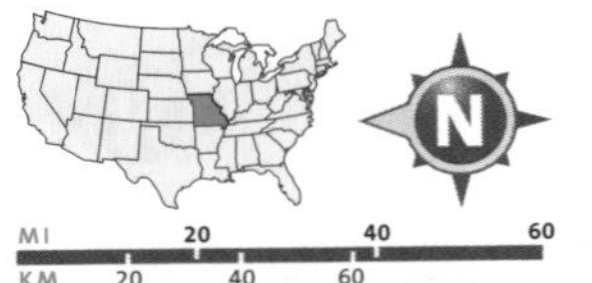

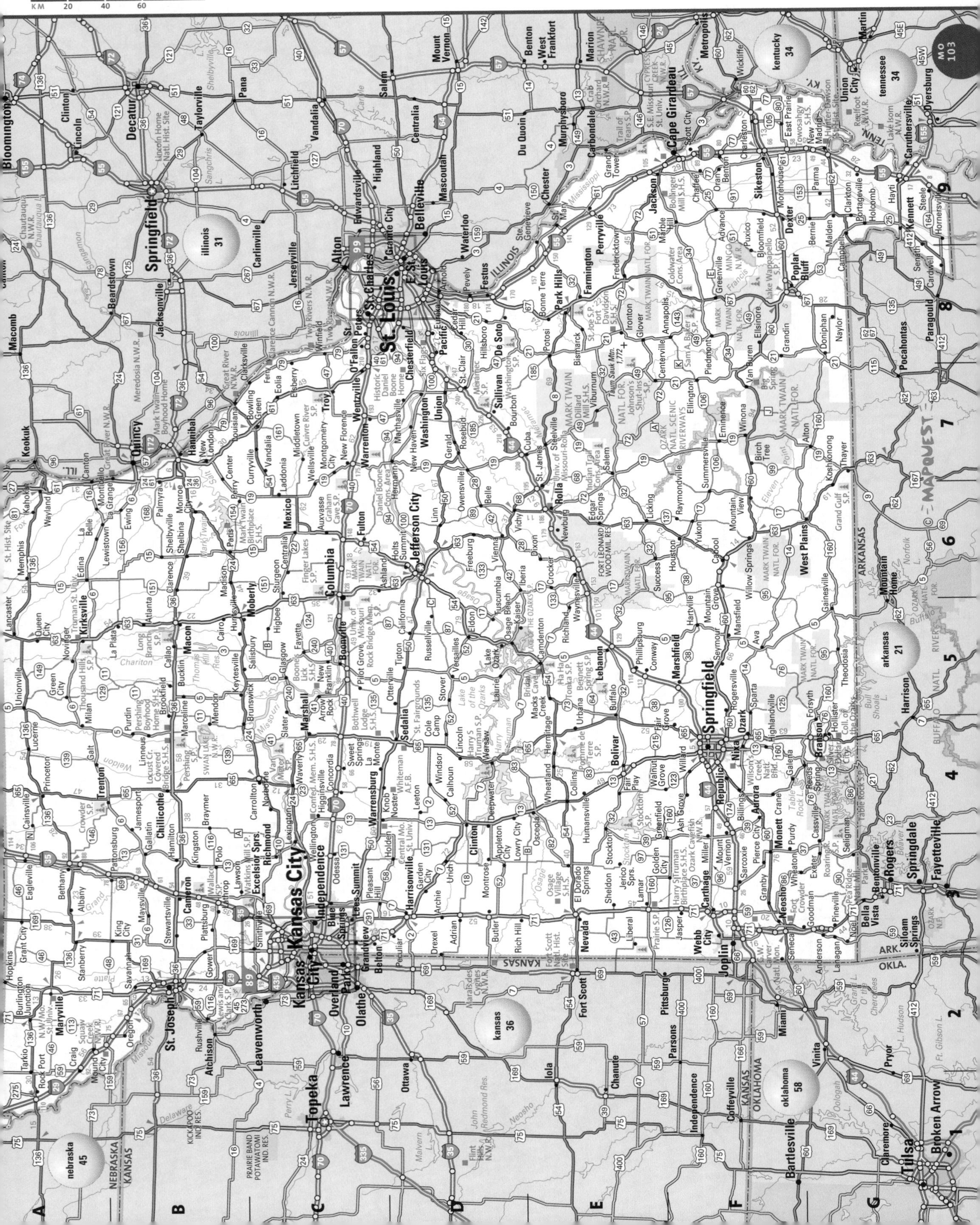

Montana

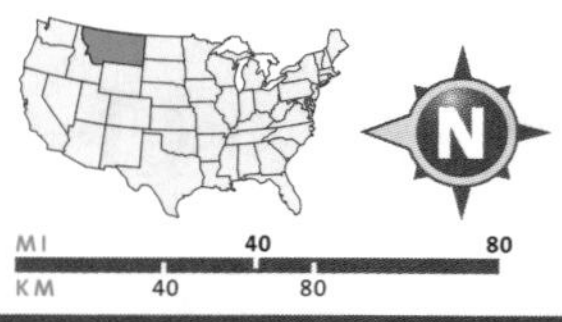

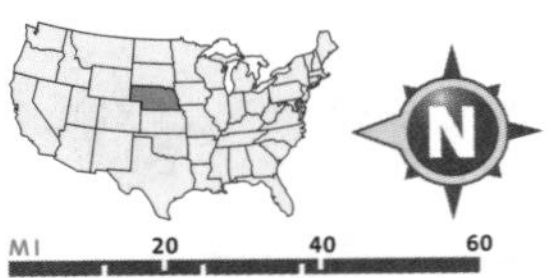
N
MI 20 40 60
KM 20 40 60

Nevada

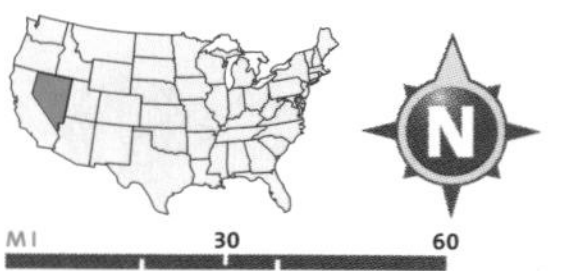

NV 103

OREGON IDAHO
FORT MCDERMITT IND. RES.
Denio
McDermitt
Three Creek
Jackpot
Owyhee
DUCK VALLEY IND. RES.
Mountain City
Jarbidge
Matterhorn 10,839
Wild Horse S.R.A.
Charleston (site)
HUMBOLDT-TOIYABE NATL. FOR.
OWYHEE DESERT
SHELDON NATL. WILDLIFE REFUGE
SUMMIT LAKE IND. RES.
Fort McDermitt Ind. Res.
Orovada
Paradise Valley
North Fork
Jack Creek
Tuscarora (site)
INDEPENDENCE MTS.
TUSCARORA MTS.
Wilkins (site)
Montello
Pilot Pk. 10,704
Oasis
Wells
Deeth
Halleck
BLACK ROCK DESERT-HIGH ROCK CANYON EMIGRANT TRAILS NATL. CONS. AREA
BLACK ROCK DESERT
DESERT VALLEY
Humboldt Mus.
Golconda
Winnemucca
Sulphur (site)
Northeastern Nevada Mus.
Elko
Spring Creek
Arthur
Lamoille
Ruby Dome 11,387
Ruby Mountains Scenic Area
West Wendover
Gerlach
Empire
Rye Patch Res.
Mill City
Imlay
Valmy
Battle Mountain
Battle Mountain Ind. Res.
Carlin
South Fork Ind. Res.
Lee
Beowawe
RYE PATCH ST. REC. AREA
Unionville
Mt. Tobin 9,775
Mt. Lewis 9,680
SHOSHONE RANGE
Jiggs
Ruby Valley
RUBY MTS.
RUBY LAKE N.W.R.
Currie
Oreana
PYRAMID LAKE IND. RES.
SIERRA ARMY DEPOT
Lovelock
Pyramid L.
ANAHO N.W.R.
Tufa Formations
Sutcliffe
Nixon
Wadsworth
GREAT BASIN
Goshute L.
Lages
Goshute Canyon and Cave
Cherry Creek
Tippett
GOSHUTE IND. RES.
Ibapah
Goshute
Ibapah Pk. 12,087
Dixie Valley (site)
Fallon Paiute-Shoshone Ind. Res.
STILLWATER N.W.R.
Stillwater
Hickison Petroglyph B.L.M. Rec. Area
Austin
Eureka
SHOSHONE MOUNTAINS
TOIYABE RANGE
Sparks
Reno
Patrick
Fernley
Verdi
Sierraville
Blairsden
Steamboat
Virginia City
Silver Springs
Fallon
Fallon N.A.S.
Sand Mountain B.L.M. Rec. Area
Pony Express Station
Stokes Castle
North Toiyabe Pk. 10,793
Kingston Canyon
Kingston
Summit Mtn. 10,461
McGill
Ruth
Ely
Nev. Northern Railway Mus.
North Schell Pk. 11,883
Mt. Moriah 12,067
Cave Lake S.P.
Truckee
Incline Village
Carson City
Dayton
Tahoe City
Lake Tahoe
South Lake Tahoe
Zephyr Cove
Campbell Ranch
Minden
Yerington Ind. Res.
Yerington
Gardnerville
WASHOE IND. RES.
Middlegate
FALLON N.A.S.
WALKER RIVER IND. RES.
Schurz
Yomba Ind. Res.
Ione
Berlin-Ichthyosaur S.P.
Gabbs
Arc Dome 11,773
Carvers
Mt. Jefferson 11,949
Round Mountain
Hadley
Duckwater
Duckwater Ind. Res.
Preston
Lund
Ward Charcoal Ovens S.H.P.
Majors Place
Baker
Wheeler Pk. 13,063
Lehman Caves
GREAT BASIN N.P.
Shoshone
Wellington
Markleeville
Topaz Lake
Walker Lake
Walker Lake S.R.A.
Mt. Grant 11,239
HAWTHORNE ARMY DEPOT
Hawthorne
Luning
Belmont Courthouse S.H.P.
Manhattan
Lunar Crater Volcanic Field Natl. Natural Landmark
Currant
Sunnyside
Bridgeport
Mina
Warm Springs (site)
Nyala (site)
Troy Pk. 11,298
GRANT RANGE
Mt. Wilson 9,296
Spring Valley S.P.
Basalt (site)
Coaldale
Tonopah
Lee Vining
Mono Lake
YOSEMITE NATL. PARK
Sonora
Groveland
Boundary Pk. 13,140
Benton
Silver Peak
Dyer
Goldfield
TONOPAH TEST RANGE
EXTRATERRESTRIAL HIGHWAY
Rachel
Hiko
Pioche
Ursine
Echo Canyon S.P.
Cathedral Gorge S.P.
Panaca
Caliente
Kershaw-Ryan S.P.
Uvada
Enterprise
Yosemite Village
Mt. Ritter 13,157
Mammoth Lakes
Devils Postpile Natl. Mon.
White Mtn. Pk. 14,246
Mariposa
Merced
Oakhurst
Mono Hot Springs
Mt. Morgan 13,748
Bishop
Lida
Gold Point
Scotty's Junction
NELLIS AIR FORCE RANGE COMPLEX
Ash Springs
Alamo
PAHRANAGAT N.W.R.
Elgin
Beaver Dam S.P.
Chowchilla
Madera
Eagle Pk. 10,318
Waucoba Mtn. 11,123
Grapevine Pk. 8,738
Rhyolite Ghost Town
NEVADA TEST SITE
Shoshone Pk. 7,058
Beatty
DESERT NATL. WILDLIFE RANGE
Carp
St. George
Clovis
Fresno
Squaw Valley
KINGS CANYON N.P.
SIERRA NEVADA
Independence
Manzanar Natl. Hist. Site
Lone Pine
Mt. Whitney 14,494
DEATH VALLEY NATIONAL PARK
Amargosa Valley
Mercury
Indian Springs
Hayford Pk. 9,912
Glendale
MOAPA RIVER IND. RES.
Overton
Lost City Mus.
VALLEY OF FIRE S.P.
Mesquite
Mt. Bangs 8,012
Reedley
Selma
Visalia
Hanford
Tulare
Exeter
Death Valley
Ash Meadows N.W.R.
Devils Hole (Death Valley Natl. Park)
SPRING MOUNTAINS N.R.A.
Charleston Pk. 11,918
Floyd Lamb S.P.
North Las Vegas
Las Vegas
Henderson
Boulder City
Coalinga
Corcoran
Porterville
Olancha
Death Valley Junction
Telescope Pk. 11,049
Pahrump
Blue Diamond
RED ROCK CANYON N.C.A.
LAKE MEAD NATL. REC. AREA
GRAND CANYON-PARASHANT NATL. MON.
Avenal
TULE RIVER IND. RES.
Earlimart
Delano
McFarland
CHINA LAKE NAVAL AIR WEAPONS STATION
Trona
Shoshone
Sloan
Jean
SLOAN CANYON N.C.A.
Nelson
Primm
Cottonwood Cove
GRAND CANYON NATL. PARK
Lake Isabella
Ridgecrest
FORT IRWIN NATIONAL TRAINING CTR.
Searchlight
Mt. Tipton 7,148
BLACK MTS.
Machesna Mtn. 4061
McKittrick
Bakersfield
Taft
Maricopa
CARRIZO PLAIN NATL. MON.
LOS PADRES NATL. FOR.
Tehachapi
Mojave
MOJAVE DESERT
Baker
MOJAVE NATL. PRESERVE
Cal Nev Ari
Laughlin
Bullhead City
Kingman
Alturas
Cedar Pass 6,305
MODOC NATL. FOR.
Eagle Pk. 9,892
Termo
PLUMAS NATL. FOR.
TAHOE N.F.
ELDORADO N.F.
STANISLAUS NATL. FOR.
SIERRA NATL. FOR.
SEQUOIA NATL. PARK
GIANT SEQUOIA NATL. MON.
INYO NATL. FOR.
CALIFORNIA
UTAH
ARIZONA
PACIFIC TIME ZONE
MOUNTAIN TIME ZONE
UTAH TEST AND TRAINING RANGE
GREAT SALT LAKE DESERT
DESERT RANGE EXP. STA.
INDIAN PEAK RANGE
DIXIE NATL. FOR.
PAIUTE IND. RES.
utah 64
california 22
arizona 20
© MAPQUEST
B C D E F G H J K
1 2 3 4 5 6 7

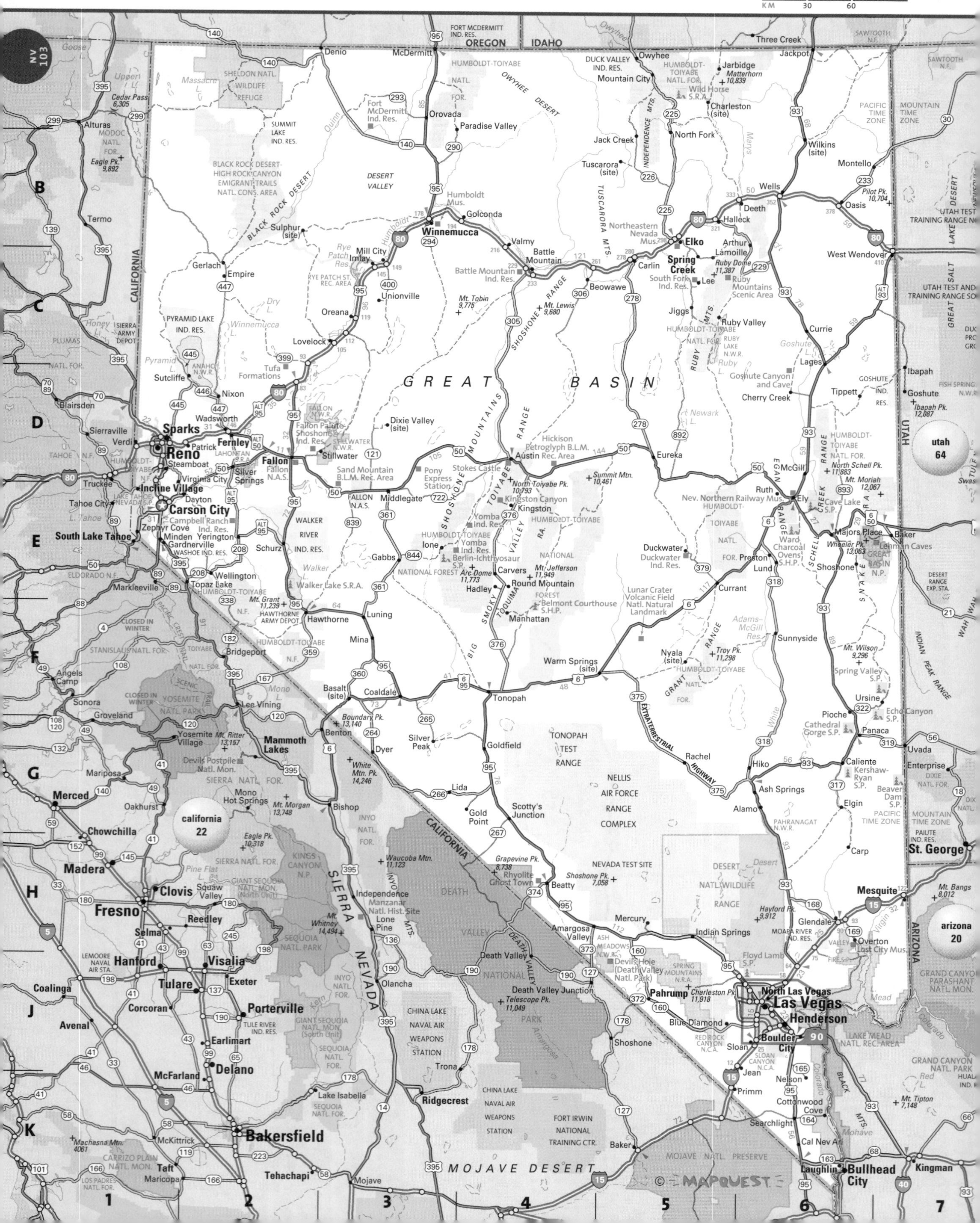

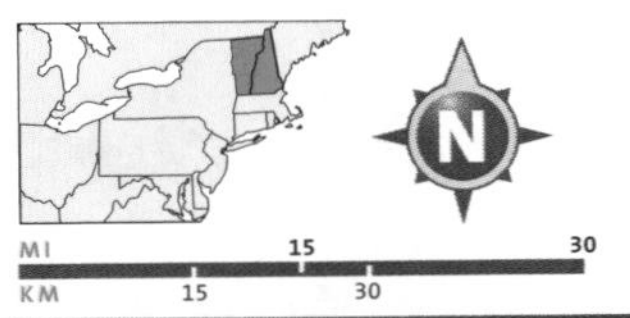

St-Jean-sur-Richelieu
Iberville
Farnham
Cowansville
Lac-Brome
Magog
Coaticook
Bedford
Sutton
Memphrémagog L.
Massawippi L.
Lacolle
CANADA
U.S.
QUÉBEC
québec 78
CONNECTICUT LAKES ST. FOR.
Second Connecticut L.
First Connecticut L.
L. Francis S.P.
Pittsburg
Norton
Beecher Falls
Stewartstown
Coleman S.P.
Colebrook
Beaver Brook Falls Wayside Nat. Area
Dixville Notch
Dixville Notch S.P.
Errol
Umbagog Lake S.P.
Umbagog L.
Aziscohos L.
Rangeley
Rangeley L.
Wilsons Mills
Saddleback Mtn. 4,116
Snow Mtn. 3,948
Mooselookmeguntic L.
Richardson Lakes
Rumford
Old Speck Mtn. 4,180
Bethel
Androscoggin
NH 103
VT 106
Alburg
Highgate Center
Swanton
Richford
North Troy
Newport
Derby Line
Enosburg Falls
Sheldon
St. Albans
Troy
Orleans
Irasburg
Lowell
Island Pond
Brighton S.P.
Bloomfield
North Stratford
NASH STREAM ST. FOR.
Mollidgewock S.P.
Crystal Lake S.P.
Barton
Albany
Eden
WILLOUGHBY ST. FOR.
West Burke
East Haven
Maidstone S.P.
Guildhall
Groveton
West Milan
Milan Hill S.P.
Milan
Nansen Wayside Park
Berlin
Shelburne Birches
Gorham
Mt. Cabot 4,160
WHITE MOUNTAIN NATL. FOR.
Lancaster
John W. Weeks S.H.S.
Santa's Village
Moose Brook S.P.
Whitefield
Forest Lake S.P.
Plattsburgh
Grand Isle
South Hero
Milton
Fairfax
Cambridge
Jeffersonville
Johnson
Hyde Park
North Wolcott
Wolcott
Mt. Mansfield 4,393
Morrisville
Smugglers Notch S.P.
Elmore S.P.
East Hardwick
Hardwick
Lyndon
Lyndonville
East Burke
VICTORY ST. FOR.
St. Johnsbury
Fairbanks Mus. and Planetarium
Concord
Danville
Cabot
Maple Grove Maple Mus.
Colchester
Winooski
Burlington
Essex Jct.
South Burlington
Univ. of Vermont
Underhill S.P.
Jericho
Stowe
MOUNT MANSFIELD S.F.
C.C. PUTNAM ST. FOR.
Waterbury Res.
Little River S.P.
Richmond
Old Round Church
Shelburne Farms
Shelburne Mus.
Shelburne
Hinesburg
Waterbury
Worcester
Marshfield
Montpelier
East Montpelier
Plainfield
GROTON S.F.
Groton
Barnet
Littleton
Bethlehem
Six Gun City
Mt. Washington Cog Railway
Mt. Washington S.P.
Mt. Washington 6,288
Twin Mountain
Glen Ellis Falls
Essex
Charlotte
Mount Philo S.P.
CAMEL'S HUMP S.F.
Vermont Wildflower Farm
Kingsland Bay S.P.
Rokeby Mus.
Lake Champlain Maritime Mus.
Vergennes
Button Bay S.P.
Waitsfield
Irasville
Northfield
Barre
South Barre
Rock of Ages Quarry
West Topsham
Williamstown
Lisbon
Franconia
The Frost Place
New England Ski Mus.
Eisenhower Mem. Wayside Park
WHITE MOUNTAIN NATIONAL FOREST
Silver Cascade
CRAWFORD NOTCH S.P.
Old Man of the Mountain Collapse
FRANCONIA NOTCH S.P.
The Basin
The Flume
Jackson
Glen
Heritage New Hampshire
Story Land
Intervale
Cathedral Ledge
North Conway
Conway Scenic R.R.
Echo L. S.P.
Bartlett
Lower Falls
maine 38
South Paris
WHITE MOUNTAIN NATIONAL FOREST
Bridgton
Fryeburg
Addison
Bristol
Warren
ROXBURY ST. FOR.
Allis S.P.
Woodsville
Wells River
Newbury
Lincoln
North Woodstock
Lost River Res.
Middlebury
D.A.R. S.P.
Morgan Horse Farm
Middlebury Coll.
GREEN MOUNTAIN NATIONAL FOREST
East Middlebury
Hancock
Randolph
East Randolph
Chelsea
Haverhill
Bradford
Warren
Waterville Valley
Swift
Conway
Madison Boulder Nat. Area
Madison
Chocorua
West Ossipee
Sebago L.
Shoreham
Branbury S.P.
Justin Smith Morrill Homestead
South Royalton
Joseph Smith Mem.
Thetford Hill S.P.
Fairlee
Wentworth
Campton
North Sandwich
White Lake S.P.
Squam L.
South Tamworth
Cornish
Ticonderoga
Orwell
Brandon
Bethel
Lyme
Hubbardton Bfld. S.H.S.
New England Maple Mus.
Silver Lake S.P.
Norwich
Dartmouth Coll.
Hanover
Mary Baker Eddy Home
Plymouth
Science Ctr. of N.H.
Ashland
Moultonborough
Castle in the Clouds
Center Ossipee
PINE RIVER S.F.
Ossipee
Half Moon Pond S.P.
Bomoseen S.P.
L. Bomoseen
Gifford Woods S.P.
Killington Pk. 4,235
Marsh-Billings Rockefeller N.H.P.
Quechee Gorge
White River Junction
Newfound L.
CARDIGAN S.P.
Wellington St. Park
New Hampton
Meredith
L. Winnipesaukee
Endicott Rock
Libby Mus.
Wentworth S.P.
Proctor
West Rutland
Rutland
Castleton
Fair Haven
COOLIDGE S.F.
Woodstock
Vermont Raptor Ctr.
Enfield
Lower Shaker Village
Lebanon
Canaan
Canaan Hist. Mus.
Bristol
Ellacoya S.P.
Wolfeboro
Governor Wentworth S.H.S.
Shapleigh
Whitehall
Poultney
Wilson Castle
Plymouth
Coolidge S.P.
Pres. Calvin Coolidge S.H.S.
Hartland
Plainfield
Saint-Gaudens Natl. Hist. Site
Grafton
Danbury
Laconia
Gunstock R.A.
Union
Sanbornville
Lake St. Catherine S.P.
Wallingford
Camp Plymouth S.P.
Old Constitution House
Windsor
Grantham
GILES S.F.
Franklin
Tilton
Belmont
Alton
N.H. Farm Mus.
Milton
Sanford
Ascutney S.P.
Georges Mills
New London
Andover
Daniel Webster Birthplace S.H.S.
Northfield
Canterbury Shaker Village
N.H. Intl. Speedway
Farmington
Danby
WHITE ROCKS NATL. REC. AREA
OKEMO S.F.
Ludlow
Wilgus S.P.
Ascutney
Claremont
Newport
Sunapee
North Sutton
KEARSARGE MTN S.F.
Rollins S.P.
Boscawen
Canterbury Center
Pittsfield
Rochester
West Pawlet
Weston
Chester
Springfield
Goshen
MT. SUNAPEE S.P.
Warner
Hannah Duston Mem. S.H.S.
Somersworth
Rollinsford
new york 50
Emerald Lake S.P.
Dorset
Peru
Londonderry
Toll
Charlestown
Fort at No. 4
PILLSBURY S.P.
Contoocook
Hopkinton
Concord
Northwood
Dover
Manchester Center
Manchester
Hildene
Historic Grafton Village
Grafton
Washington
Fox S.F.
Franklin Pierce Homestead S.H.S.
Henniker
BEAR BROOK S.P.
Suncook
Hooksett
PAWTUCKAWAY S.P.
Durham
Univ. of N.H.
Kittery
NEW YORK
Arlington
East Arlington
Jamaica S.P.
Jamaica
Bellows Falls
Westminster
Walpole
Marlow
Stoddard
Hillsborough
Weare
Clough S.P.
South Hooksett
Raymond
Newmarket
Epping
Portsmouth
Lake Shaftsbury S.P.
Shaftsbury
GREEN MOUNTAIN NATIONAL FOREST
Townshend
Townshend S.P.
Newfane
Putney
Gilsum
Antrim
Bennington
Goffstown
Pinardville
Manchester
New Hamp. Coll.
Fremont
Exeter
Rye
Rye Harbor S.P.
Rye Beach
North Bennington
Hoosick Falls
West Dover
West Dummerston
Keene
Hancock
Dublin
Greenfield S.P.
Greenfield
Peterborough
Wapack N.W.R.
New Boston
Merrimack
Kingston S.T. Park
Kingston
Hampton
Hampton Beach S.P.
Seabrook
ATLANTIC OCEAN
Bennington
Southern Vt. Coll.
Bennington Battle Mon.
Wilmington
Molly Stark S.P.
Brattleboro
Chesterfield
PISGAH S.P.
Marlborough
MONADNOCK S.P.
West Swanzey
Swanzey
Rhododendron S.P.
Miller S.P.
Wilton
Amherst
Milford
Londonderry
Derry
Robert Frost Farm S.H.S.
Plaistow
Amesbury
Newburyport
PARKER RIVER N.W.R.
Pownal
Readsboro
Ft. Dummer S.P.
Jacksonville
Stamford
Brigham Young Mem.
Hinsdale
Winchester
Troy
Fitzwilliam
Jaffrey
Greenville
Rindge
EVERETT TPK
Nashua
Hudson
Salem
Haverhill
Lawrence
Thatcher Island N.W.R.
Cape Ann
Rockport
MASSACHUSETTS
MONROE S.F.
North Adams
Mt. Greylock 3,491
Adams
MT. GREYLOCK RES.
SAVOY MTN. S.F.
MOHAWK TRAIL S.F.
DUBUQUE MEM. S.F.
massachusetts 26
MT. GRACE S.F.
ERVING S.F.
Athol
OTTER RIVER S.F.
Gardner
Fitchburg
Brookline
Chelmsford
Lowell
Andover
HAROLD PARKER S.F.
Danvers
Gloucester
Manchester-by-the-sea
Greenfield
WENDELL S.F.
MAPQUEST
1 2 3 4 5 6 7
B C D E F G H J K

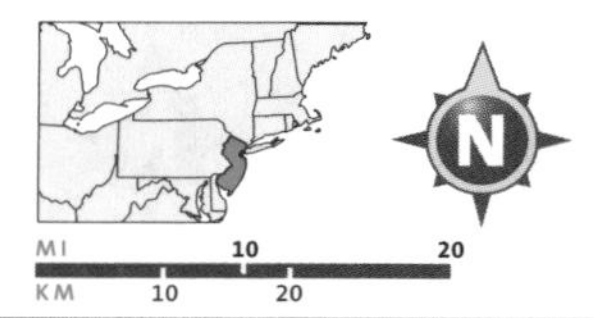

Philadelphia
New York
Newark
Trenton
Atlantic City
Allentown
Paterson
Elizabeth
Camden
Wilmington
Reading
ATLANTIC OCEAN
Delaware Bay
pennsylvania 60
new york 50
maryland 25
delaware 25
NJ 103

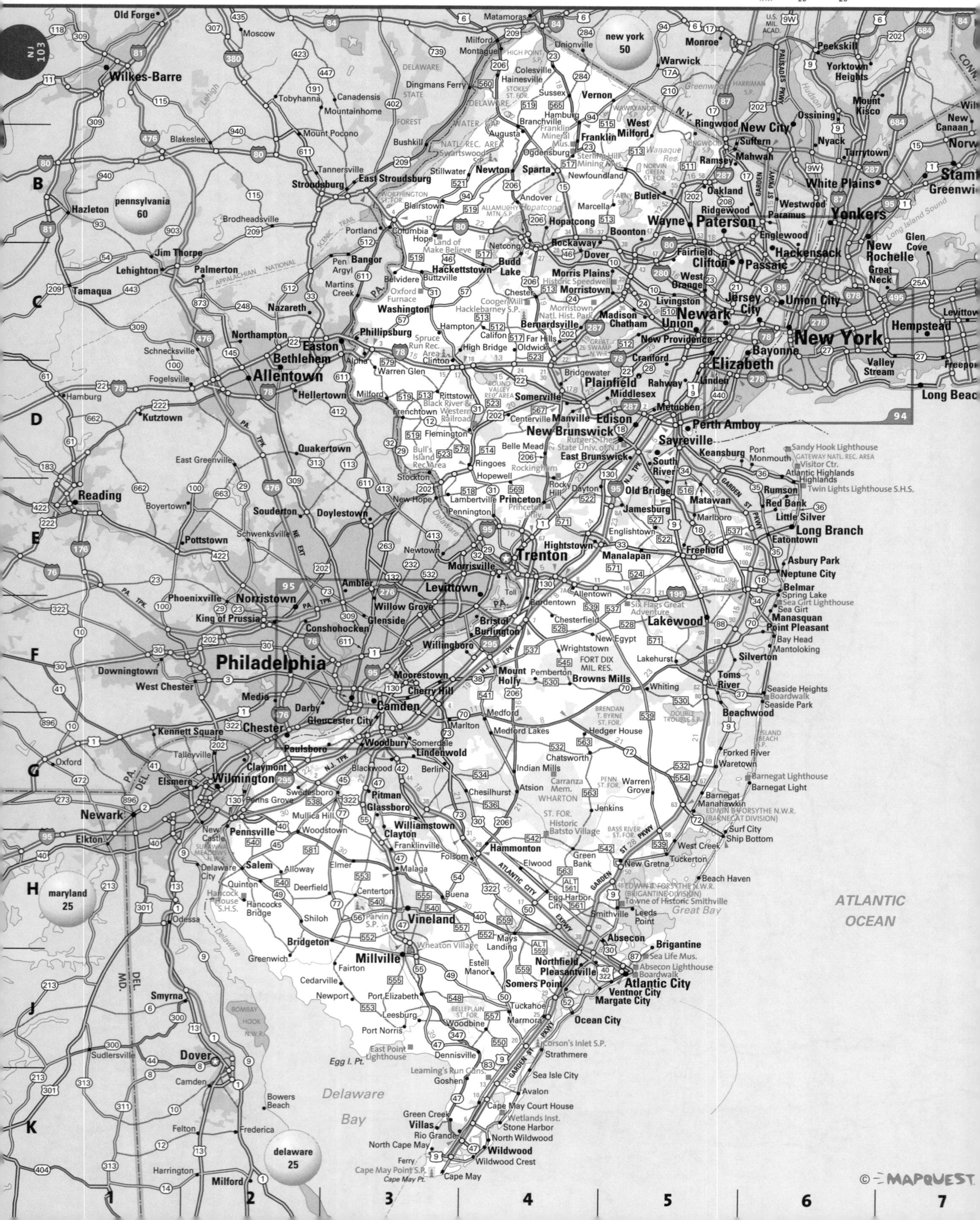

1 2 3 4 5 6 7
B C D E F G H J K

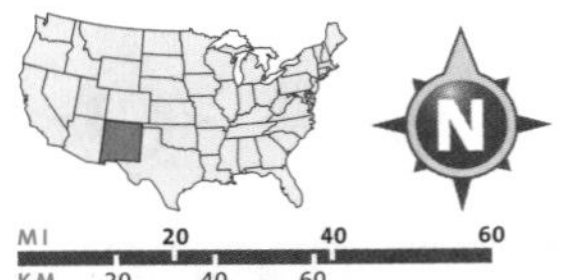

colorado 24
oklahoma 58
texas 62
mexico 82
NM 104

COLORADO
ARIZONA
UTAH
TEXAS
OKLA.
CHIHUAHUA
SONORA
U.S.
MEXICO

Alamosa
Cortez
Durango
Pagosa Springs
Wolf Creek Pass Tunnel
Rio Grande Montezuma Pk. 13,150
Monte Vista N.W.R.
San Juan Natl. For.
Southern Ute Ind. Res.
Ute Mountain Ind. Res.
Mesa Verde Natl. Park
Canyons of the Ancients Natl. Mon.
Antonito
San Luis
Trinidad
Fort Carson Mil. Res.
Kim
Comanche Natl. Grassland
San Isabel Natl. For.

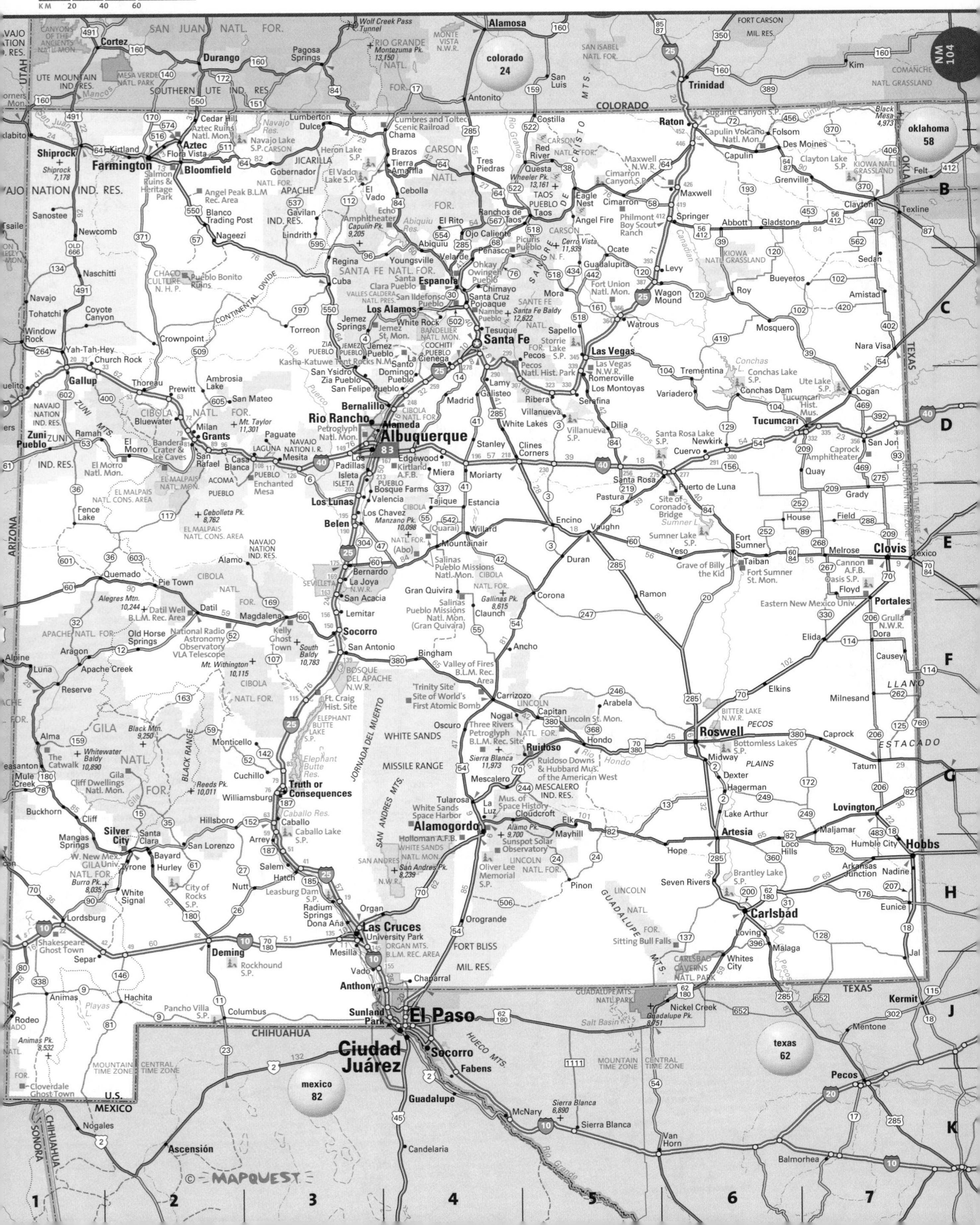

Raton
Shiprock
Farmington
Kirtland
Aztec
Flora Vista
Bloomfield
Cedar Hill
Aztec Ruins Natl. Mon.
Navajo Lake S.P.
Lumberton
Dulce
Chama
Cumbres and Toltec Scenic Railroad
Costilla
Red River
Questa
Wheeler Pk. 13,161
Taos Pueblo
Taos
Eagle Nest
Cimarron
Maxwell
Springer
Folsom
Capulin Volcano Natl. Mon.
Capulin
Des Moines
Clayton
Clayton Lake S.P.
Kiowa Natl. Grassland
Grenville
Felt
Texline
Abbott
Gladstone
Angel Fire
Philmont Boy Scout Ranch
Tres Piedras
Tierra Amarilla
Brazos
Heron Lake S.P.
El Vado Lake S.P.
Cebolla
Gobernador
Jicarilla Apache Ind. Res.
Angel Peak B.L.M. Rec. Area
Blanco Trading Post
Salmon Ruins & Heritage Park
Navajo Nation Ind. Res.
Sanostee
Newcomb
Nageezi
Gavilan
Lindrith
El Rito
Abiquiu
Echo Amphitheater
Capulin Pk. 9,205
Ojo Caliente
Ranchos de Taos
Picuris Pueblo
Penasco
Velarde
Ohkay Owingeh Pueblo
Española
Chimayo
Santa Cruz
Pojoaque
Nambe Pueblo
Santa Fe Baldy 12,622
Santa Clara Pueblo
San Ildefonso Pueblo
Los Alamos
White Rock
Bandelier Natl. Mon.
Valles Caldera Natl. Pres.
Jemez Springs
Jemez Pueblo
Zia Pueblo
Cochiti Pueblo
Kasha-Katuwe Tent Rocks N.M.
Santo Domingo Pueblo
San Felipe Pueblo
San Ysidro
Tesuque
Santa Fe
La Cienega
Cuba
Regina
Youngsville
Santa Fe Natl. For.
Carson Natl. For.
Ocate
Guadalupita
Mora
Fort Union Natl. Mon.
Wagon Mound
Watrous
Sapello
Las Vegas
Las Vegas N.W.R.
Romeroville
Los Montoyas
Storrie Lake S.P.
Pecos
Pecos Natl. Hist. Park
Lamy
Galisteo
Ribera
Villanueva
Villanueva S.P.
Serafina
Levy
Roy
Bueyeros
Sedan
Amistad
Mosquero
Nara Visa
Logan
Ute Lake S.P.
Conchas Lake S.P.
Conchas Dam
Trementina
Variadero
Tucumcari
Tucumcari Hist. Mus.
San Jon
Caprock Amphitheater
Quay
Grady
Newkirk
Cuervo
Santa Rosa
Santa Rosa Lake S.P.
Dilia
Puerto de Luna
Pastura
Site of Coronado's Bridge
Sumner Lake S.P.
Vaughn
Encino
Fort Sumner
Yeso
Grave of Billy the Kid
Taiban
Fort Sumner St. Mon.
House
Field
Melrose
Clovis
Cannon A.F.B.
Oasis S.P.
Floyd
Portales
Eastern New Mexico Univ.
Grulla N.W.R.
Dora
Elida
Causey
Texico

Chaco Culture N.H.P.
Pueblo Bonito Ruins
Naschitti
Navajo
Tohatchi
Coyote Canyon
Window Rock
Yah-Tah-Hey
Church Rock
Gallup
Crownpoint
Torreon
Continental Divide
Thoreau
Prewitt
Ambrosia Lake
San Mateo
Mt. Taylor 11,301
Cibola Natl. For.
Bluewater
Milan
Grants
Zuni Pueblo
Zuni Ind. Res.
Ramah
El Morro
El Morro Natl. Mon.
Bandera Crater & Ice Caves
San Rafael
Casa Blanca
Laguna
Paguate
Mesita
Acoma Pueblo
El Malpais Natl. Mon.
El Malpais Natl. Cons. Area
Cebolleta Pk. 8,762
Fence Lake
Bernalillo
Rio Rancho
Petroglyph Natl. Mon.
Alameda
Albuquerque
Isleta Pueblo
Padillas
Kirtland A.F.B.
Edgewood
Madrid
Stanley
Clines Corners
Moriarty
Miera
Bosque Farms
Los Lunas
Los Chavez
Valencia
Belen
Tajique
Estancia
Manzano Pk. 10,098
Willard
Mountainair
Salinas Pueblo Missions Natl. Mon.
Bernardo
La Joya
San Acacia
Sevilleta N.W.R.
Lemitar
Socorro
San Antonio
Gran Quivira
Claunch
Gallinas Pk. 8,615
Corona
Duran
Ramon
Alamo
Navajo Nation Ind. Res.
Quemado
Pie Town
Datil
Datil Well B.L.M. Rec. Area
Alegres Mtn. 10,244
Magdalena
National Radio Astronomy Observatory VLA Telescope
Kelly Ghost Town
South Baldy 10,783
Old Horse Springs
Aragon
Apache Creek
Apache Natl. For.
Mt. Withington 10,115
Luna
Reserve
Alpine
Bingham
Valley of Fires B.L.M. Rec. Area
Bosque del Apache N.W.R.
Carrizozo
'Trinity Site' Site of World's First Atomic Bomb
Ft. Craig Hist. Site
Elephant Butte Lake S.P.
Jornada del Muerto
White Sands Missile Range
Oscuro
Nogal
Capitan
Lincoln
Lincoln St. Mon.
Arabela
Hondo
Three Rivers Petroglyph B.L.M. Rec. Site
Ruidoso
Ruidoso Downs & Hubbard Mus. of the American West
Sierra Blanca 11,973
Mescalero
Mescalero Ind. Res.
Tularosa
White Sands Space Harbor
La Luz
Mus. of Space History
Cloudcroft
Alamogordo
Holloman A.F.B.
White Sands Natl. Mon.
Alamo Pk. 9,700
Sunspot Solar Observatory
Mayhill
Elk
Oliver Lee Memorial S.P.
Pinon
San Andres Mts.
San Andres Pk. 8,239
Roswell
Bitter Lake N.W.R.
Bottomless Lakes S.P.
Midway
Dexter
Hagerman
Lake Arthur
Artesia
Hope
Elkins
Milnesand
Caprock
Tatum
Lovington
Maljamar
Loco Hills
Humble City
Hobbs
Arkansas Junction
Nadine
Eunice
Jal
Seven Rivers
Brantley Lake S.P.
Carlsbad
Loving
Malaga
Whites City
Carlsbad Caverns Natl. Park
Sitting Bull Falls
Lincoln Natl. For.
Guadalupe Mts.
Llano Estacado
Pecos Plains

Alma
Whitewater Baldy 10,890
The Catwalk
Gila Natl. For.
Black Mtn. 9,250
Black Range
Gila Cliff Dwellings Natl. Mon.
Mule Creek
Glenwood
Buckhorn
Cliff
Monticello
Cuchillo
Reeds Pk. 10,011
Williamsburg
Truth or Consequences
Caballo Res.
Caballo
Caballo Lake S.P.
Hillsboro
Arrey
Salem
Hatch
Silver City
Santa Clara
Bayard
Hurley
Tyrone
Mangas Springs
W. New Mex. Univ.
Burro Pk. 8,035
White Signal
City of Rocks S.P.
San Lorenzo
Nutt
Leasburg Dam S.P.
Radium Springs
Dona Aña
Organ
Las Cruces
University Park
Mesilla
Organ Mts. B.L.M. Rec. Area
Fort Bliss Mil. Res.
Orogrande
Vado
Anthony
Chaparral
Sunland Park
El Paso
Lordsburg
Shakespeare Ghost Town
Separ
Deming
Rockhound S.P.
Animas
Hachita
Playas L.
Rodeo
Animas Pk. 8,532
Pancho Villa S.P.
Columbus
Cloverdale Ghost Town

Ciudad Juárez
Socorro
Fabens
Hueco Mts.
Guadalupe
McNary
Sierra Blanca
Sierra Blanca 6,890
Van Horn
Salt Basin
Nickel Creek
Guadalupe Mts. Natl. Park
Guadalupe Pk. 8,751
Kermit
Mentone
Pecos
Balmorhea
Nogales
Ascensión
Candelaria
Mountain Time Zone
Central Time Zone

© MAPQUEST

A B C D E F G H J K
1 2 3 4 5 6 7

New York

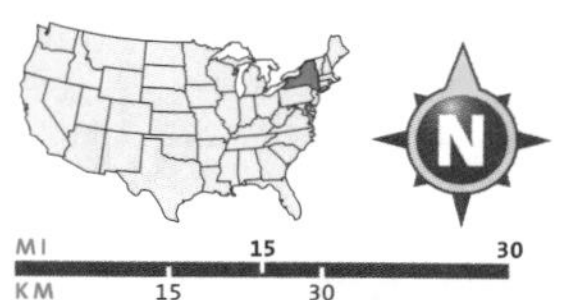

SOUTHERN NEW YORK

NY 104

connecticut 26

new jersey 48

ontario 76

pennsylvania 60

Toronto 98

Buffalo 83

94

Hartford, West Hartford, New Britain, Bristol, Waterbury, Meriden, Middletown, Norwich, New London, New Haven, West Haven, Hamden, Milford, Bridgeport, Norwalk, Stamford, Greenwich, Danbury, Torrington, Poughkeepsie, New Paltz, Newburgh, Middletown, Monticello, Port Jervis, White Plains, Yonkers, New Rochelle, Paterson, Passaic, Newark, Elizabeth, Plainfield, New York, Hempstead, Hicksville, Levittown, Brentwood, Riverhead, Stony Brook, Huntington Station

Long Island Sound, LONG ISLAND, ATLANTIC OCEAN

Toronto, Mississauga, Milton, Oakville, Burlington, Hamilton, St. Catharines, Niagara Falls, Welland, Buffalo, Cheektowaga, North Tonawanda, Tonawanda, West Seneca, Lockport, Batavia, Rochester, Irondequoit, Greece, Brockport, Albion, Medina, Geneseo, Canandaigua, Geneva, Penn Yan, Bath, Hornell, Corning, Elmira, Olean, Salamanca, Jamestown, Dunkirk, Fredonia, Erie

LAKE ONTARIO, LAKE ERIE, CANADA, U.S., ONTARIO, PENNSYLVANIA

B C D E F G H J K

1 2 3 4 5 6 7

NY 104
ontario 76
vermont 47
massachusetts 26
connecticut 26
QUÉBEC
CANADA
U.S.
ONTARIO
VERMONT
MASS.
CONN.
PENNSYLVANIA
ADIRONDACK
MOUNTAINS
PARK
ADIRONDACK
CATSKILL PARK
CATSKILL MTS.
Mt. Marcy 5,344
Slide Mtn. 4,204
FORT DRUM MIL. RES.
ST. REGIS MOHAWK IND. RES.
ONONDAGA IND. RES.
Oneida Ind. Res.
Lanark
Kemptville
Perth
Smiths Falls
Spencerville
Toledo
Brockville
Perth Road
Lansdowne
Kingston
Morrisburg
Cornwall
Hogansburg
Fort Covington
Massena
Waddington
Coles Creek S.P.
Norfolk
Norwood
Brasher Falls
Brushton
Malone
Burke
Chateaugay
Hemmingford
Champlain
Mooers
Altona
Chazy
Rouses Pt.
Alburg
St. Albans
Madrid
Potsdam
Nicholville
St. Regis Falls
Parishville
Santa Clara
Hannawa Falls
Colton
South Colton
Higley Flow S.P.
Ogdensburg
Remington Art Mus.
Heuvelton
Eel Weir S.P.
Canton
Rensselaer Falls
Morristown
Jacques Cartier S.P.
Hermon
Hammond
Kring Point S.P.
Richville
Russell
Gouverneur
Edwards
Fowler
Fine
Boldt Castle
Alexandria Bay
Wellesley Island S.P.
Thousand Islands
Grass Point S.P.
Clayton
Theresa
Antwerp
Newton Falls
Star Lake
Harrisville
Carry Falls Res.
Childwold
Piercefield
Tupper Lake
Cranberry L.
Sabattis
Lyon Mountain
Merrill
Dannemora
Morrisonville
Plattsburgh
S.U.N.Y. at Plattsburgh
Schuyler Falls
Saranac
Redford
Macomb Reservation S.P.
Peru
Ausable Chasm
Keeseville
Port Kent
Loon Lake
Paul Smiths
Lake Clear Junction
Saranac Lake
Lake Placid
John Brown Farm St. Hist. Site
Wilmington
Au Sable Forks
Jay
Keene
Keene Valley
Elizabethtown
Lewis
Essex
Willsboro
Westport
Winooski
Essex Junction
Burlington
South Burlington
Vergennes
Middlebury
Mineville
Port Henry
North Hudson
Crown Point
Ticonderoga
Seasonal Ferry
Severance
Schroon Lake
Hague
Pottersville
Brant Lake
Natural Stone Br. and Caves
Minerva
Newcomb
Long Lake
Adirondack Museum
Blue Mountain Lake
Raquette Lake
Indian Lake
Sabael
North Creek
Bakers Mills
Johnsburg
The Glen
Warrensburg
Bolton Landing
Whitehall
Hampton
Fair Haven
Diamond Point
Lake George
Fort Wm. Henry
Great Escape
Lake Luzerne
Hadley
Glens Falls
Hudson Falls
Fort Edward
Fort Ann
Comstock
Granville
Hartford
Argyle
Salem
Corinth
Moreau Lake S.P.
Grants Cottage St. Hist. Site
Northville
Great Sacandaga L.
Saratoga Springs
Broadalbin
Galway
Ballston Spa
Victory Mills
Schuylerville
Greenwich
Cambridge
Bennington Bfld. St. Hist. Site
Hoosick Falls
Bennington
Stillwater
Mechanicville
Round Lake
Saratoga Natl. Hist. Park
Schaghticoke
Grafton Lakes S.P.
Clifton Park
Melrose
Cohoes
Schenectady
Scotia
Amsterdam
Hagaman
Johnstown
Johnson Hall S.H.S.
Guy Park S.H.S.
Mayfield
Caroga Lake
Speculator
Lake Pleasant
Piseco L.
Higgins Bay
Wells
Hoffmeister
Big Moose
Inlet
Old Forge
Thendara
Enchanted Forest/ Water Safari
Dolgeville
Little Falls
St. Johnsville
Fonda
Palatine Bridge
Fort Plain
Canajoharie
Herkimer
Herkimer Home S.H.S.
Ilion
Mohawk
Frankfort
Middleville
Newport
Poland
Cold Brook
Watertown
Evans Mills
Calcium
Black River
Carthage
West Carthage
Natural Bridge
Castorland
Croghan
Copenhagen
Lowville
Glenfield
Whetstone Gulf S.P.
Lyons Falls
Port Leyden
Turin
Constableville
West Leyden
Boonville
Alder Creek
Pixley Falls S.P.
Delta Lake S.P.
Steuben Mem. S.H.S.
Remsen
Prospect
Hinckley Res.
Chaumont
Cape Vincent
Long Point S.P.
Brownville
Dexter
Sackets Harbor
Sackets Harbor Bfld. S.H.S.
Galloo I.
Stony I.
Stony Pt.
Henderson
Westcott Beach S.P.
Adams Center
Adams
Lorraine
Southwick Beach S.P.
Ellisburg
Mannsville
Sandy Creek
Lacona
Selkirk Shores S.P.
Mexico Bay
Pulaski
Salmon River Res.
Redfield
Altmar
Osceola
Fort Ontario St. Hist. Site
Oswego
New Haven
Mexico
Williamstown
Parish
Battle Island S.P.
Minetto
Fulton
Camden
Central Square
Constantia
Ft. Stanwix Natl. Mon.
Brewerton
Phoenix
Cleveland
Rome
Holland Patent
Oriskany
Sylvan Beach
Oneida L.
Erie Canal
Bridgeport
Cicero
Baldwinsville
North Syracuse
Whitesboro
Utica
Oneida
Sherrill
Canastota
Minoa
Fayetteville
Chittenango
Clinton
New Hartford
Clayville
Syracuse
Fairmount
Weedsport
Elbridge
Skaneateles
Manlius
Munnsville
Oriskany Falls
Waterville
Sangerfield
Morrisville
Cazenovia
Auburn
LaFayette
Lorenzo S.H.S.
Madison
Bridgewater
West Winfield
Richfield Springs
Fabius
Hamilton
Leonardsville
Owasco L.
Skaneateles L.
Tully
De Ruyter
Georgetown
Earlville
Glimmerglass S.P.
Cherry Valley
Cooperstown
National Baseball Hall of Fame
Sharon Springs
Sloansville
Esperance
Howe Caverns
Central Bridge
Cobleskill
Altamont
Colonie
Troy
Albany
Rensselaer
Petersburg
Berlin
Cherry Plain S.P.
Fillmore Glen S.P.
Preble
Moravia
Truxton
Otselic
South Otselic
Smyrna
Sherburne
Edmeston
Gilbert Lake S.P.
Hartwick
Worcester
Schoharie
John Boyd Thacher S.P.
Voorheesville
Delmar
Castleton-on-Hudson
Stephentown
Nassau
Homer
Cortland
S.U.N.Y. Coll. at Cortland
McGraw
Groton
Freeville
Lansing
Ithaca
Cornell Univ.
Robert H. Treman S.P.
Dryden
Harford
Marathon
Richford
Lisle
Cincinnatus
Bowman Lake S.P.
Norwich
Willet
Oxford
New Berlin
Hunts Pond S.P.
Morris
South New Berlin
Gilbertsville
Laurens
S.U.N.Y. Coll. at Oneonta
Oneonta
Natl. Soccer Hall of Fame
Mt. Upton
Otego
Milford
Schenevus
Richmondville
Middleburgh
Max V. Shaul S.P.
Clarksville
Westerlo
Ravena
Valatie
New Lebanon
Pittsfield
Kinderhook
Lenox
Davenport
East Meredith
Stamford
Hobart
Mine Kill S.P.
Schoharie Res.
Grand Gorge
Prattsville
Greenville
Martin Van Buren N.H.S.
Coxsackie
Hudson Riv. Is. S.P.
Chatham
Columbiaville
Philmont
Athens
Hudson
Claverack
Great Barrington
Unadilla
Sidney
Franklin
Sidney Center
John Burroughs Memorial St. Hist. Site
Roxbury
Delhi
Bainbridge
Afton
Masonville
Chenango Valley S.P.
Whitney Point
Greene
Berkshire
Candor
Newfield
Spencer
Newark Valley
Johnson City
Endwell
Endicott
Owego
Binghamton
S.U.N.Y. at Binghamton
Apalachin
Nichols
Waverly
Sayre
Harpursville
Windsor
Oquaga Creek S.P.
Cannonsville Res.
Walton
De Lancey
Andes
Pepacton Res.
Downsville
Deposit
East Branch
Hancock
Roscoe
Livingston Manor
Hallstead
Susquehanna
New Milford
Margaretville
Fleischmanns
Big Indian
Shandaken
Phoenicia
Boiceville
Hunter
Tannersville
Palenville
Cairo
Leeds
Catskill
Olana S.H.S.
Hillsdale
Taconic S.P.
Saugerties
Clermont S.H.S.
Tivoli
L. Taghkanic S.P.
Woodstock
W. Hurley
Hurley
Kingston
Ashokan Res.
Red Hook
Old Rhinebeck Aerodrome
Rhinebeck
Senate House S.H.S.
Millerton
Amenia
Canaan
MAPQUEST
8 9 10 11 12 13 14
B C D E F G H J K

North & South Carolina

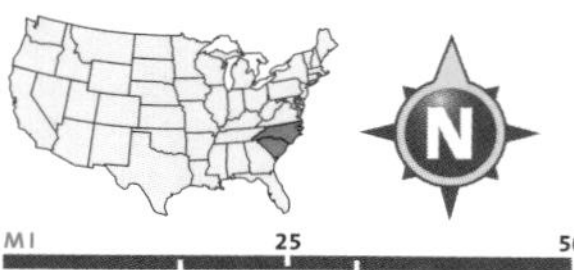

NC 104
SC 105
tennessee 34
georgia 29

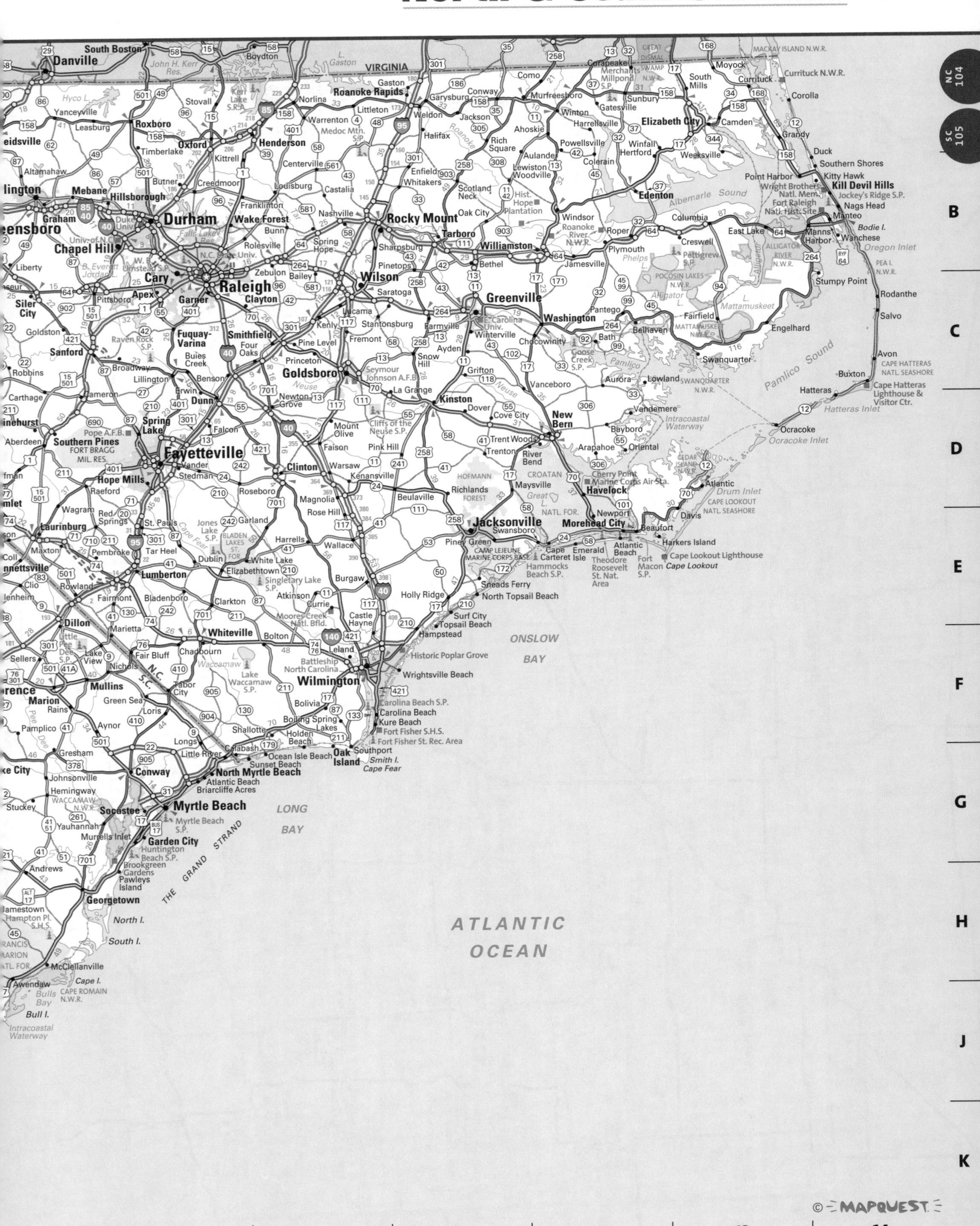
VIRGINIA
Danville
South Boston
Boydton
John H. Kerr Res.
L. Gaston
Gaston
Roanoke Rapids
Como
Corapeake
Great Dismal Swamp N.W.R.
Merchants Millpond S.P.
Mackay Island N.W.R.
Moyock
Currituck
Currituck N.W.R.
Corolla
South Mills
Yanceyville
Leasburg
Roxboro
Stovall
Kerr Lake S.R.A.
Norlina
Warrenton
Littleton
Medoc Mtn. S.P.
Weldon
Garysburg
Conway
Jackson
Murfreesboro
Winton
Gatesville
Sunbury
Harrellsville
Elizabeth City
Camden
Grandy
Reidsville
Timberlake
Oxford
Henderson
Halifax
Ahoskie
Rich Square
Aulander
Powellsville
Colerain
Winfall
Hertford
Weeksville
Duck
Southern Shores
Kitty Hawk
Kill Devil Hills
Point Harbor
Wright Brothers Natl. Mem.
Jockey's Ridge S.P.
Nags Head
Fort Raleigh Natl. Hist. Site
Manteo
Altamahaw
Kittrell
Centerville
Enfield
Whitakers
Scotland Neck
Lewiston Woodville
Hist. Hope Plantation
Edenton
Albemarle Sound
Mebane
Hillsborough
Butner
Creedmoor
Franklinton
Louisburg
Castalia
Nashville
Rocky Mount
Oak City
Windsor
Roanoke River N.W.R.
Roper
Columbia
East Lake
Manns Harbor
Wanchese
Bodie I.
Oregon Inlet
Greensboro
Graham
Durham
Duke Univ.
Wake Forest
Bunn
Tarboro
Williamston
Plymouth
Creswell
Pettigrew S.P.
Alligator River N.W.R.
Chapel Hill
Univ. of N.C.
Falls Lake
N.C. State Univ.
Rolesville
Spring Hope
Sharpsburg
Pinetops
Bethel
Jamesville
Phelps L.
Pocosin Lakes N.W.R.
Pea I. N.W.R.
Liberty
B. Everett Jordan L.
W.B. Umstead S.P.
Cary
Zebulon
Bailey
Wilson
Stumpy Point
Rodanthe
Siler City
Pittsboro
Apex
Garner
Raleigh
Clayton
Saratoga
Greenville
Washington
Pantego
Alligator L.
L. Mattamuskeet
Salvo
Goldston
Sanford
Raven Rock S.P.
Fuquay-Varina
Smithfield
Four Oaks
Kenly
Lucama
Stantonsburg
Farmville
E. Carolina Univ.
Winterville
Chocowinity
Bath
Belhaven
Fairfield
Mattamuskeet N.W.R.
Engelhard
Avon
Cape Hatteras Natl. Seashore
Buies Creek
Pine Level
Fremont
Snow Hill
Ayden
Goose Creek S.P.
Pamlico
Swanquarter
Pamlico Sound
Robbins
Broadway
Lillington
Benson
Princeton
Goldsboro
Seymour Johnson A.F.B.
Grifton
Vanceboro
Aurora
Lowland
Swanquarter N.W.R.
Buxton
Hatteras
Cape Hatteras Lighthouse & Visitor Ctr.
Carthage
Cameron
Erwin
Dunn
Newton Grove
La Grange
Kinston
Dover
Cove City
New Bern
Vandemere
Intracoastal Waterway
Hatteras Inlet
Pinehurst
Pope A.F.B.
Spring Lake
Falcon
Mount Olive
Cliffs of the Neuse S.P.
Trent Woods
Bayboro
Ocracoke
Ocracoke Inlet
Aberdeen
Southern Pines
Fort Bragg Mil. Res.
Fayetteville
Vander
Faison
Pink Hill
Trenton
River Bend
Arapahoe
Oriental
Hope Mills
Stedman
Clinton
Warsaw
Kenansville
Hofmann Forest
Croatan Natl. For.
Maysville
Cherry Point Marine Corps Air Sta.
Havelock
Cedar Island N.W.R.
Atlantic
Drum Inlet
Raeford
Roseboro
Magnolia
Beulaville
Richlands
Great L.
Cape Lookout Natl. Seashore
Hamlet
Wagram
Red Springs
Rose Hill
Jacksonville
Swansboro
Newport
Morehead City
Beaufort
Davis
Laurinburg
St. Pauls
Jones Lake S.P.
Garland
Bladen Lakes St. For.
Harrells
Wallace
Piney Green
Camp Lejeune Marine Corps Base
Cape Carteret
Emerald Isle
Atlantic Beach
Harkers Island
Maxton
Pembroke
Tar Heel
Dublin
White Lake
Hammocks Beach S.P.
Theodore Roosevelt St. Nat. Area
Fort Macon S.P.
Cape Lookout Lighthouse
Cape Lookout
Bennettsville
Clio
Rowland
Lumberton
Elizabethtown
Singletary Lake S.P.
Burgaw
Sneads Ferry
North Topsail Beach
Fairmont
Bladenboro
Clarkton
Atkinson
Currie
Moores Creek Natl. Bfld.
Holly Ridge
Surf City
Topsail Beach
Dillon
Marietta
Whiteville
Bolton
Castle Hayne
Hampstead
Onslow Bay
Little Pee Dee S.P.
Lake View
Fair Bluff
Chadbourn
Lake Waccamaw S.P.
Leland
Battleship North Carolina
Historic Poplar Grove
Sellers
Nichols
N.C.
S.C.
Mullins
Tabor City
Wilmington
Wrightsville Beach
Florence
Marion
Rains
Green Sea
Loris
Bolivia
Carolina Beach S.P.
Carolina Beach
Kure Beach
Fort Fisher S.H.S.
Fort Fisher St. Rec. Area
Pamplico
Aynor
Shallotte
Boiling Spring Lakes
Holden Beach
Southport
Gresham
Longs
Little River
Calabash
Ocean Isle Beach
Sunset Beach
Oak Island
Smith I.
Cape Fear
Johnsonville
Conway
North Myrtle Beach
Atlantic Beach
Briarcliffe Acres
Hemingway
Waccamaw N.W.R.
Stuckey
Socastee
Myrtle Beach
Myrtle Beach S.P.
Long Bay
Yauhannah
Murrells Inlet
Garden City
Huntington Beach S.P.
Brookgreen Gardens
Pawleys Island
The Grand Strand
Andrews
Georgetown
Jamestown
Hampton Pl. S.H.S.
North I.
South I.
Francis Marion Natl. For.
McClellanville
Awendaw
Cape I.
Cape Romain N.W.R.
Bulls Bay
Bull I.
Intracoastal Waterway
Atlantic Ocean
NC 104
SC 105
B
C
D
E
F
G
H
J
K
8
9
10
11
12
13
14
© MAPQUEST

North Dakota

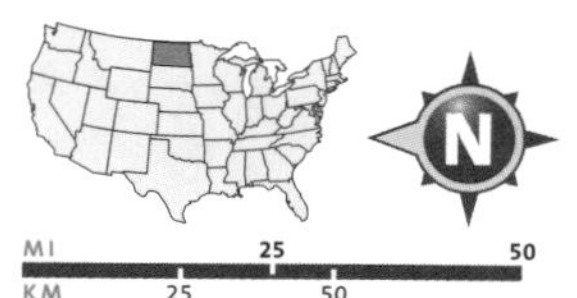

N
MI 25 50
KM 25 50 75

NORTH DAKOTA
NEBRASKA
MONTANA
WYOMING
MINN.
IOWA
minnesota 39
north dakota 54
nebraska 45
montana 44
SD 105
Pierre
Sioux Falls
Rapid City
Aberdeen
Watertown
Brookings
Huron
Mitchell
Yankton
Vermillion
Madison
Spearfish
Sturgis
Mobridge
Wahpeton
Sioux City
South Sioux City
Chadron
Valentine
O'Neill
Wayne
STANDING ROCK IND. RES.
CHEYENNE RIVER IND. RES.
PINE RIDGE IND. RES.
ROSEBUD IND. RES.
BADLANDS NATL PARK
BLACK HILLS
SAND HILLS
MOUNTAIN TIME ZONE
CENTRAL TIME ZONE
MAPQUEST

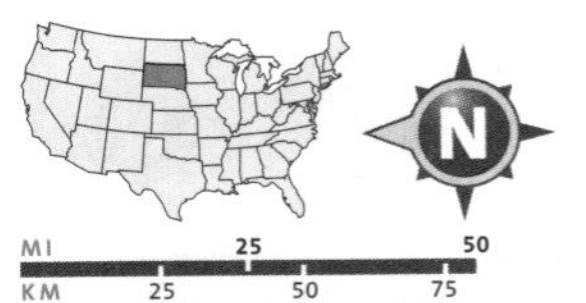

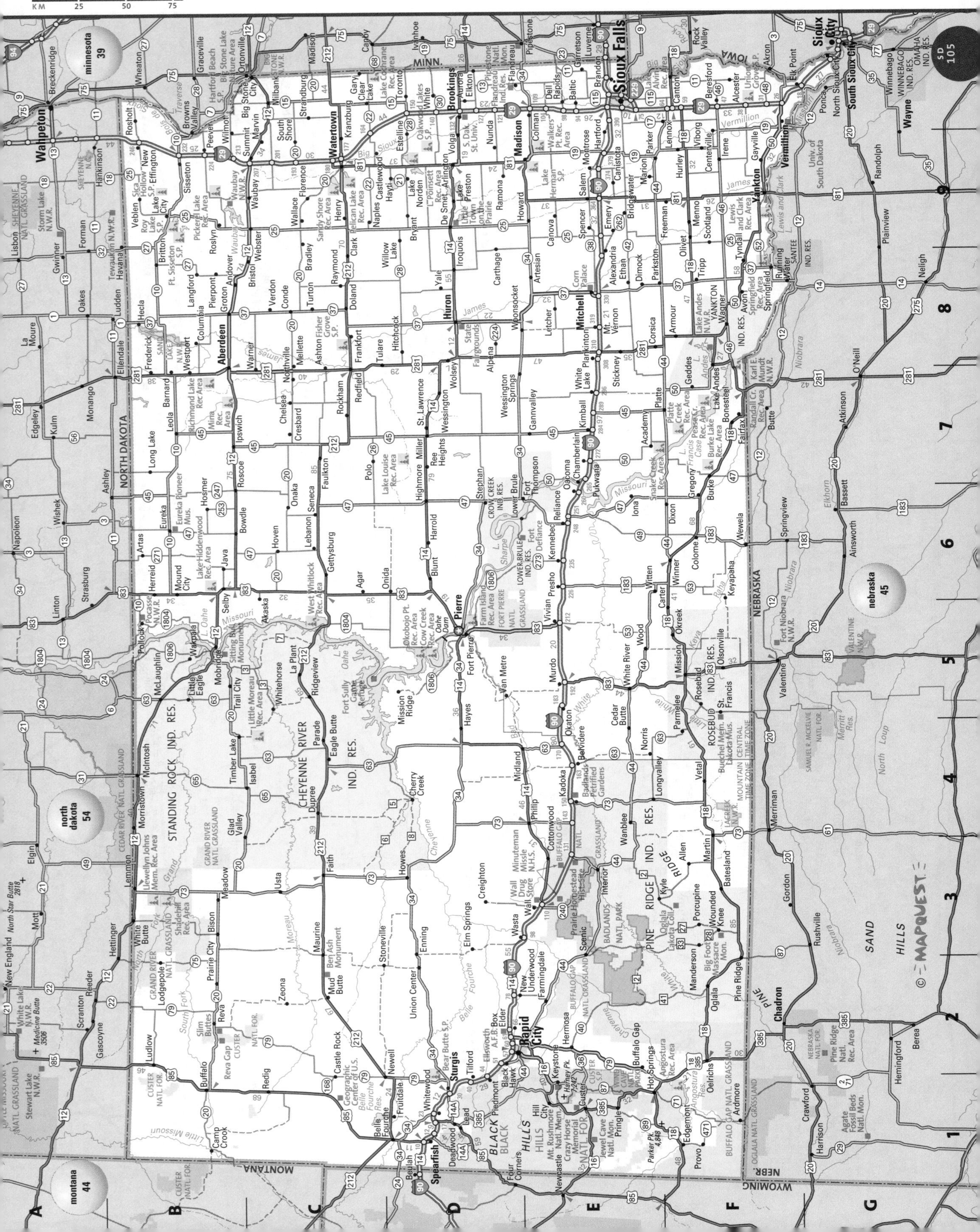

MI 15 30
KM 15 30
OH 104
LAKE ERIE
ONTARIO
MICHIGAN
PENNSYLVANIA
INDIANA
CANADA
U.S.
Toledo
Cleveland
Detroit
Windsor
Akron
Canton
Youngstown
Lansing
Ann Arbor
London
Sandusky
Mansfield
Lima
Findlay
Warren
Sarnia
Chatham
ontario 76
michigan 40

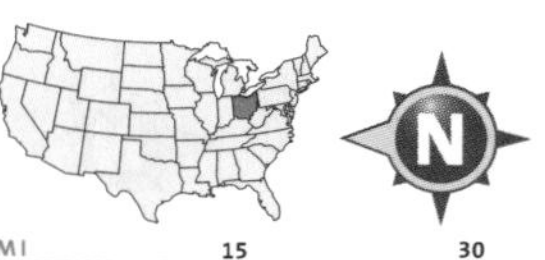

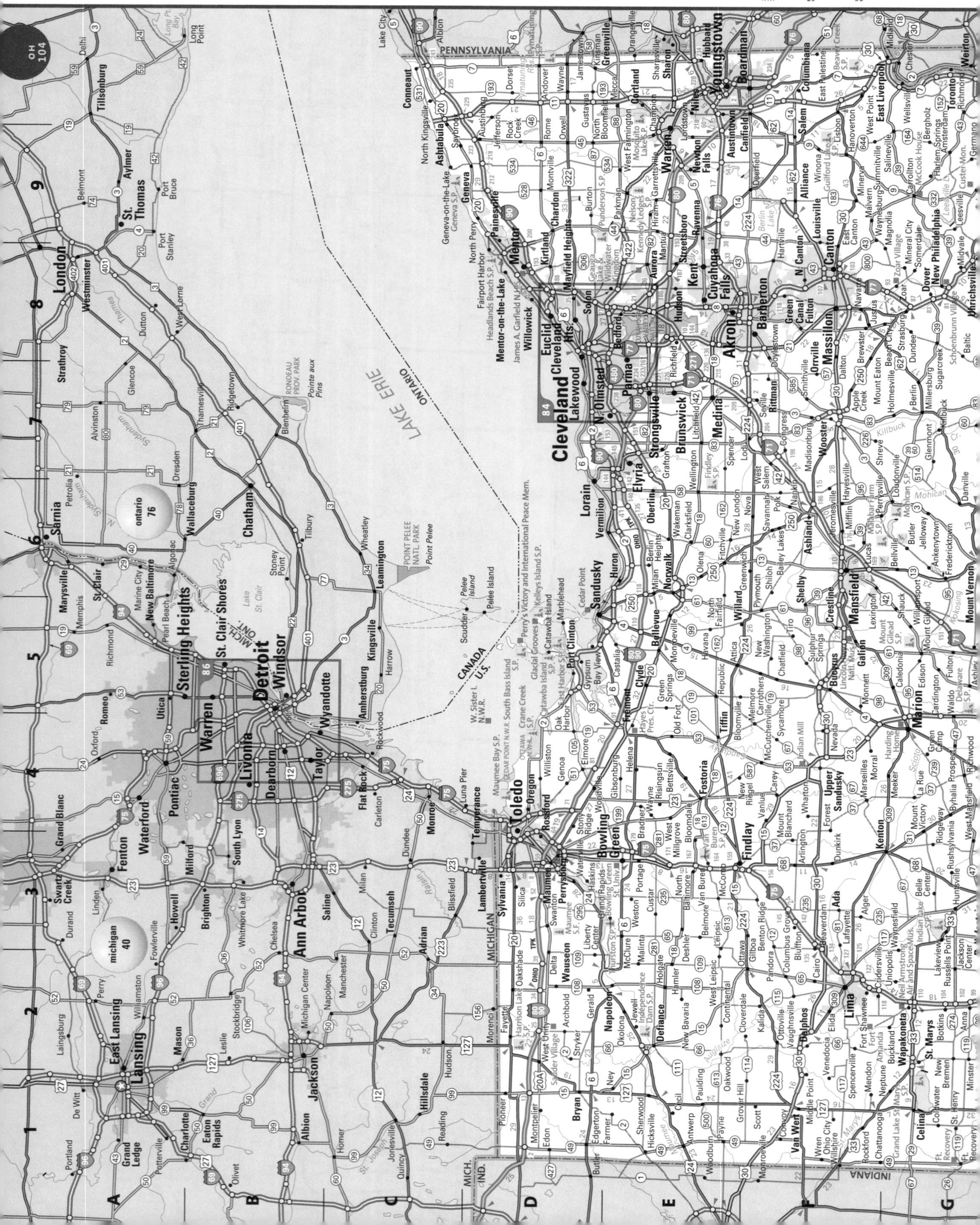

OH 104
Columbus
Dayton
Cincinnati
Covington
Springfield
Hamilton
Middletown
Zanesville
Newark
Lancaster
Chillicothe
Athens
Marietta
Parkersburg
Wheeling
Charleston
Huntington
Ashland
Portsmouth
Lexington
Frankfort
Richmond
Beckley
west virginia 66
kentucky 34
WAYNE N.F.
DANIEL BOONE N.F.
MONONGAHELA NATL. FOR.
INDIANA
KENTUCKY
W. VA.
PA.
© MAPQUEST

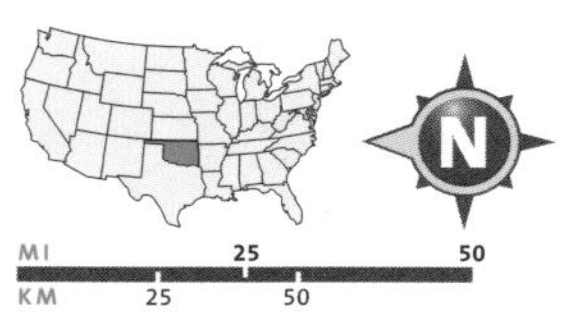

OKLAHOMA PANHANDLE

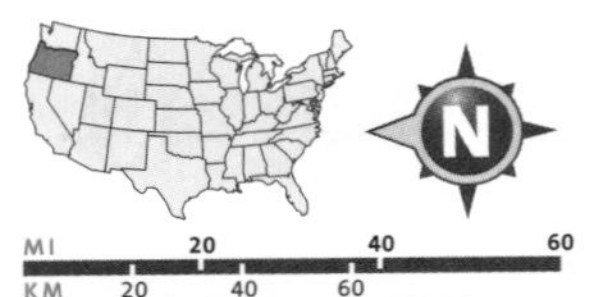
N
MI 20 40 60
KM 20 40 60

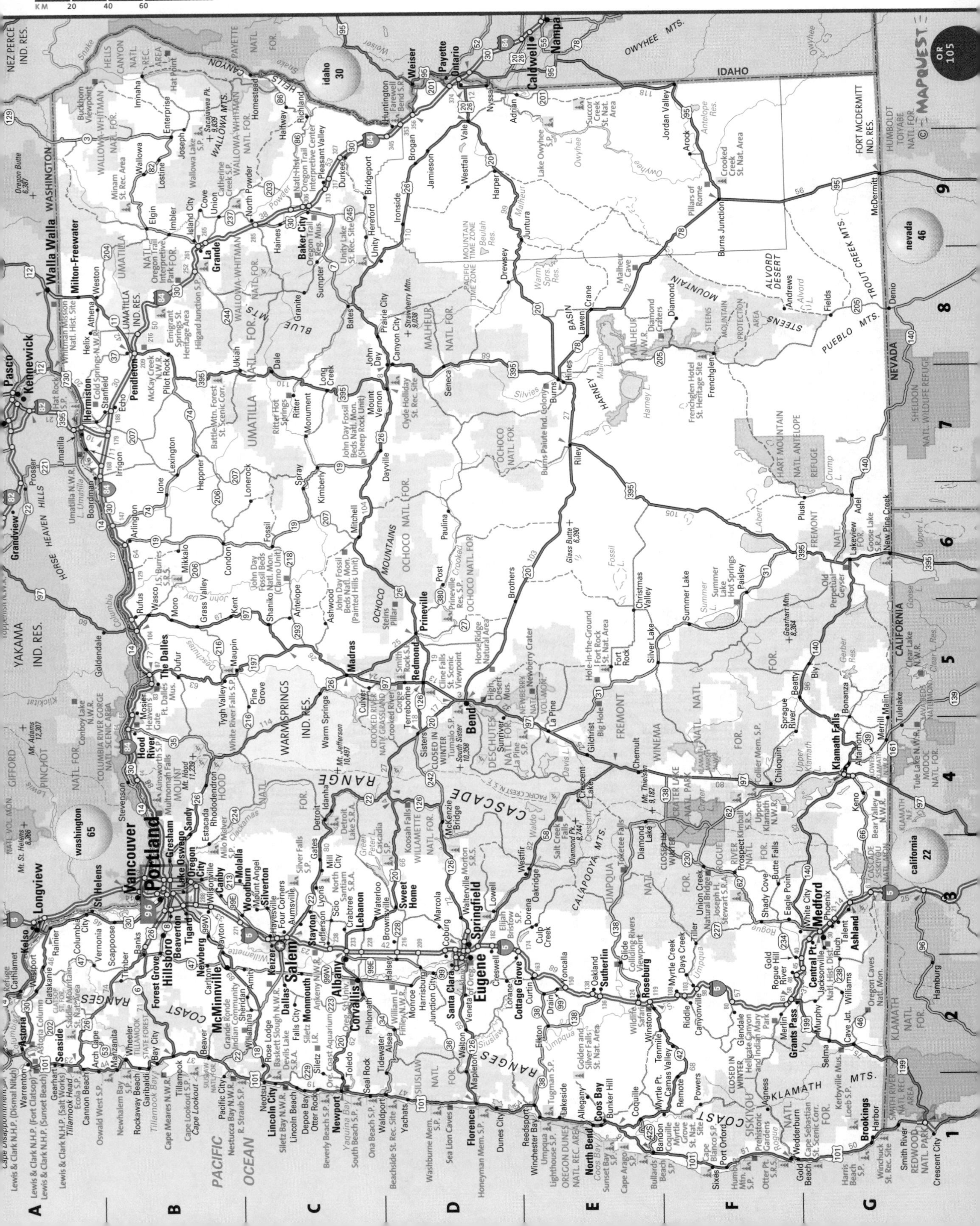

Pennsylvania

MI 15 30
KM 15 30

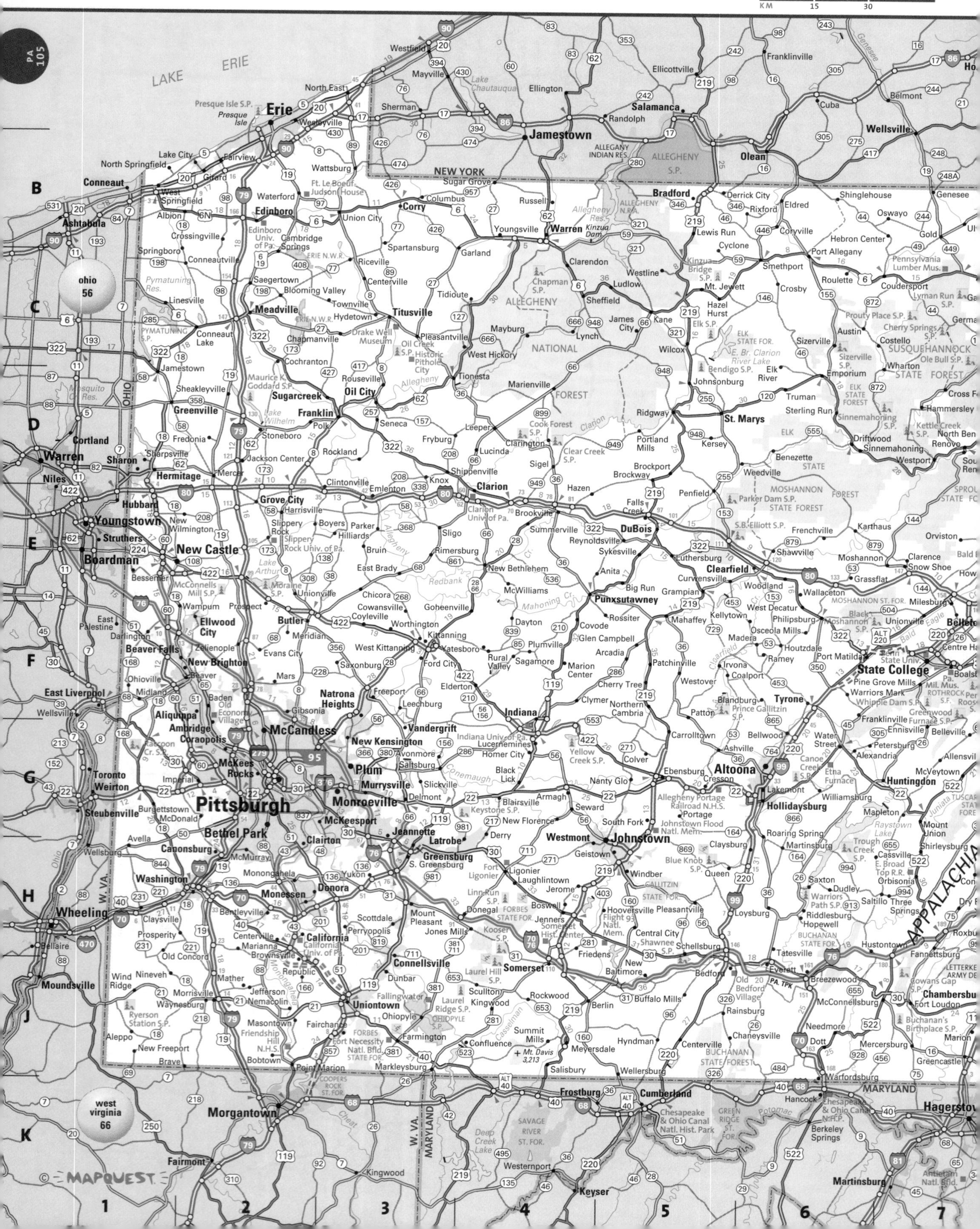

PA 105

LAKE ERIE

NEW YORK

ohio 56

west virginia 66

MARYLAND

W. VA.

OHIO

Erie
Jamestown
Salamanca
Olean
Wellsville
Bradford
Warren
Meadville
Titusville
Oil City
Franklin
Clarion
DuBois
St. Marys
Clearfield
State College
Altoona
Johnstown
Indiana
Butler
New Castle
Youngstown
Warren
Boardman
Pittsburgh
McCandless
Bethel Park
Monroeville
Washington
Wheeling
Steubenville
Greensburg
Uniontown
Somerset
Bedford
Huntingdon
Chambersburg
Morgantown
Cumberland
Hagerstown
Martinsburg

ALLEGHENY NATIONAL FOREST
SUSQUEHANNOCK STATE FOREST
MOSHANNON STATE FOREST
APPALACHIA

© MAPQUEST

1 2 3 4 5 6 7

PA 105
new york 50
new jersey 48
maryland 25
delaware 25
NEW YORK
MARYLAND
Binghamton
Elmira
Corning
Horseheads
Bath
Johnson City
Endwell
Endicott
Owego
Waverly
Sayre
Athens
Towanda
Mansfield
Wellsboro
Williamsport
South Williamsport
Lock Haven
Scranton
Wilkes-Barre
Kingston
Pittston
Carbondale
Honesdale
Stroudsburg
East Stroudsburg
Hazleton
Bloomsburg
Berwick
Sunbury
Shamokin
Pottsville
Allentown
Bethlehem
Easton
Reading
Lebanon
Hershey
Harrisburg
Carlisle
Mechanicsburg
Lancaster
York
Gettysburg
Hanover
Chambersburg
Shippensburg
Norristown
King of Prussia
Philadelphia
Camden
Chester
Wilmington
Newark
West Chester
Trenton
Levittown
Doylestown
Pottstown
Phoenixville
New Brunswick
Princeton
Morristown
Dover
Port Jervis
Milford
Monticello
Vineland
Bridgeton
Glassboro
Elkton
Bel Air
Aberdeen
Havre de Grace
Westminster
Thurmont
Waynesboro
CATSKILL PARK
CATSKILL MTS.
Pepacton Res.
Cannonsville Res.
TIADAGHTON STATE FOREST
DELAWARE STATE FOREST
BALD EAGLE STATE FOREST
PA. TURNPIKE
B
C
D
E
F
G
H
J
K
8
9
10
11
12
13
14

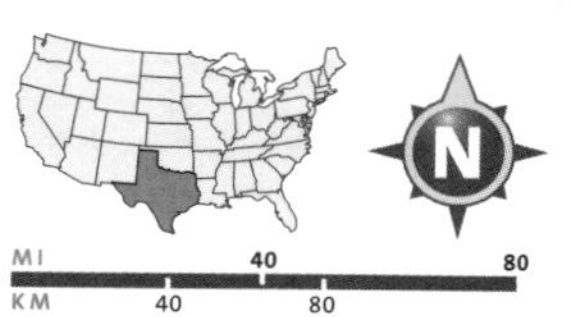

TEXAS PANHANDLE

new mexico 49

oklahoma 58

mexico 82

TX 105

NEW MEXICO
CHIHUAHUA
COAHUILA
OKLAHOMA
LLANO ESTACADO
PECOS PLAINS
STOCKTON PLATEAU
SIERRA GRANDE
SIERRA DEL CARMEN
WHITE SANDS MISSILE RANGE
FORT BLISS MIL. RES.
GILA NATL. FOR.
CIBOLA NATL. FOR.
LINCOLN NATL. FOR.
BIG BEND NATL. PARK
CARLSBAD CAVERNS NATL. PARK
MOUNTAIN TIME ZONE
CENTRAL TIME ZONE

El Paso
Ciudad Juárez
Las Cruces
Alamogordo
Roswell
Carlsbad
Hobbs
Lubbock
Midland
Odessa
Big Spring
Pecos
Fort Stockton
Alpine
Marfa
Van Horn
Presidio
Ojinaga
Del Rio
Ciudad Acuña
Monclova
Nueva Rosita
San Juan de Sabinas
Amarillo
Wichita Falls
Lawton
Clovis
Dalhart
Borger
Pampa
Plainview
Childress
Vernon

Wichita Falls
Abilene
Ft. Worth
Dallas
Arlington
Waco
Austin
San Antonio
Houston
Galveston
Beaumont
Corpus Christi
Laredo
Nuevo Laredo
McAllen
Brownsville
Matamoros
Reynosa
Monterrey
Tyler
Shreveport
Texarkana
Lake Charles
San Angelo
Victoria
OKLAHOMA
ARKANSAS
LOUISIANA
MEXICO
arkansas 21
louisiana 37
TX 105
GULF OF MEXICO
PADRE ISLAND NATL. SEASHORE
EDWARDS PLATEAU
B
C
D
E
F
G
H
J
K
8
9
10
11
12
13
14
© MAPQUEST

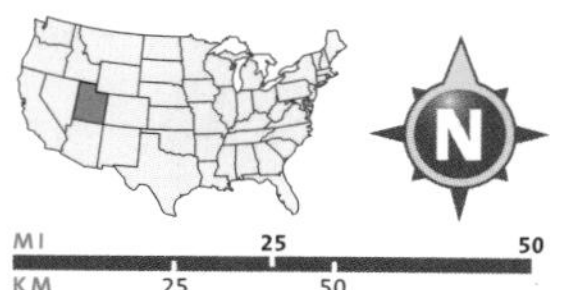

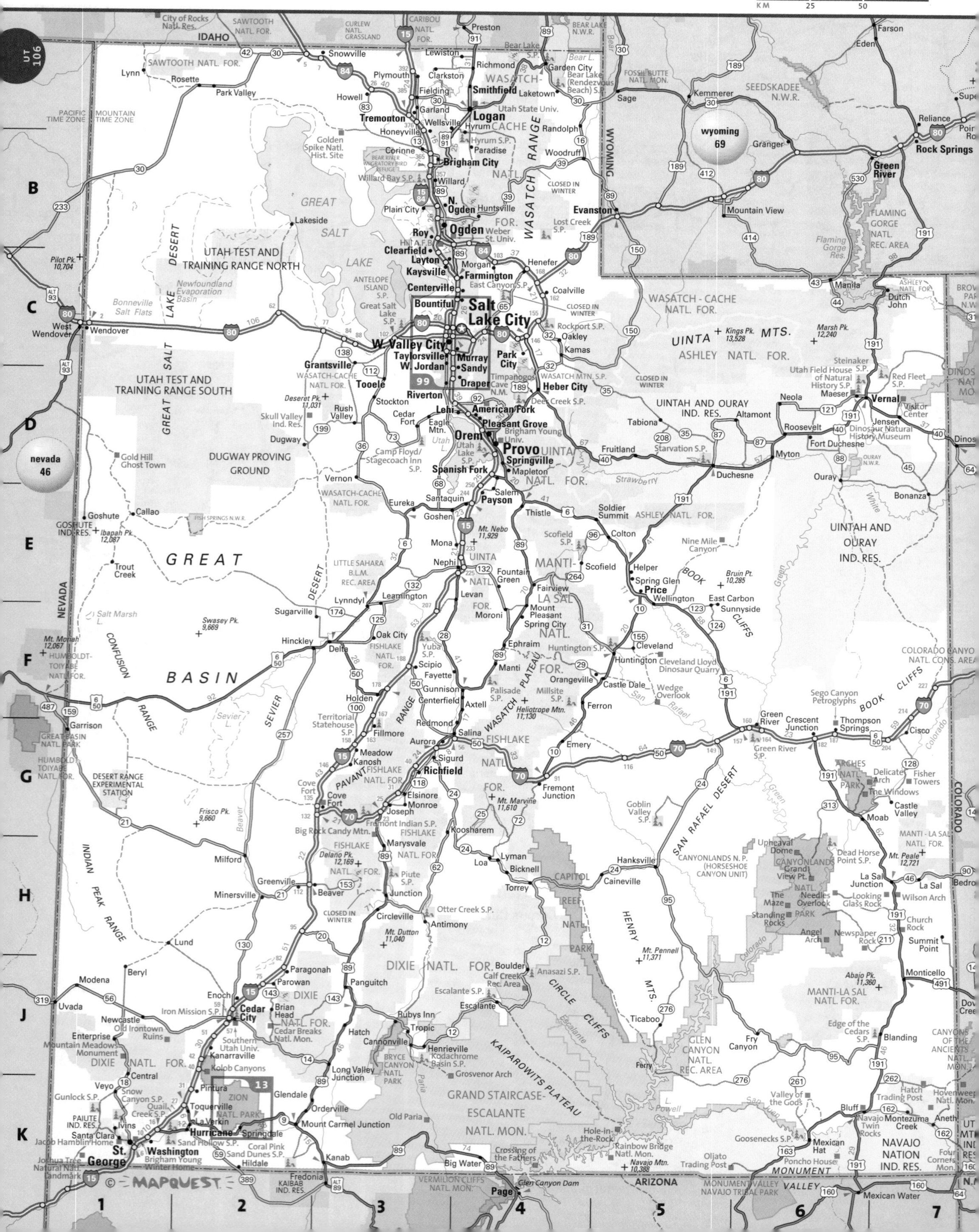

UT 106

City of Rocks Natl. Res.
SAWTOOTH NATL. FOR.
CURLEW NATL. GRASSLAND
CARIBOU NATL. FOR.
Preston
BEAR LAKE N.W.R.
Farson
Eden
IDAHO
Snowville
Lewiston
Bear Lake S.P.
Garden City
Bear Lake (Rendezvous Beach) S.P.
Lynn
Rosette
Park Valley
Plymouth
Clarkston
Richmond
WASATCH-
Smithfield
Laketown
FOSSIL BUTTE NATL. MON.
Sage
Kemmerer
SEEDSKADEE N.W.R.
Howell
Fielding
Garland
Logan
Utah State Univ.
CACHE
Randolph
Reliance
Rock Springs
PACIFIC TIME ZONE
MOUNTAIN TIME ZONE
Tremonton
Honeyville
Wellsville
Hyrum
Hyrum S.P.
Paradise
Woodruff
wyoming 69
Granger
Golden Spike Natl. Hist. Site
Corinne
BEAR RIVER MIGRATORY BIRD REFUGE
Brigham City
NATL.
Green River
Willard Bay S.P.
Willard
CLOSED IN WINTER
WYOMING
RANGE
WASATCH
B
GREAT
N. Ogden
Huntsville
Evanston
Mountain View
FLAMING GORGE NATL. REC. AREA
Flaming Gorge Res.
Plain City
Lakeside
SALT
Roy
Ogden
Weber St. Univ.
FOR.
Lost Creek S.P.
DESERT
UTAH TEST AND TRAINING RANGE NORTH
LAKE
Hill A.F.B.
Clearfield
Layton
Kaysville
Morgan
Henefer
Pilot Pk. 10,704
Newfoundland Evaporation Basin
ANTELOPE ISLAND S.P.
Farmington
Centerville
East Canyon S.P.
Coalville
CLOSED IN WINTER
Manila
ASHLEY NATL. FOR.
Dutch John
WASATCH - CACHE NATL. FOR.
C
Bonneville Salt Flats
Great Salt Lake S.P.
Bountiful
Salt Lake City
Rockport S.P.
Oakley
Kings Pk. 13,528
UINTA MTS.
Marsh Pk. 12,240
West Wendover
Wendover
W. Valley City
Taylorsville
W. Jordan
Murray
Sandy
Draper
Park City
Kamas
ASHLEY NATL. FOR.
Steinaker S.P.
Red Fleet S.P.
Grantsville
WASATCH-CACHE NATL. FOR.
Tooele
Timpanogos Cave N.M.
WASATCH MTN. S.P.
Heber City
CLOSED IN WINTER
Utah Field House of Natural History S.P.
Maeser
Vernal
Visitor Center
UTAH TEST AND TRAINING RANGE SOUTH
Deseret Pk. 11,031
Riverton
Stockton
Lehi
American Fork
Deer Creek S.P.
UINTAH AND OURAY IND. RES.
Neola
Altamont
Jensen
Dinosaur Natural History Museum
D
Skull Valley Ind. Res.
Rush Valley
Cedar Fort
Eagle Mtn.
Pleasant Grove
Brigham Young Univ.
Tabiona
Roosevelt
Fort Duchesne
Dugway
Orem
Utah Lake S.P.
Provo
Springville
Starvation S.P.
Fruitland
Myton
OURAY N.W.R.
nevada 46
Gold Hill Ghost Town
DUGWAY PROVING GROUND
Camp Floyd/Stagecoach Inn S.P.
Spanish Fork
Mapleton
UINTA NATL. FOR.
Strawberry
Duchesne
Ouray
Bonanza
Vernon
WASATCH-CACHE NATL. FOR.
Eureka
Santaquin
Salem
Payson
Thistle
Soldier Summit
ASHLEY NATL. FOR.
Goshute
Callao
FISH SPRINGS N.W.R.
GOSHUTE IND. RES.
Ibapah Pk. 12,087
Goshen
Mt. Nebo 11,929
Scofield S.P.
Colton
UINTAH AND OURAY IND. RES.
E
GREAT
Trout Creek
LITTLE SAHARA B.L.M. REC. AREA
Mona
Nephi
UINTA
Nine Mile Canyon
Scofield
Helper
Fountain Green
MANTI-
Spring Glen
Price
BOOK
Bruin Pt. 10,285
Wellington
East Carbon
Sunnyside
CLIFFS
NEVADA
Salt Marsh L.
Swasey Pk. 9,669
DESERT
Sugarville
Lynndyl
Leamington
Levan
NATL.
FOR.
Moroni
Fairview
LA SAL
Mount Pleasant
Spring City
NATL.
Mt. Moriah 12,067
HUMBOLDT-TOIYABE NATL. FOR.
CONFUSION
Hinckley
Delta
Oak City
FISHLAKE NATL. FOR.
Yuba S.P.
Ephraim
Huntington S.P.
Cleveland
Huntington
Cleveland Lloyd Dinosaur Quarry
COLORADO CANYON NATL. CONS. AREA
F
BASIN
Scipio
Fayette
Manti
FOR.
Orangeville
Castle Dale
Wedge Overlook
Gunnison
Centerfield
Axtell
Palisade S.P.
Millsite S.P.
Sego Canyon Petroglyphs
BOOK CLIFFS
Garrison
RANGE
Sevier L.
SEVIER
Holden
Territorial Statehouse S.P.
Fillmore
RANGE
WASATCH PLATEAU
Heliotrope Mtn. 11,130
Ferron
Green River
Crescent Junction
Thompson Springs
Cisco
GREAT BASIN NATL. PARK
Redmond
Salina
FISHLAKE
Emery
Green River S.P.
HUMBOLDT-TOIYABE NATL. FOR.
Meadow
Kanosh
Aurora
Sigurd
Richfield
NATL.
ARCHES NATL. PARK
Delicate Arch
Fisher Towers
G
DESERT RANGE EXPERIMENTAL STATION
Cove Fort
PAVANT
FISHLAKE NATL. FOR.
Cove Fort
Elsinore
Monroe
Joseph
FOR.
Mt. Marvine 11,610
Fremont Junction
Goblin Valley S.P.
SAN RAFAEL DESERT
The Windows
Castle Valley
Moab
COLORADO
Frisco Pk. 9,660
Beaver
Big Rock Candy Mtn.
Fremont Indian S.P.
FISHLAKE
Marysvale
Koosharem
Upheaval Dome
CANYONLANDS
MANTI - LA SAL NATL. FOR.
INDIAN
Milford
Delano Pk. 12,169
NATL. FOR.
Loa
Lyman
Bicknell
Hanksville
CANYONLANDS N.P. (HORSESHOE CANYON UNIT)
Grand View Pt.
Dead Horse Point S.P.
Mt. Peale 12,721
H
PEAK
Minersville
Greenville
Beaver
Piute S.P.
Junction
Torrey
CAPITOL
REEF
Caineville
La Sal Junction
La Sal
Bedrock
The Maze
Needles Overlook
Looking Glass Rock
Wilson Arch
RANGE
CLOSED IN WINTER
Circleville
Otter Creek S.P.
Antimony
NATL.
HENRY
Standing Rocks
PARK
Angel Arch
Newspaper Rock
Church Rock
Lund
Mt. Dutton 11,040
PARK
Mt. Pennell 11,371
Summit Point
Modena
Beryl
Paragonah
DIXIE NATL. FOR.
Boulder
Anasazi S.P.
Calf Creek Rec. Area
MTS.
Abajo Pk. 11,360
Monticello
Parowan
DIXIE
Panguitch
Escalante S.P.
CIRCLE
MANTI-LA SAL NATL. FOR.
J
Uvada
Iron Mission S.P.
Enoch
Cedar City
Brian Head
Escalante
CLIFFS
Ticaboo
Dove Creek
Newcastle
Old Irontown Ruins
NATL. FOR.
Cedar Breaks Natl. Mon.
Rubys Inn
Tropic
Escalante
Edge of the Cedars S.P.
Blanding
Enterprise
Mountain Meadows Monument
Southern Utah Univ.
Kanarraville
Hatch
Cannonville
Henrieville
Kodachrome Basin S.P.
KAIPAROWITS PLATEAU
GLEN CANYON NATL. REC. AREA
Fry Canyon
CANYONS OF THE ANCIENTS NATL. MON.
DIXIE NATL. FOR.
Central
Kolob Canyons
BRYCE CANYON NATL. PARK
Long Valley Junction
Grosvenor Arch
Ferry
Veyo
Snow Canyon S.P.
Pintura
GRAND STAIRCASE-ESCALANTE NATL. MON.
L. Powell
Valley of the Gods
Hatch Trading Post
Hovenweep Natl. Mon.
Gunlock S.P.
Quail Creek S.P.
Toquerville
ZION NATL. PARK
Glendale
Orderville
Old Paria
San Juan
Bluff
PAIUTE IND. RES.
Ivins
La Verkin
Springdale
Mount Carmel Junction
Navajo Twin Rocks
Montezuma Creek
Aneth
K
Santa Clara
Jacob Hamblin Home
Hurricane
Sand Hollow S.P.
Coral Pink Sand Dunes S.P.
Hole-in-the-Rock
Rainbow Bridge Natl. Mon.
Goosenecks S.P.
Mexican Hat
NAVAJO NATION IND. RES.
Four Corners Mon.
Joshua Tree Natural Landmark
St. George
Washington
Brigham Young Winter Home
Hildale
Kanab
Big Water
Crossing of the Fathers
Navajo Mtn. 10,388
Oljato Trading Post
Poncho House
MONUMENT
© MAPQUEST
KAIBAB IND. RES.
Fredonia
VERMILION CLIFFS NATL. MON.
Page
Glen Canyon Dam
ARIZONA
MONUMENT VALLEY NAVAJO TRIBAL PARK
VALLEY
Mexican Water

1 2 3 4 5 6 7

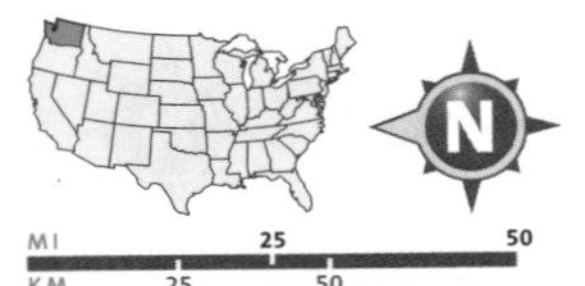
N
MI 25 50
KM 25 50

Virginia & West Virginia

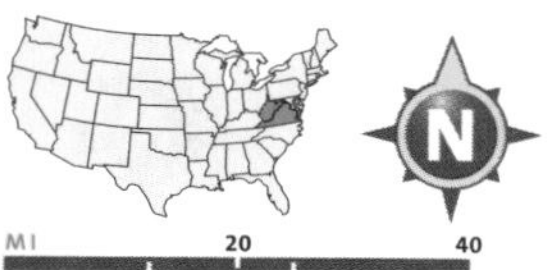

VA 106
WV 106
ohio 56
kentucky 34
tennessee 34
north carolina 52

Columbus
Pittsburgh
Wheeling
Zanesville
Lancaster
Newark
Parkersburg
Marietta
Morgantown
Clarksburg
Fairmont
Charleston
South Charleston
Huntington
Ashland
Portsmouth
Beckley
Bluefield
Princeton
Blacksburg
Roanoke
Salem
Christiansburg
Radford
Wytheville
Marion
Abingdon
Bristol
Kingsport
Johnson City
Elizabethton
Danville
Martinsville
Galax
Mount Airy
Pikeville
Hazard
Morehead
Maysville
Middlesboro
Lexington
Covington
Elkins
Buckhannon
Weirton
Steubenville
Washington
Uniontown

pennsylvania 60
maryland 25
new jersey 48
delaware 25
VA 106
WV 106
Indiana
Altoona
Huntingdon
Lewistown
Mifflintown
Millersburg
Pottsville
Allentown
Bethlehem
Flemington
Quakertown
Kutztown
Reading
Doylestown
Princeton
Lambertville
Trenton
Hollidaysburg
Johnstown
Windber
Blain
Harrisburg
Lebanon
Hershey
Carlisle
Ephrata
Pottstown
Norristown
Lancaster
Downingtown
Dillsburg
Shippensburg
York
Philadelphia
Kennett Square
Bedford
Breezewood
Chambersburg
Gettysburg
Hanover
Red Lion
Wilmington
Meyersdale
Waynesboro
Cumberland
Hagerstown
Newark
Elkton
Salem
Vineland
Hammonton
Bel Air
Aberdeen
Reisterstown
Bridgeton
Millville
Martinsburg
Frederick
Baltimore
Tuckahoe
Keyser
Smyrna
Harpers Ferry
Charles Town
Damascus
Columbia
Chestertown
Dover
Dover A.F.B.
Glen Burnie
Winchester
Leesburg
Gaithersburg
Centreville
Delaware Bay
North Cape May
Wildwood
Annapolis
Bowie
Reston
Front Royal
Middleburg
Washington
Arlington
Alexandria
Fairfax
Manassas
Warrenton
Milford
Cape May
Denton
Lewes
Dewey Beach
Easton
Upper Marlboro
Woodstock
Edinburg
Luray
Dale City
Woodbridge
St. Charles
Tilghman
Seaford
Bethany Beach
Cambridge
New Market
LaPlata
Harrisonburg
Bridgewater
Culpeper
Stafford
Salisbury
Ocean City
Fredericksburg
Spotsylvania
Staunton
Waynesboro
Charlottesville
Orange
Gordonsville
Crisfield
Chincoteague
Tangier
Tappahannock
Reedville
Ashland
Kilmarnock
Onancock
Richmond
Lynchburg
Farmville
Petersburg
Hopewell
Williamsburg
Yorktown
Hampton
Newport News
Portsmouth
Norfolk
Virginia Beach
Chesapeake
Suffolk
Emporia
Franklin
South Boston
Roanoke Rapids
Clarksville
Roxboro
Murfreesboro
Gatesville
Camden
Currituck
Chesapeake Bay
ATLANTIC OCEAN
© MAPQUEST
B
C
D
E
F
G
H
J
K
8
9
10
11
12
13
14

Wisconsin

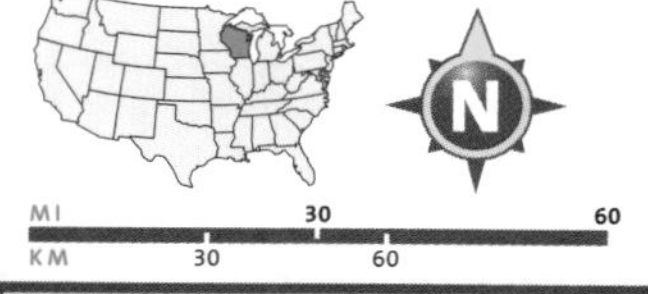

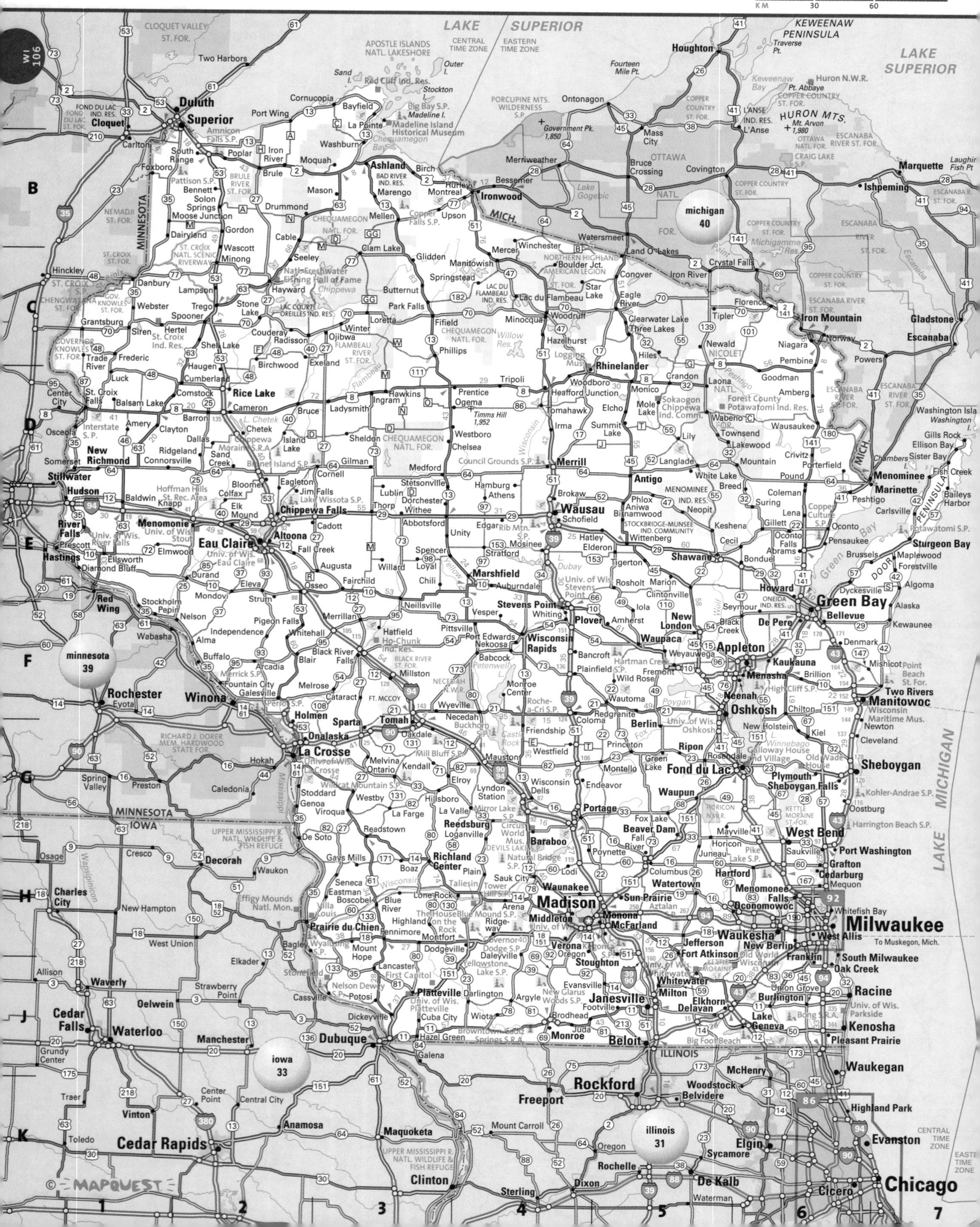

N
MI 30 60
KM 30 60

WI 106
LAKE SUPERIOR
KEWEENAW PENINSULA
LAKE SUPERIOR
APOSTLE ISLANDS NATL. LAKESHORE
CENTRAL TIME ZONE
EASTERN TIME ZONE
CLOQUET VALLEY ST. FOR.
Two Harbors
Duluth
Superior
Cloquet
Carlton
Houghton
Traverse Pt.
Huron N.W.R.
Pt. Abbaye
COPPER COUNTRY ST. FOR.
HURON MTS.
Mt. Arvon +1,980
L'Anse
Ontonagon
PORCUPINE MTS. WILDERNESS S.P.
Government Pk. 1,850
Fourteen Mile Pt.
Mass City
Bayfield
La Pointe
Madeline Island Historical Museum
Red Cliff Ind. Res.
Cornucopia
Port Wing
Washburn
Ashland
Iron River
Brule
Moquah
Poplar
South Range
Mason
Marengo
Mellen
Hurley
Montreal
Ironwood
Bessemer
Wakefield
Merriweather
Bruce Crossing
Covington
Marquette
Ishpeming
Laughing Fish Pt.
MICH.
michigan 40
Watersmeet
Land O'Lakes
Crystal Falls
Iron River
Conover
Eagle River
Florence
Iron Mountain
Norway
Gladstone
Escanaba
Manistique
Mercer
Winchester
Boulder Jct.
Manitowish
Springstead
Lac du Flambeau
Minocqua
Woodruff
Star Lake
Hazelhurst
Three Lakes
Clearwater Lake
Tipler
Niagara
Pembine
Powers
Rhinelander
Crandon
Laona
Goodman
Amberg
Hinckley
Grantsburg
Siren
Webster
Danbury
Frederic
Luck
Trade River
St. Croix Falls
Balsam Lake
Center City
Osceola
Amery
Cumberland
Rice Lake
Barron
Cameron
Chetek
Hayward
Seeley
Cable
Spooner
Shell Lake
Trego
Minong
Gordon
Solon Springs
Dairyland
Stone Lake
Couderay
Radisson
Ojibwa
Winter
Exeland
Birchwood
Park Falls
Butternut
Glidden
Clam Lake
Fifield
Phillips
Prentice
Ogema
Tripoli
Tomahawk
Irma
Merrill
Timms Hill 1,952
Ladysmith
Bruce
Hawkins
Ingram
Sheldon
Gilman
Medford
Westboro
Chelsea
Stillwater
Hudson
New Richmond
Somerset
River Falls
Prescott
Hastings
Ellsworth
Menomonie
Eau Claire
Altoona
Chippewa Falls
Cornell
Bloomer
Stanley
Cadott
Thorp
Abbotsford
Colby
Wausau
Schofield
Mosinee
Antigo
Shawano
Marinette
Menominee
Peshtigo
Oconto
Green Bay
Sturgeon Bay
Algoma
Kewaunee
De Pere
Appleton
Kaukauna
Neenah
Menasha
Oshkosh
Manitowoc
Two Rivers
Sheboygan
Fond du Lac
Red Wing
Wabasha
Durand
Mondovi
Alma
Arcadia
Whitehall
Black River Falls
Neillsville
Marshfield
Stevens Point
Plover
Wisconsin Rapids
Waupaca
New London
Rochester
Winona
La Crosse
Onalaska
Sparta
Tomah
Mauston
Wisconsin Dells
Portage
Baraboo
Reedsburg
Richland Center
Viroqua
Prairie du Chien
Dodgeville
Platteville
Madison
Middleton
Waunakee
Sun Prairie
Stoughton
Janesville
Beloit
Monroe
Watertown
Oconomowoc
Waukesha
Milwaukee
West Allis
Racine
Kenosha
Dubuque
Decorah
Cresco
Waterloo
Cedar Falls
Cedar Rapids
Clinton
Maquoketa
Freeport
Rockford
Belvidere
Elgin
Dixon
De Kalb
Sterling
Waukegan
Evanston
Chicago
Cicero
LAKE MICHIGAN
MINNESOTA
IOWA
ILLINOIS
minnesota 39
iowa 33
illinois 31
CENTRAL TIME ZONE
EASTERN TIME ZONE
To Muskegon, Mich.
MAPQUEST
B
C
D
E
F
G
H
J
K
1
2
3
4
5
6
7

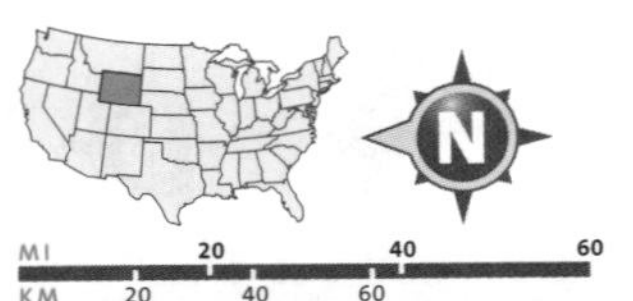
N
MI 20 40 60
KM 20 40 60

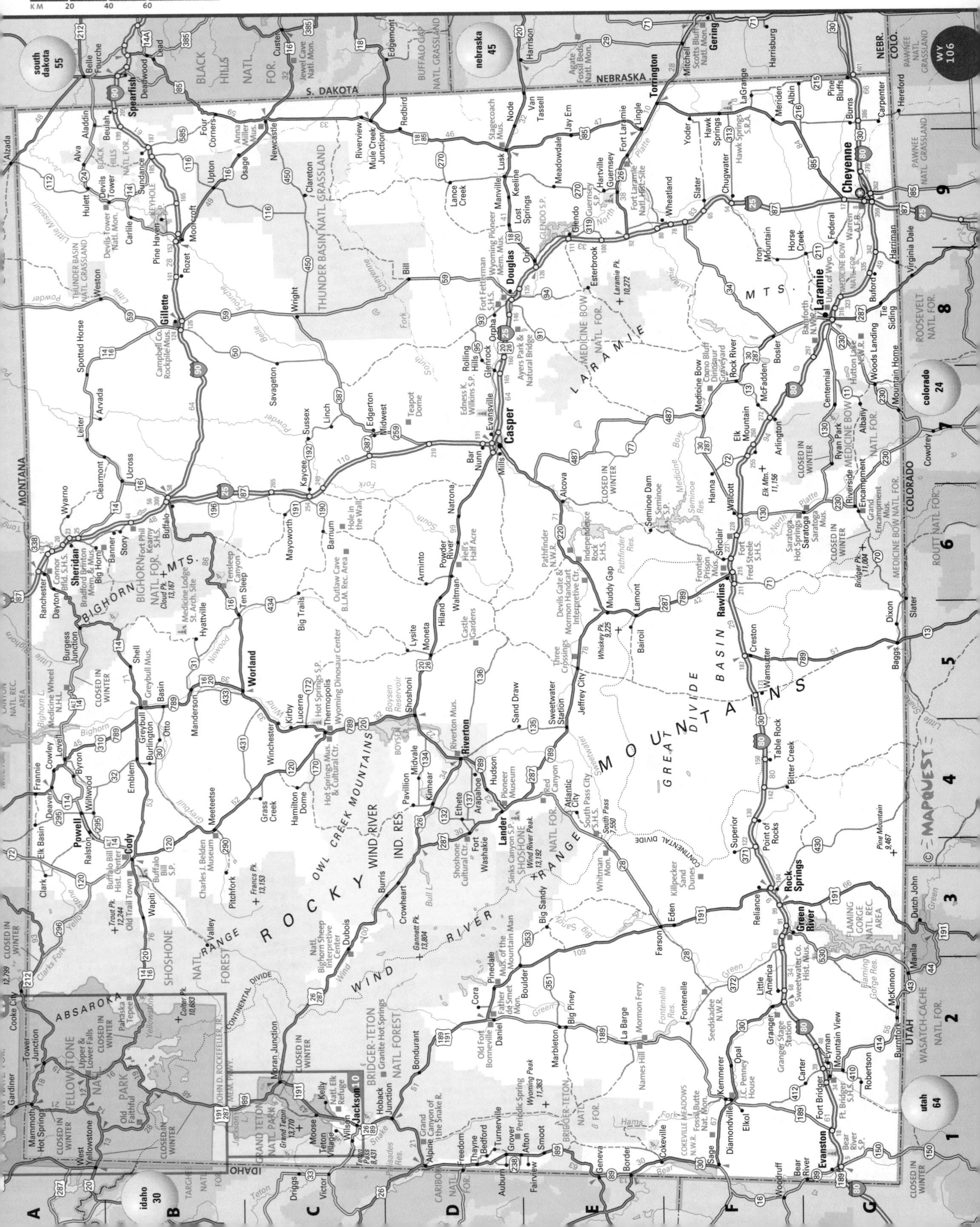

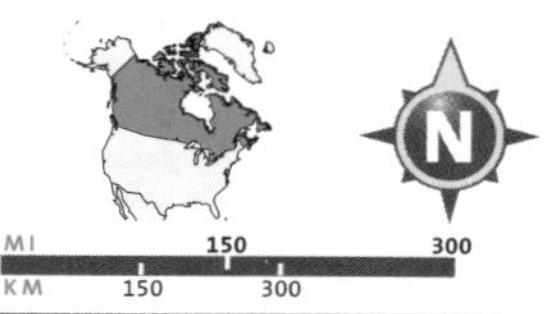
MI 150 300
KM 150 300
N

CAN 107
B
C
D
E
F
G
H
J
K
1 2 3 4 5 6 7
UNITED STATES
ALASKA
YUKON TERRITORY
NORTHWEST TERRITORIES
BRITISH COLUMBIA
ALBERTA
SASKATCHEWAN
MANITOBA
ROCKY MOUNTAINS
COAST MOUNTAINS
MACKENZIE MOUNTAINS
PACIFIC OCEAN
Gulf of Alaska
VICTORIA ISLAND
BANKS ISLAND
PACIFIC TIME ZONE
MOUNTAIN TIME ZONE
CENTRAL TIME ZONE
ALASKA TIME ZONE
6 a.m.
7 a.m.
8 a.m.
9 a.m.
Anchorage
Fairbanks
Seward
Whitehorse
Yellowknife
Edmonton
Calgary
Vancouver
Victoria
Saskatoon
Regina
Winnipeg
Seattle
Portland
WASH.
OREGON
IDAHO
MONTANA
WYOMING
NEVADA
UTAH
CALIFORNIA
NORTH DAKOTA
SOUTH DAKOTA
NEBRASKA
MINNESOTA
IOWA
UNITED STATES

DISTANCES BETWEEN CITIES ARE COMPUTED IN KILOMETERS OVER MAIN HIGHWAYS AND INCLUDE FERRY DISTANCES

	BOSTON, MA	BRANDON, MB	CALGARY, AB	CHARLOTTETOWN, PE	CHICAGO, IL	DAWSON CREEK, BC	EDMONTON, AB	FREDERICTON, NB	HALIFAX, NS	KENORA, ON	MINNEAPOLIS, MN	MONTRÉAL, QC	NEW YORK, NY	NORTH BAY, ON	OTTAWA, ON	PRINCE GEORGE, BC	QUÉBEC, QC	REGINA, SK	ST. JOHN'S, NL	SASKATOON, SK	SAULT STE. MARIE, ON	SEATTLE, WA	THUNDER BAY, ON	TORONTO, ON	VANCOUVER, BC	VICTORIA, BC	WHITEHORSE, YT	WINDSOR, ON	WINNIPEG, MB
BANFF, AB	4434	1234	128	4681	2811	1001	412	4432	4802	1648	2156	3652	4104	3137	3500	637	3888	856	6032	729	2725	977	2105	3642	819	874	2219	3280	1429
BOSTON, MA		3220	4318	1049	1614	4950	4353	690	1149	2639	2280	504	346	1036	665	5093	634	3577	2379	3840	1572	4941	2187	917	5156	5235	6268	1181	3006
BRANDON, MB			1117	3468	1598	1749	1152	3217	3589	434	943	2438	2889	1923	2287	1894	2675	377	4817	639	1510	2041	892	2427	2016	2108	3067	2066	216
CALGARY, AB				4566	2696	885	296	4315	4686	1530	2041	3536	3986	3021	3384	755	3772	740	5914	613	2607	1093	1989	3524	900	991	2203	3162	1313
CHARLOTTETOWN, PE					2382	5198	4601	354	322	3035	3048	1030	1381	1574	1204	5341	819	3825	1376	4088	1997	5708	2583	1561	5924	6003	6516	1925	3241
CHICAGO, IL						3328	2731	2134	2504	1577	658	1353	1283	1138	1252	3471	1604	1955	3734	2216	896	3318	1521	821	3534	3613	4646	460	1384
DAWSON CREEK, BC							597	4947	5319	2165	2673	4168	4620	3653	4017	406	4405	1373	6548	1112	3241	1283	2622	4158	1184	1181	1318	3796	1946
EDMONTON, AB								4350	4722	1566	2076	3571	4022	3056	3420	740	3806	776	5950	513	2642	1308	2024	3560	1115	1207	1915	3198	1347
FREDERICTON, NB									452	2784	2797	779	1022	1323	953	5092	568	3574	1688	3837	1746	5457	2333	1310	5673	5752	6265	1674	2990
HALIFAX, NS										3156	3169	1151	1481	1695	1324	5462	940	3946	1402	4208	2118	5829	2704	1682	6045	6123	6637	2045	3362
KENORA, ON											668	2005	2622	1489	1854	2308	2240	792	4384	1052	1077	2456	459	1814	2432	2522	3483	1640	208
MINNEAPOLIS, MN												2020	1949	1802	1918	2816	2271	1299	4398	1561	1173	2662	547	1487	2877	2956	3989	1125	727
MONTRÉAL, QC													616	544	194	4311	250	2795	2379	3058	967	4678	1553	531	4894	4973	5486	895	2211
NEW YORK, NY														999	703	4764	838	3248	2710	3508	1545	4609	2171	816	4825	4905	5938	1001	2675
NORTH BAY, ON															364	3796	795	2280	2924	2541	423	4464	1072	336	3920	4012	4971	679	1696
OTTAWA, ON																4160	444	2644	2552	2906	787	4578	1401	431	4792	4873	5335	793	2060
PRINCE GEORGE, BC																	4548	1516	6691	1255	3384	922	2765	4302	778	821	1580	3940	2089
QUÉBEC, QC																		3032	2168	3293	1218	4929	1790	782	5143	5224	5723	1144	2448
REGINA, SK																			5176	261	1868	1664	1249	2786	1640	1732	2691	2424	573
ST. JOHN'S, NL																				5436	3346	7058	3933	2910	7272	7353	7866	3273	4590
SASKATOON, SK																					2129	1823	1511	3046	1630	1722	2430	2684	834
SAULT STE. MARIE, ON																						4223	649	674	3508	3598	4559	563	1283
SEATTLE, WA																							2913	4147	225	177	2504	3787	2237
THUNDER BAY, ON																								1355	2889	2980	3940	1699	665
TORONTO, ON																									4363	4443	5476	364	2213
VANCOUVER, BC																										93	2311	4001	2213
VICTORIA, BC																											2401	4081	2305
WHITEHORSE, YT																												5114	3264
WINDSOR, ON																													1852

British Columbia

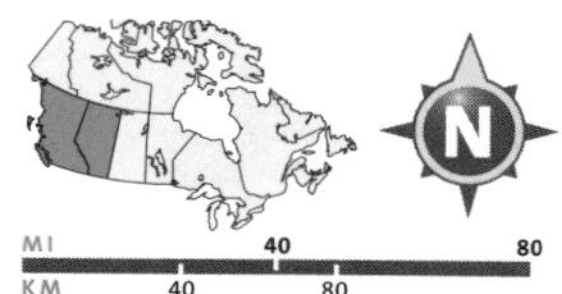

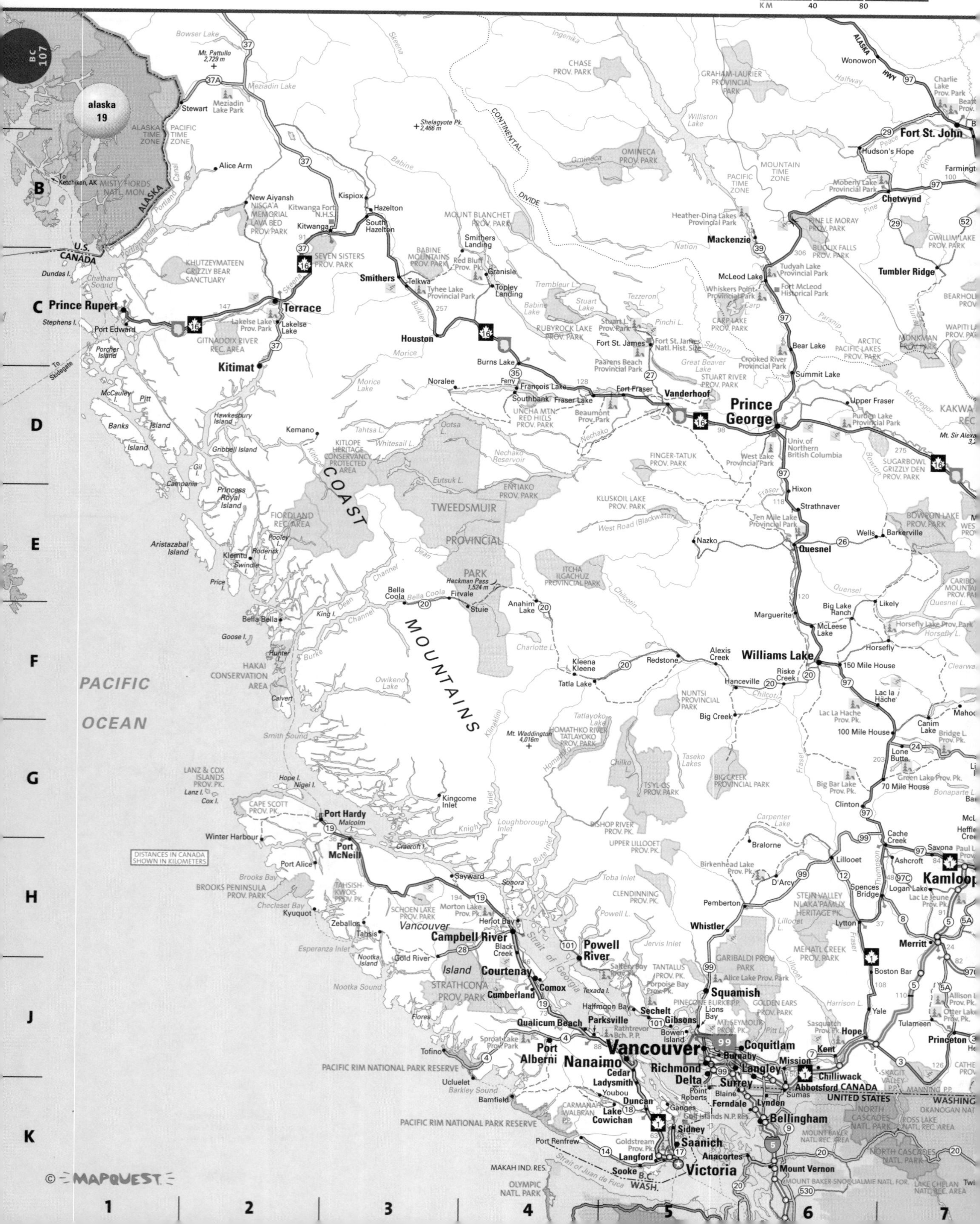

BC
107

alaska
19

Bowser Lake
Mt. Pattullo
2,729 m
Meziadin Lake
Stewart
Meziadin Lake Park
ALASKA TIME ZONE
PACIFIC TIME ZONE
Alice Arm
To Ketchikan, AK
MISTY FIORDS NATL. MON.
ALASKA
Portland Canal
New Aiyansh
NISGA'A MEMORIAL LAVA BED PROV. PARK
Kitwanga Fort N.H.S.
Kitwanga
Kispiox
Hazelton
South Hazelton
SEVEN SISTERS PROV. PARK
U.S.
CANADA
Dundas I.
Chatham Sound
KHUTZEYMATEEN GRIZZLY BEAR SANCTUARY
Prince Rupert
Stephens I.
Port Edward
Terrace
Lakelse Lake Prov. Park
Lakelse Lake
GITNADOIX RIVER REC. AREA
Kitimat
Porcher Island
To Skidegate
McCauley I.
Pitt
Banks
Island
Hawkesbury Island
Gribbell Island
Gil I.
Campania
Princess Royal Island
Aristazabal Island
Klemtu
Roderick I.
Swindle I.
Pooley I.
Price I.
Bella Bella
Goose I.
Hunter I.
HAKAI CONSERVATION AREA
Calvert I.
PACIFIC
OCEAN
Smith Sound
LANZ & COX ISLANDS PROV. PK.
Lanz I.
Cox I.
Hope I.
Nigei I.
CAPE SCOTT PROV. PK.
Port Hardy
Malcolm
Winter Harbour
DISTANCES IN CANADA SHOWN IN KILOMETERS
Port McNeill
Cracroft I.
Port Alice
Brooks Bay
BROOKS PENINSULA PROV. PARK
Checleset Bay
Kyuquot
TAHSISH-KWOIS PROV. PK.
Zeballos
Tahsis
Esperanza Inlet
Nootka Island
Gold River
Nootka Sound
Flores
Tofino
PACIFIC RIM NATIONAL PARK RESERVE
Ucluelet
Barkley Sound
Bamfield
Port Alberni
Sproat Lake Prov. Park

Skeena
Shelagyote Pk. 2,466 m
Babine
CONTINENTAL DIVIDE
MOUNT BLANCHET PROV. PARK
Smithers Landing
BABINE MOUNTAINS PROV. PARK
Red Bluff Prov. Pk.
Granisle
Topley Landing
Smithers
Telkwa
Tyhee Lake Provincial Park
Bulkley
Houston
Morice
Morice Lake
Noralee
Burns Lake
Ferry
François Lake
Southbank
Fraser Lake
UNCHA MTN RED HILLS PROV. PARK
Kemano
Tahtsa L.
Whitesail L.
KITLOPE HERITAGE CONSERVANCY PROTECTED AREA
Kitlope
Ootsa L.
Nechako Reservoir
Eutsuk L.
COAST
MOUNTAINS
FIORDLAND REC. AREA
TWEEDSMUIR PROVINCIAL PARK
ENTIAKO PROV. PARK
Dean
Dean Channel
Heckman Pass 1,524 m
Bella Coola
Firvale
Stuie
King I.
Burke Channel
Anahim Lake
Charlotte L.
Owikeno Lake
Klinaklini
Mt. Waddington 4,016m
Kingcome Inlet
Knight Inlet
Loughborough Inlet
Bute Inlet
Sayward
Sonora
SCHOEN LAKE PROV. PARK
Morton Lake Prov. Pk.
Heriot Bay
Vancouver Island
Campbell River
Black Creek
Courtenay
Comox
Cumberland
STRATHCONA PROV. PARK
Texada I.
Strait of Georgia
Powell River
Qualicum Beach
Parksville
Nanaimo
Cedar
Ladysmith
Youbou
Duncan
Lake Cowichan
CARMANAH WALBRAN P.P.
Port Renfrew
Goldstream Prov. Pk.
Langford
Sooke
Victoria
Strait of Juan de Fuca
MAKAH IND. RES.
OLYMPIC NATL. PARK
B.C.
WASH.

Ingenika
CHASE PROV. PARK
Omineca
OMINECA PROV. PARK
GRAHAM-LAURIER PROVINCIAL PARK
Williston Lake
PACIFIC TIME ZONE
MOUNTAIN TIME ZONE
Heather-Dina Lakes Provincial Park
Mackenzie
Nation
Tremblear L.
Stuart Lake
Babine Lake
Tezzeron L.
Pinchi L.
Stuart L. Prov. Park
RUBYROCK LAKE PROV. PARK
Fort St. James
Fort St. James Natl. Hist. Site
Paarens Beach Provincial Park
Great Beaver Lake
STUART RIVER PROV. PARK
Fort Fraser
Vanderhoof
Beaumont Prov. Park
Nechako
Prince George
McLeod Lake
Whiskers Point Provincial Park
Fort McLeod Historical Park
Carp
CARP LAKE PROV. PARK
Tudyah Lake Provincial Park
Bear Lake
Crooked River Provincial Park
Summit Lake
Salmon
Parsnip
FINGER-TATUK PROV. PARK
West Lake Provincial Park
Univ. of Northern British Columbia
KLUSKOIL LAKE PROV. PARK
West Road (Blackwater)
Nazko
Hixon
Strathnaver
Ten Mile Lake Provincial Park
Quesnel
ITCHA ILGACHUZ PROVINCIAL PARK
Chilcotin
Marguerite
Alexis Creek
Redstone
Kleena Kleene
Tatla Lake
Williams Lake
Riske Creek
Hanceville
NUNTSI PROVINCIAL PARK
Big Creek
Tatlayoko Lake
HOMATHKO RIVER TATLAYOKO PROV. PARK
Homathko
Chilko L.
Taseko Lakes
TS'YL-OS PROV. PARK
BIG CREEK PROVINCIAL PARK
BISHOP RIVER PROV. PARK
UPPER LILLOOET PROV. PK.
Carpenter Lake
Bralorne
Birkenhead Lake Prov. Pk.
D'Arcy
Toba Inlet
CLENDINNING PROV. PK.
Powell L.
Pemberton
Whistler
Jervis Inlet
GARIBALDI PROV. PARK
Saltery Bay Prov. Pk.
TANTALUS PROV. PK.
Porpoise Bay Prov. Pk.
Alice Lake Prov. Park
Squamish
Halfmoon Bay
Sechelt
Gibsons
PINECONE BURKE P.P.
GOLDEN EARS PROV. PARK
Lions Bay
MT. SEYMOUR PROV. PK.
Rathtrevor Bch. P. P.
Bowen Island
Vancouver
Burnaby
Coquitlam
Richmond
Delta
Langley
Surrey
Point Roberts
Blaine
Ferndale
Lynden
Gulf Islands N.P. Res.
Ganges
Sidney
Saanich
Anacortes
Bellingham
Mount Vernon
Pitt L.

Alaska Hwy
Wonowon
Halfway
Charlie Lake Prov. Park
Fort St. John
Hudson's Hope
Peace
Farmington
Moberly Lake Provincial Park
Chetwynd
Pine
PINE LE MORAY PROV. PARK
BIJOUX FALLS PROV. PARK
GWILLIM LAKE PROV. PARK
Tumbler Ridge
BEARHOLE PROV.
WAPITI LAKE PROV. PARK
MONKMAN PROV. PARK
ARCTIC PACIFIC LAKES PROV. PARK
Murray
McGregor
Upper Fraser
Purden Lake Provincial Park
KAKWA REC.
Mt. Sir Alexander
Bowron
SUGARBOWL GRIZZLY DEN PROV. PARK
BOWRON LAKE PROV. PARK
Wells
Barkerville
Quesnel
Likely
Big Lake Ranch
McLeese Lake
Horsefly Lake Prov. Park
Horsefly L.
Horsefly
150 Mile House
Clearwater
Lac la Hache
Lac La Hache Prov. Pk.
Canim Lake
100 Mile House
Bridge L. Prov. Pk.
Mahood
Lone Butte
Green Lake Prov. Pk.
70 Mile House
Big Bar Lake Prov. Pk.
Bonaparte L.
Clinton
Cache Creek
Savona
Ashcroft
Kamloops
Lillooet
Thompson
Spences Bridge
Logan Lake
Lac Le Jeune Prov. Pk.
STEIN VALLEY NLAKA'PAMUX HERITAGE PK.
Lillooet
Lytton
MEHATL CREEK PROV. PARK
Fraser
Merritt
Boston Bar
Harrison L.
Yale
Tulameen
Sasquatch Prov. Pk.
Hope
Princeton
Kent
Mission
Chilliwack
Abbotsford
CANADA
UNITED STATES
Sumas
SKAGIT VALLEY P.P.
MANNING P.P.
WASHINGTON
OKANOGAN NAT.
NORTH CASCADES NATL. PARK
ROSS LAKE NATL. REC. AREA
MOUNT BAKER NATL. REC. AREA
MOUNT BAKER-SNOQUALMIE NATL. FOR.
LAKE CHELAN NATL. REC. AREA
Twisp
Allison Lake Prov. Pk.
Otter Lake Prov. Pk.

B
C
D
E
F
G
H
J
K

1
2
3
4
5
6
7

Fort McMurray
Wood Buffalo
Peace River
Grimshaw
Fairview
Manning
High Prairie
Slave Lake
Grande Prairie
Valleyview
Fox Creek
Whitecourt
Swan Hills
Athabasca
Lac La Biche
Cold Lake
Bonnyville
St. Paul
Westlock
Barrhead
Morinville
St. Albert
Ft. Saskatchewan
Edmonton
Spruce Grove
Stony Plain
Devon
Leduc
Edson
Hinton
Grande Cache
Jasper
Vegreville
Vermilion
Lloydminster
Camrose
Wetaskiwin
Ponoka
Wainwright
Drayton Valley
Lacombe
Sylvan Lake
Red Deer
Rocky Mountain House
Innisfail
Olds
Three Hills
Drumheller
Hanna
Didsbury
Airdrie
Cochrane
Canmore
Banff
Calgary
Strathmore
Okotoks
High River
Brooks
Medicine Hat
Redcliff
Claresholm
Fort Macleod
Lethbridge
Taber
Coaldale
Pincher Creek
Cardston
Raymond
Golden
Revelstoke
Salmon Arm
Vernon
Kelowna
Penticton
Cranbrook
Fernie
Sparwood
Invermere
Kimberley
Nelson
Castlegar
Trail
Rossland
Creston
ROCKY MOUNTAINS
JASPER NATIONAL PARK
BANFF NATIONAL PARK
COLD LAKE AIR WEAPONS RANGE
SASKATCHEWAN
CANADA
UNITED STATES
MONTANA
IDAHO
WASH.
washington 65
idaho 30
montana 44
saskatchewan 59
AB 107
Kalispell
Whitefish
Columbia Falls
Shelby
Cut Bank
Conrad
Omak
Colville
Sandpoint
Libby
B
C
D
E
F
G
H
J
K
8
9
10
11
12
13
14

Saskatchewan

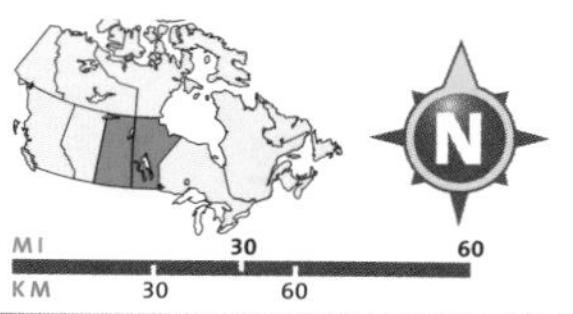

SK 107

COLD LAKE AIR WEAPONS RANGE

MEADOW LAKE PROV. PARK

PRINCE ALBERT NATL. PARK

LAC LA RONGE PROV. PARK

NARROW HILLS PROV. PARK

CLARENCE-STEEPBANK LAKES PROV. WILDERNESS PARK

MAKWA LAKE PROV. PARK

C.F.B WAINWRIGHT

C.F.B SUFFIELD

CYPRESS HILLS INTERPROV. PARK

Cypress Hills Highest Pt. in Sask. 1392 m

GRASSLANDS NATL. PARK

GREAT SAND HILLS

MOSTOOS HILLS

WAPANEKA HILLS

MOOSE MTN.

MOUNTAIN TIME ZONE / CENTRAL TIME ZONE

alberta 73

montana 44

ALBERTA

MONTANA

CANADA

UNITED STATES

N. DAK.

Saskatoon

Regina

Prince Albert

Moose Jaw

Swift Current

North Battleford

Lloydminster

Medicine Hat

Yorkton

Estevan

Weyburn

Kindersley

Melfort

Humboldt

Melville

Nipawin

La Ronge

Meadow Lake

Assiniboia

DISTANCES IN CANADA SHOWN IN KILOMETERS

© MAPQUEST

A B C D E F G H J K

1 2 3 4 5 6 7

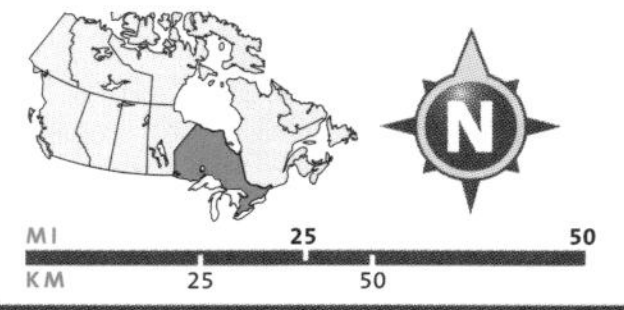

ON 107

Sault Ste. Marie Canal N.H.S.
Sault Ste. Marie
Sault Ste. Marie
Echo Bay
Ophir
Desbarats
Bruce Mines
Richards Landing
Hilton Beach
Thessalon
Sowerby
Iron Bridge
Mississagi Museum and Mineshaft
St. Joseph Island
Fort St. Joseph N.H.S.
Lake Superior St. For.
Cedarville
De Tour Village
Drummond Island
Pickford
Michigan
Elliot Lake
Mississagi Prov. Park
Blind River
Spragge
Spanish
Walford
Massey
Webbwood
Espanola
Chutes Prov. Park
McKerrow
Whitefish Falls
Nairn Centre
Whitefish
Lively
Chelmsford
Onaping
Windy Lake Prov. Park
Fairbank Prov. Park
Valley East
Sudbury
Laurentian Univ.
Greater Sudbury
Lake Panache
Estaire
Markstay-Warren
Markstay
Warren
River Valley
Field
Verner
West Nipissing
Sturgeon Falls
North Bay
Lake Nipissing
French River
Alban
Noëlville
French River Prov. Park
Restoule Prov. Park
Restoule
Powassan
Trout Creek
Loring
Port Loring
Mikisew Prov. Park
Grundy Lake Prov. Park
Britt
Sundridge
Magnetawan
Burk's Falls
Pointe au Baril Station
Sturgeon Bay Prov. Park
McKellar
Shawanaga Island
Killbear Prov. Park
Parry Sound
Oastler Lake Prov. Park
Rosseau
Massasauga Prov. Park
Windermere
MacTier
Bracebridge
Bala
Georgian Bay Islands Natl. Park
Bethune Mem. House N.H.S.
Gravenhurst
Six Mile Lake Prov. Park
Christian Island
Awenda Prov. Park
Penetanguishene
Midland
Victoria Harbour
Coldwater
North Channel
John I.
Clapperton I.
Meldrum Bay
Cockburn Island
Barrie Island
Gore Bay
Little Current
Killarney Prov. Park
McGregor Bay
Great La Cloche I.
Killarney
Northeastern Manitoulin and the Islands
Sheguiandah
M'Chigeeng
Silver Water
Evansville
Mindemoya
Spring Bay
Providence Bay
Great Duck I.
Manitowaning
Manitoulin Island
South Baymouth
Lonely Island
Fitzwilliam Island
Main Channel
Fathom Five Natl. Marine Park
Cove Island
Tobermory
Bruce Peninsula Natl. Park
Bruce Peninsula N.P.
Miller Lake
Bruce Peninsula
Georgian Bay
Lion's Head
Distances in Canada shown in kilometers
Canada
United States
Lake Huron
Michigan
South Bruce Peninsula
Wiarton
Sauble Falls Prov. Park
Sauble Beach
Hepworth
Owen Sound
Meaford
Nottawasaga Bay
Craigleith Prov. Park
Wasaga Beach
Collingwood
Thornbury
Blue Mts.
Elmvale
Bass Lake Prov. Park
Barrie
Allenford
Southampton
Saugeen Shores
Port Elgin
Tara
Chatsworth
MacGregor Point Prov. Park
Inverhuron Prov. Park
Tiverton
Paisley
Chesley
Markdale
Flesherton
Kimberley
Scenic Caves
Stayner
Angus
Earl Rowe Prov. Pk.
Kincardine
Hanover
Walkerton
Durham
Dundalk
Shelburne
Mono
Cookstown
Bradford
Alliston
Tecumseth
Newmarket
Schomberg
Point Clark Lighthouse N.H.S.
Amberley
Mildmay
Mount Forest
Clifford
Lucknow
Teeswater
Wingham
Bluevale
Minto
Harriston
Palmerston
Arthur
Grand Valley
Orangeville
Caledon
Caledon Village
Bolton
Richmond Hill
Toronto
Point Farms Prov. Park
Goderich
Blyth
Molesworth
Brussels
Walton
Listowel
North Perth
Elora
Fergus
Erin
Brampton
Halton Hills
Georgetown
Clinton
Huron East
Seaforth
Monkton
Milverton
St. Jacobs
Elmira
Univ. of Guelph
Guelph
Milton
Mississauga
Bayfield
Bluewater
Zurich
Hensall
Mitchell
Waterloo
Univ. of Waterloo
Kitchener
Cambridge
Morriston
Oakville
African Lion Safari
Burlington
Hamilton
Grand Bend
Exeter
South Huron
Stratford
New Hamburg
Tavistock
Dundas
Ancaster
Pinery Prov. Park
St. Marys
Woodstock
Paris
Brantford
Stoney Creek
Grimsby
Smithville
Lambton Shores
Thedford
Forest
Parkhill
Lucan
Thamesford
Burford
Caledonia
Plympton-Wyoming
Warwick
Arkona
Watford
Strathroy
London
Ingersoll
Salford
Brant
Norwich
Hagersville
Cayuga
Haldimand
Dunnville
Sarnia
Petrolia Discovery
Wyoming
Petrolia
St. Thomas
Tillsonburg
Delhi
Waterford
Jarvis
Simcoe
Norfolk
Port Dover
Rock Point Prov. Park
Selkirk Prov. Park
Oil Springs
Oil Mus.
Alvinston
Glencoe
Aylmer
Langton
Turkey Point Prov. Park
Vienna
Port Burwell
Port Rowan
Long Point Bay
Long Point
Long Point Prov. Park
Port Lambton
Wallaceburg
Dresden
Thamesville
Wallacetown
West Lorne
Rodney
John E. Pearce Prov. Park
Port Stanley
Southwold Earthworks N.H.S.
Port Bruce
Port Burwell Prov. Park
Lake St. Clair
Chatham-Kent
Chatham
Ridgetown
Morpeth
Blenheim
Charing Cross
Rondeau Prov. Park
Windsor
Lakeshore
Tecumseh
Belle River
Tilbury
Merlin
Essex
Fort Malden N.H.S.
Amherstburg
Bois Blanc Lighthouse N.H.S.
Kingsville
Wheatley
Wheatley Prov. Park
Leamington
Point Pelee Natl. Park
to Pelee I.
Lake Erie
Canada
United States
Erie
Girard
Conneaut
Ashtabula
Corry
N.Y.
PA.
Westfield
Dunkirk
Fredonia
Bois Blanc Island
Cheboygan
Mullett Lake
Black L.
Rogers City
Onaway
Mackinaw St. For.
Hillman
Atlanta
Alpena
Lewiston
Fairview
Harrisville
Huron Natl. For.
Oscoda
Au Sable
West Branch
East Tawas
Tawas City
Au Gres
Standish
Gladwin
michigan 40
Port Austin
Pigeon
Bad Axe
Harbor Beach
Sanford
Midland
Bay City
Cass City
Caro
Saginaw
Sandusky
Port Sanilac
Chesaning
Owosso
Flint
Davison
Lapeer
Imlay City
Port Huron
Corunna
Grand Blanc
Marysville
St. Clair
Lansing
Mason
Howell
Pontiac
New Baltimore
Sterling Hts.
Warren
Livonia
Detroit
Ann Arbor
Dearborn
Ypsilanti
Jackson
Saline
Taylor
Tecumseh
Adrian
Monroe
Mich.
Ont.

© MAPQUEST

B C D E F G H J K

1 2 3 4 5 6 7

québec 78
new york 50
minnesota 39
ON 107
LAKE ONTARIO
CANADA
UNITED STATES
NEW YORK
QUÉBEC
ALGONQUIN PROV. PARK
ADIRONDACK PARK
NORTHERN ONTARIO
LAKE SUPERIOR
Ottawa
Gatineau
Kingston
Belleville
Peterborough
Oshawa
Whitby
Bowmanville
Port Hope
Cobourg
Trenton
Brockville
Cornwall
Pembroke
Petawawa
Renfrew
Arnprior
Carleton Place
Smiths Falls
Perth
Napanee
Gananoque
Bancroft
Lindsay
Mattawa
Mont-Laurier
Hawkesbury
Salaberry-de-Valleyfield
Massena
Malone
Ogdensburg
Potsdam
Canton
Watertown
Oswego
Rome
Utica
Rochester
Irondequoit
Buffalo
Niagara Falls
Lake Placid
Saranac Lake
Thunder Bay
Kenora
Dryden
Fort Frances
International Falls
Duluth
Superior
Sault Ste. Marie
Sudbury
North Bay
Timmins
Kapuskasing
Hearst
Kirkland Lake
Rouyn-Noranda
New Liskeard
Elliot Lake
Espanola
Sturgeon Falls
Marquette
Ishpeming
Houghton
Ashland
Bemidji
Hibbing
Grand Rapids
Virginia
Cloquet
Wawa
Geraldton
Nipigon
Schreiber
Marathon
Chapleau
Cochrane
Iroquois Falls
Sault Ste. Marie
© MQST
8
9
10
11
12
13
14
B
C
D
E
F
G
H
J
K

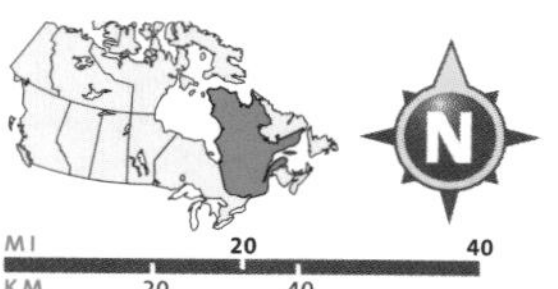

QC 107

DISTANCES IN CANADA SHOWN IN KILOMETERS

EASTERN QUÉBEC

ontario 76

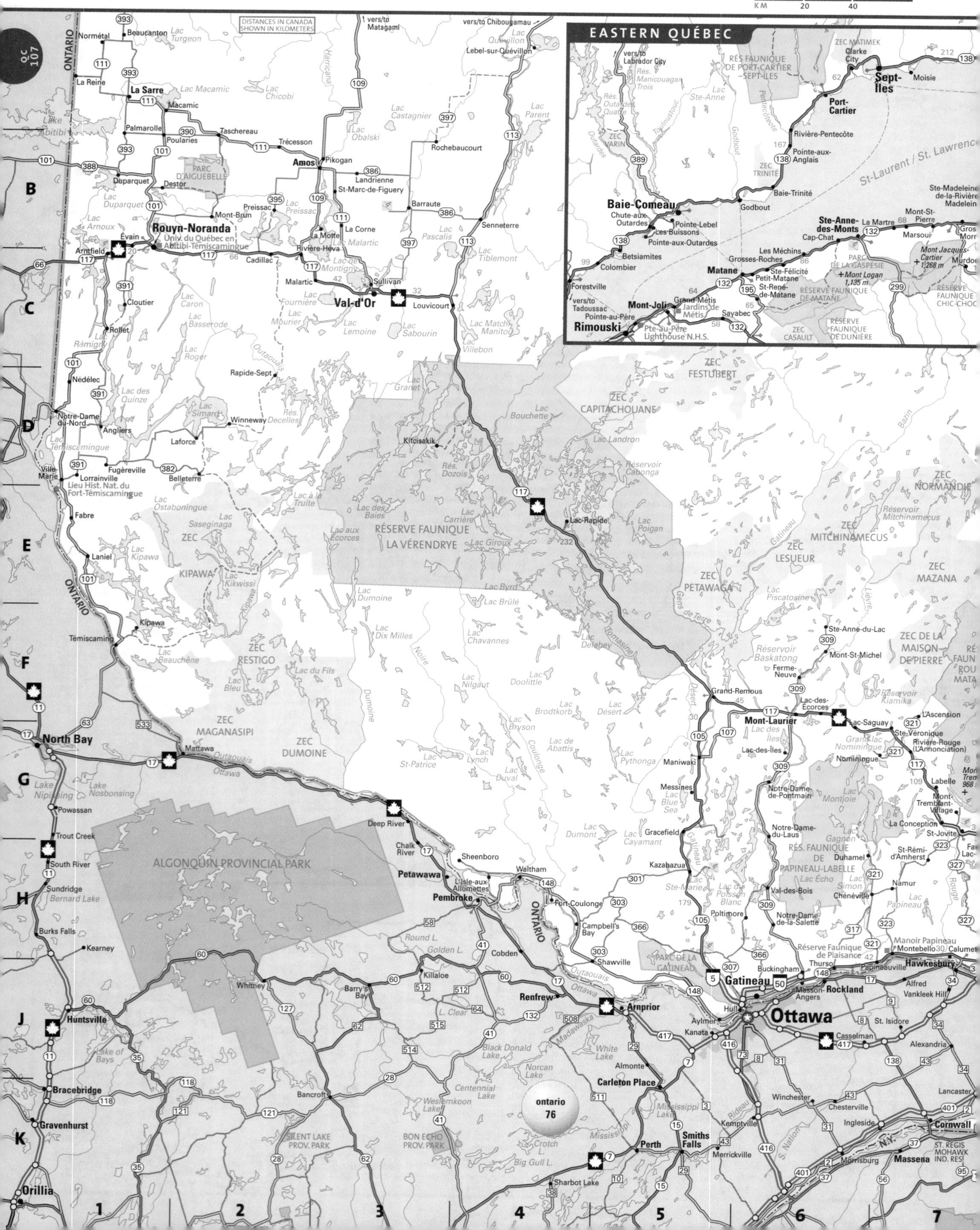

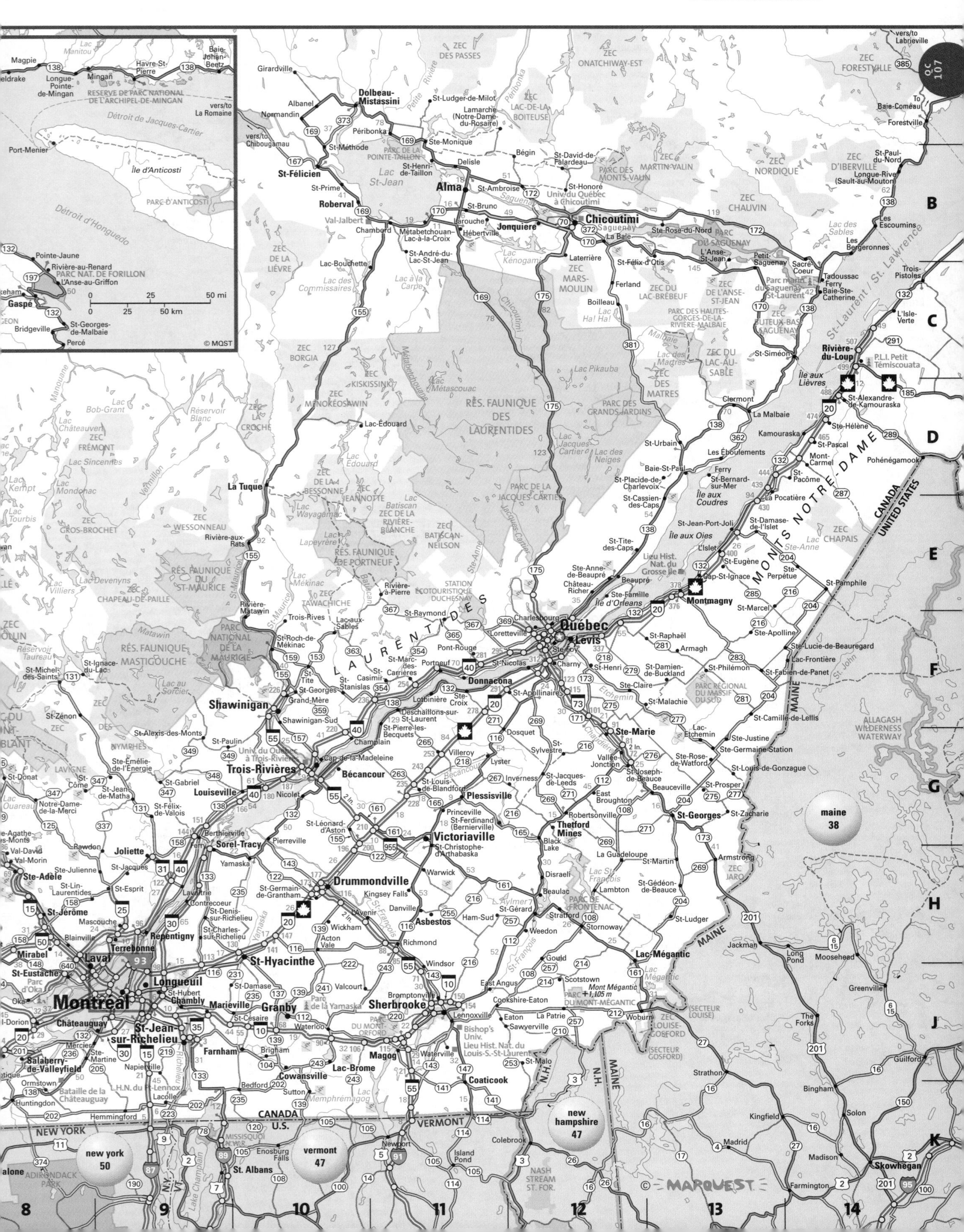

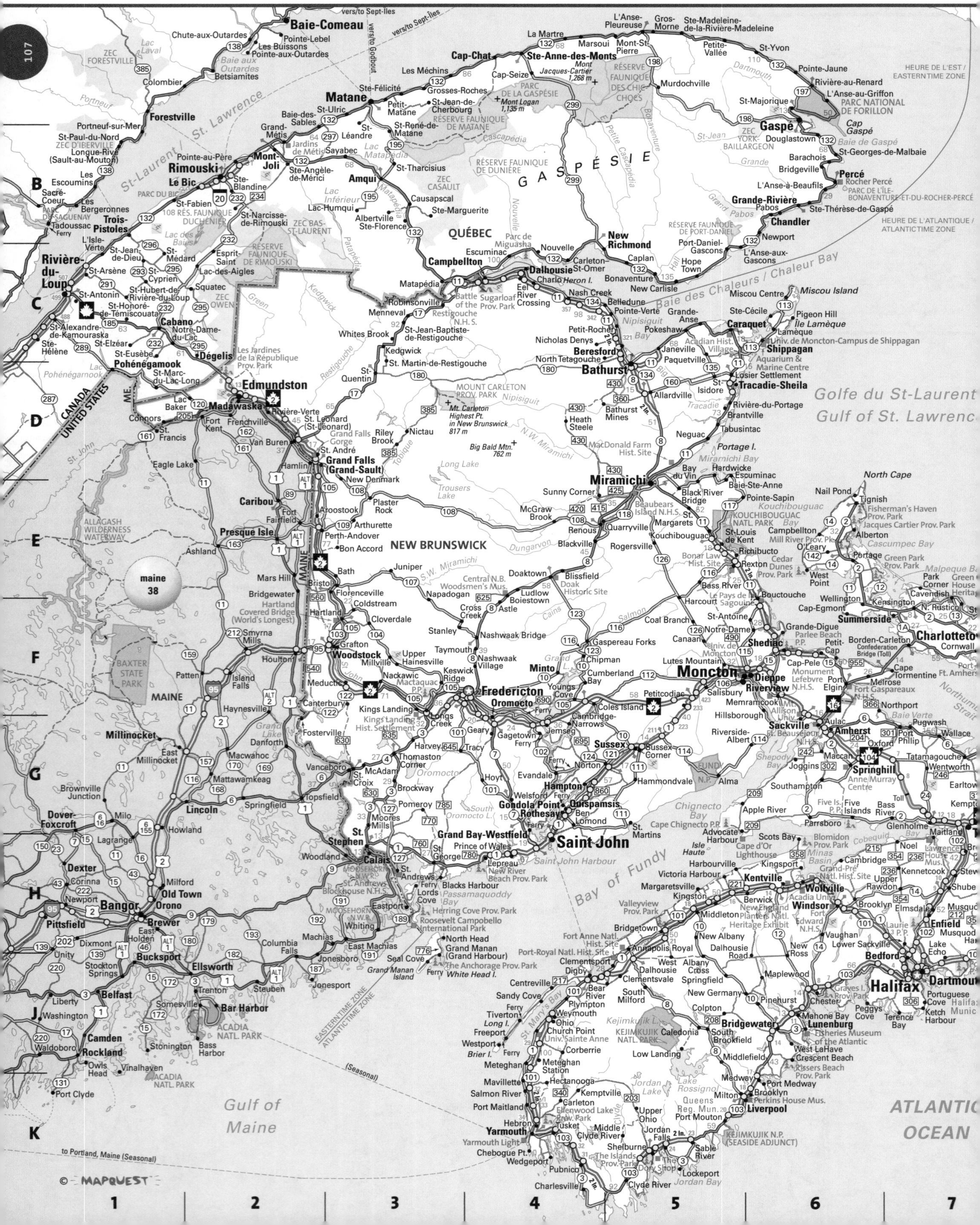

Maritimes

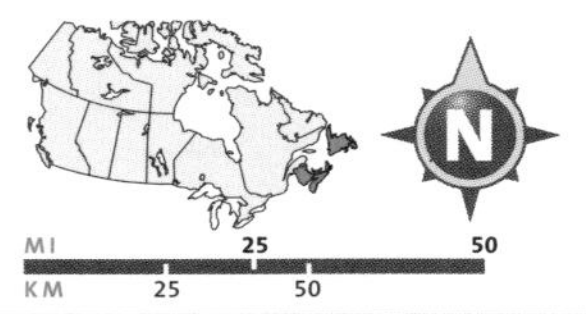

107

HEURE DE L'EST / EASTERN TIME ZONE

HEURE DE L'ATLANTIQUE / ATLANTIC TIME ZONE

EASTERN TIME ZONE / ATLANTIC TIME ZONE

QUÉBEC

G A S P É S I E

NEW BRUNSWICK

MAINE

CANADA / UNITED STATES

Golfe du St-Laurent / Gulf of St. Lawrence

Baie des Chaleurs / Chaleur Bay

Bay of Fundy

Gulf of Maine

ATLANTIC OCEAN

maine 38

B C D E F G H J K

1 2 3 4 5 6 7

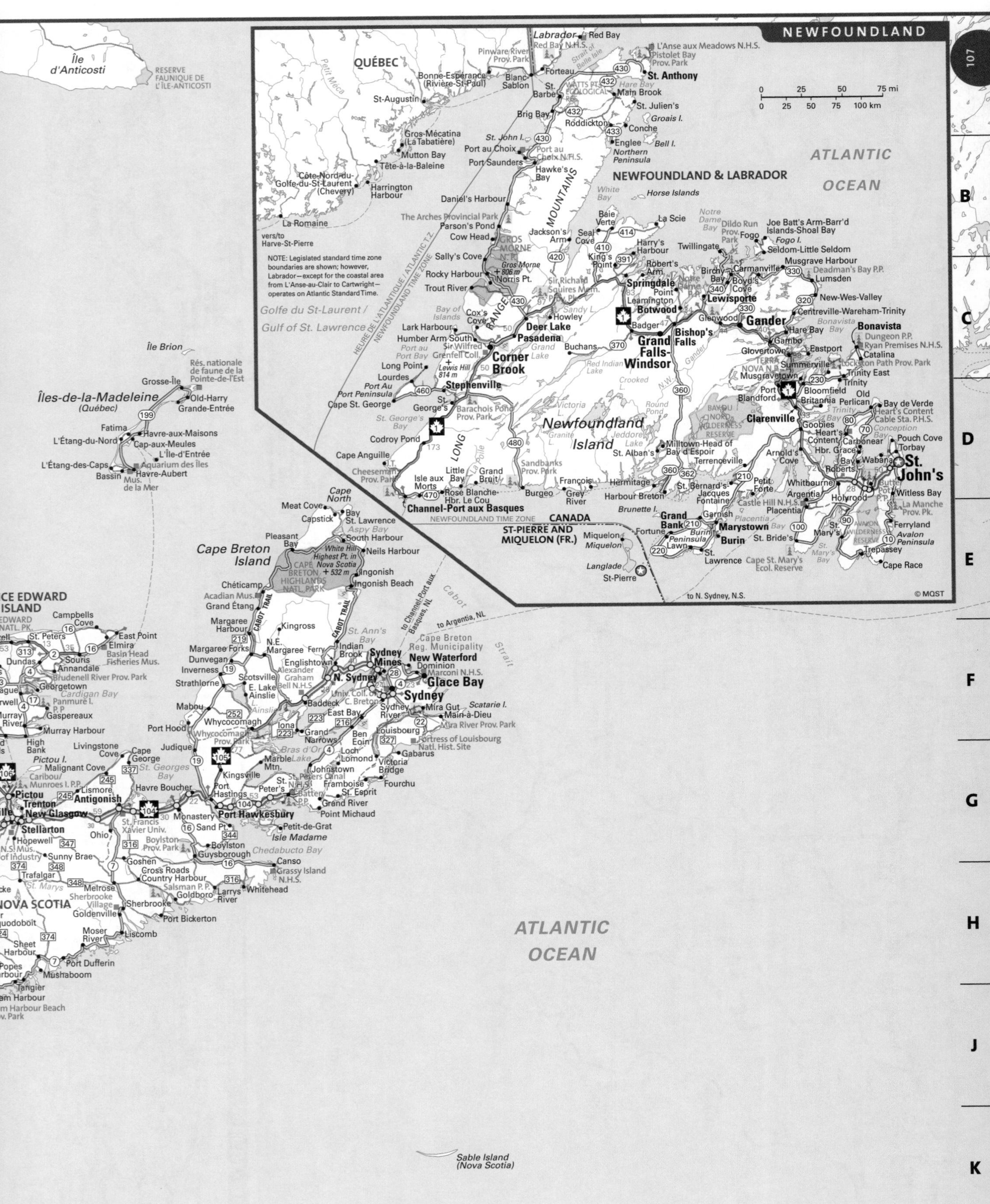

B C D E F G H J K

8 9 10 11 12 13 14

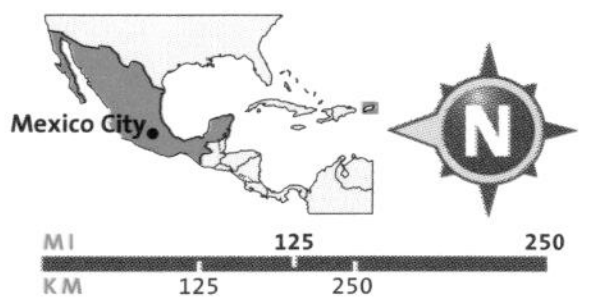
Mexico City
N
MI 125 250
KM 125 250

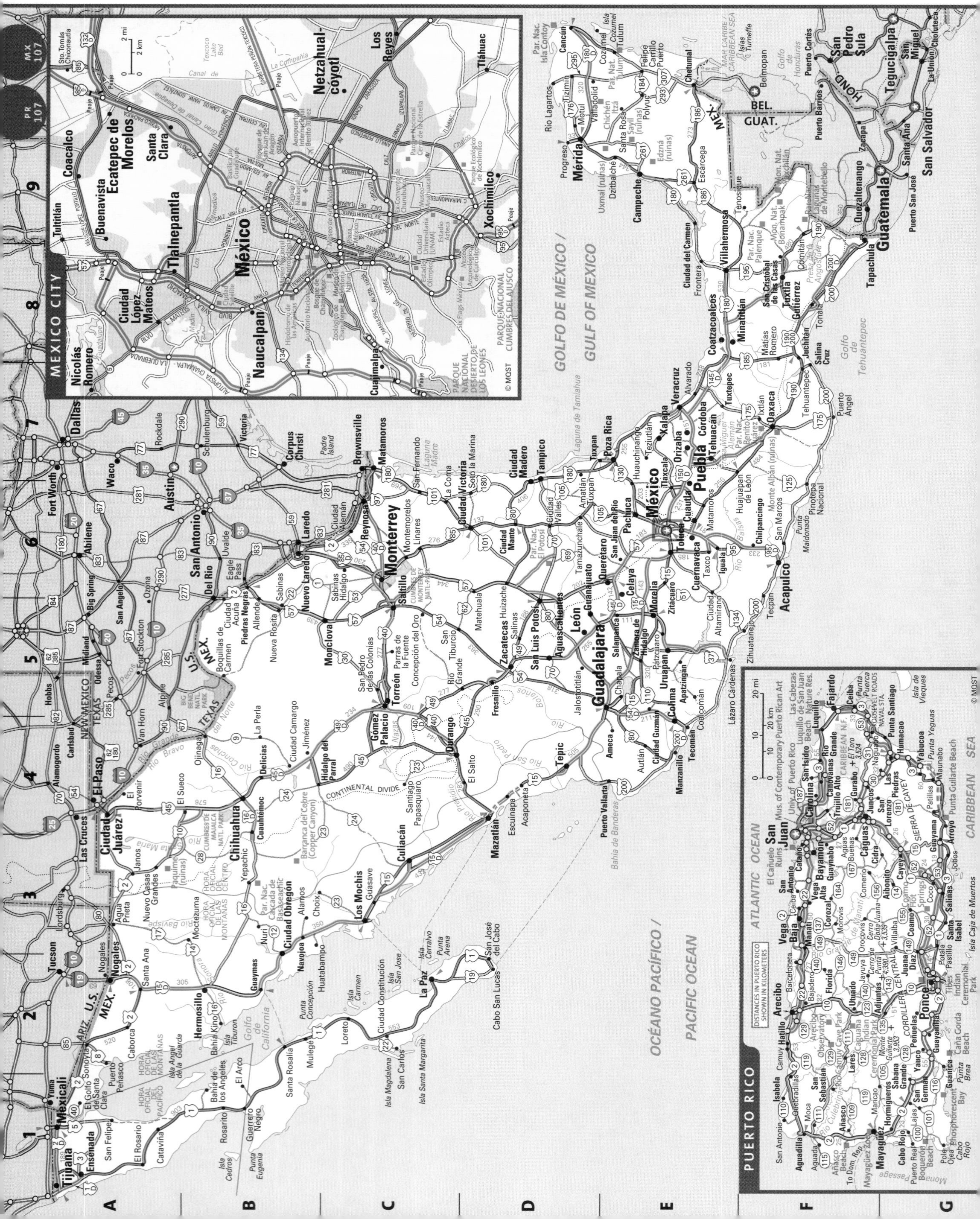

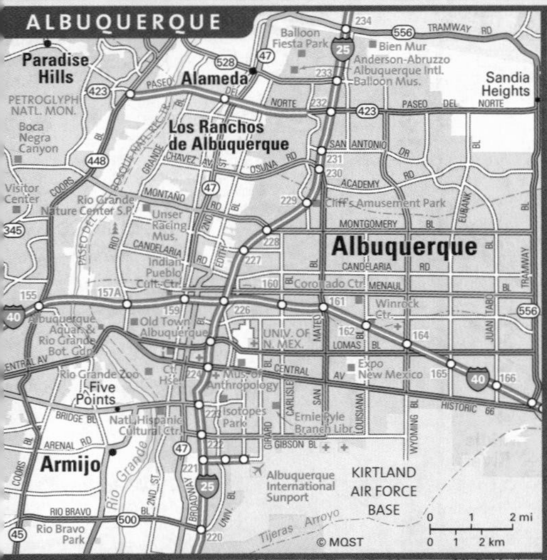

ALBUQUERQUE

Paradise Hills
Alameda
Sandia Heights
Los Ranchos de Albuquerque
Albuquerque
Five Points
Armijo
Albuquerque International Sunport
KIRTLAND AIR FORCE BASE
Rio Bravo Park
© MQST

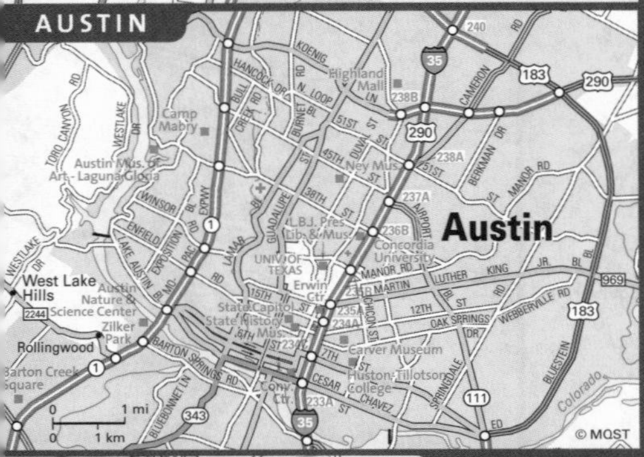

AUSTIN

Austin
West Lake Hills
Rollingwood
Barton Creek Square
© MQST

BUFFALO

Niagara Falls
Colonial Village
Sanborn
Bergholtz
St. Johnsburg
North Tonawanda
Tonawanda
Grandyle Village
GRAND ISLAND
Kenmore
Buffalo
Amherst
Williamsville
Snyder
Depew
Cheektowaga
Sloan
West Seneca
Fort Erie
Stevensville
Ridgeway
Crystal Beach
LAKE ERIE
CAN. ON U.S. NY
© MQST

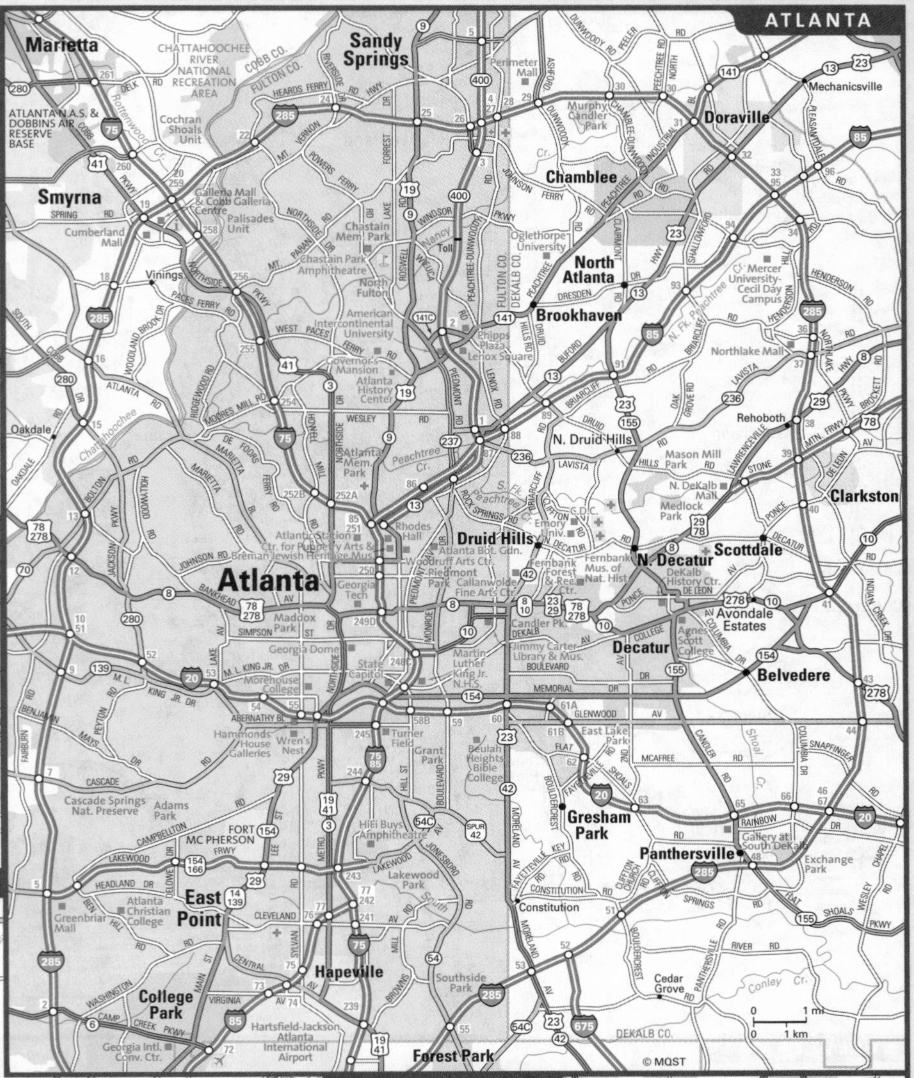

ATLANTA

Marietta
Sandy Springs
Smyrna
Doraville
Mechanicsville
Chamblee
North Atlanta
Brookhaven
Vinings
Oakdale
N. Druid Hills
Druid Hills
Clarkston
N. Decatur
Scottdale
Atlanta
Avondale Estates
Decatur
Belvedere
Gresham Park
Panthersville
East Point
Hapeville
College Park
Forest Park
Constitution
Cedar Grove
© MQST

BIRMINGHAM

Gardendale
Center Point
Fultondale
Tarrant City
Trussville
Adamsville
Forestdale
Birmingham
Irondale
Pleasant Grove
Vestavia Hills
Fairfield
Mountain Brook
Midfield
Homewood
Brighton
Lipscomb
Hoover
Bessemer
Helena
Pelham
Chelsea
© MQST

Boston
Cleveland
Columbus
Baltimore
Cincinnati
Charlotte

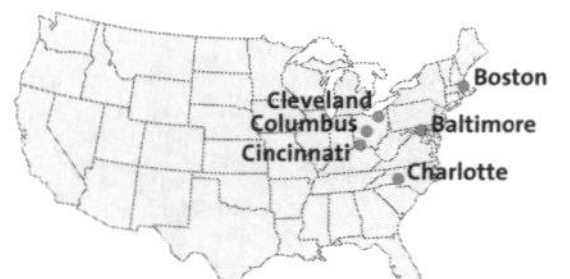

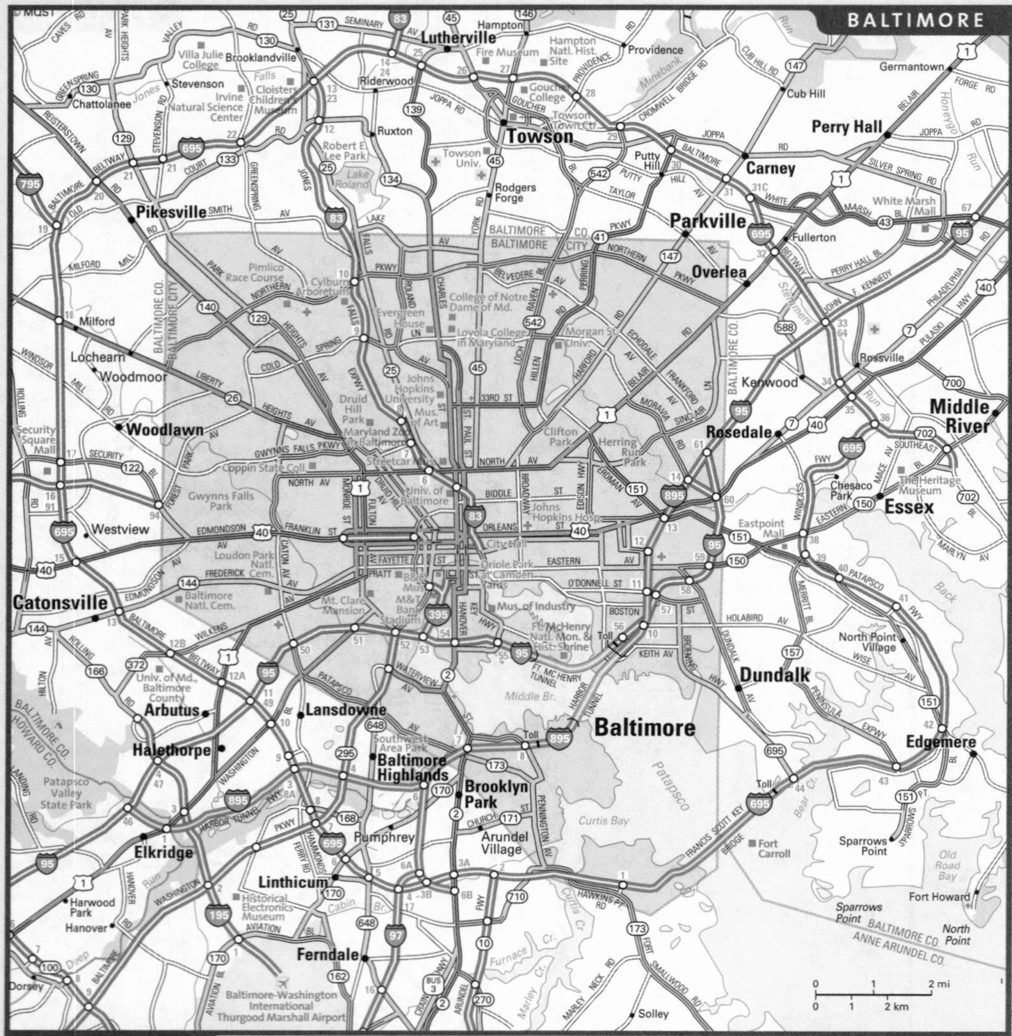
BALTIMORE
Baltimore
Towson
Lutherville
Pikesville
Parkville
Carney
Perry Hall
Overlea
Rosedale
Middle River
Essex
Dundalk
Edgemere
Catonsville
Arbutus
Halethorpe
Lansdowne
Baltimore Highlands
Brooklyn Park
Elkridge
Linthicum
Ferndale
Woodlawn
Milford
Lochearn
Woodmoor
Westview
Stevenson
Chattolanee
Ruxton
Riderwood
Germantown
Cub Hill
Fullerton
Kenwood
Rossville
Pumphrey
Arundel Village
Sparrows Point
Fort Howard
North Point
Solley
Hanover
Harwood Park
Dorsey
Baltimore-Washington International Thurgood Marshall Airport
Patapsco Valley State Park
Curtis Bay
Middle Br.
BALTIMORE CO.
ANNE ARUNDEL CO.
HOWARD CO.
0 1 2 mi
0 1 2 km
© MQST

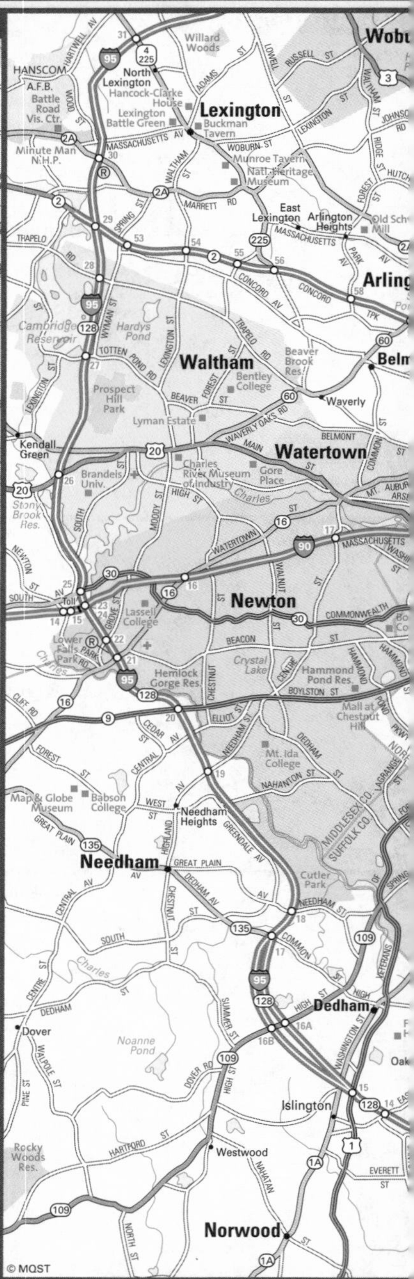
Woburn
Lexington
Waltham
Watertown
Newton
Needham
Dedham
Norwood
Arlington
Belmont
Hanscom A.F.B.
Battle Road Vis. Ctr.
Minute Man N.H.P.
Kendall Green
Brandeis Univ.
Lasell College
Babson College
Needham Heights
Islington
Westwood
Dover
Rocky Woods Res.
Noanne Pond
Cambridge Reservoir
Hardys Pond
Prospect Hill Park
Bentley College
Charles
© MQST

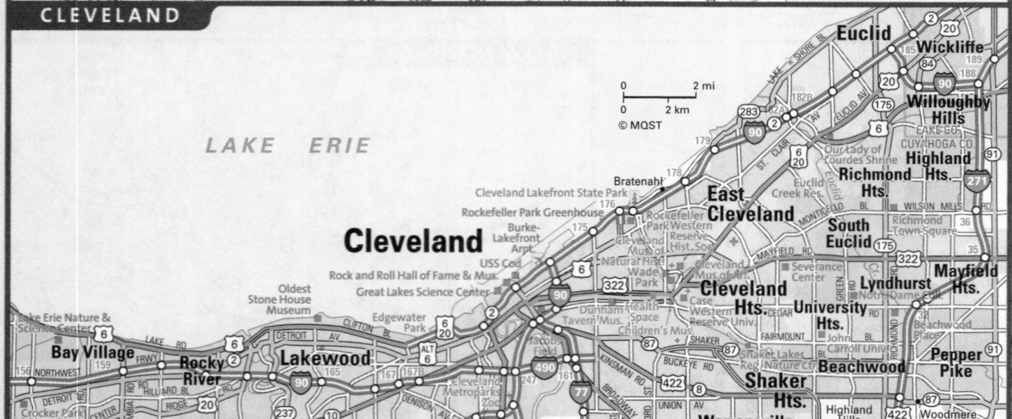
CLEVELAND
LAKE ERIE
Cleveland
East Cleveland
Euclid
Wickliffe
Willoughby Hills
Highland Hts.
Richmond Hts.
South Euclid
Lyndhurst
Mayfield Hts.
Cleveland Hts.
University Hts.
Beachwood
Pepper Pike
Shaker Hts.
Warrensville Hts.
Orange
Lakewood
Rocky River
Bay Village
Westlake
Fairview Park
North Olmsted
Brooklyn
Parma
Parma Hts.
Brook Park
Berea
Middleburg Heights
Olmsted Falls
Strongsville
North Royalton
Broadview Heights
Seven Hills
Independence
Brecksville
Garfield Hts.
Maple Hts.
Bedford
Bedford Heights
Solon
Oakwood
Glenwillow
Walton Hills
Northfield
Sagamore Hills
Macedonia
Twinsburg
Valley View
Cuyahoga Heights
Newburgh Heights
Linndale
Bratenahl
Woodmere
0 2 mi
0 2 km
© MQST

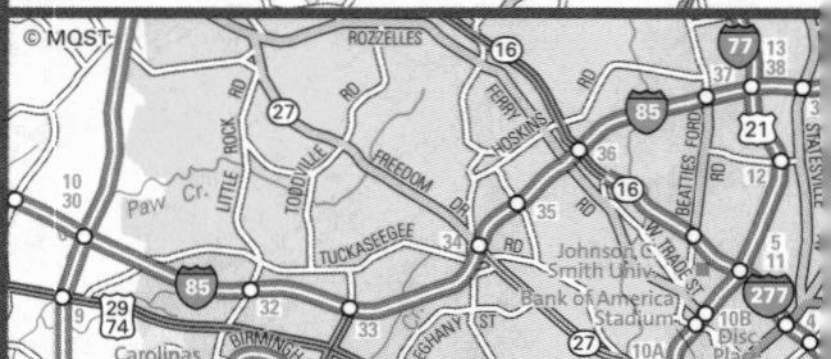
Charlotte/Douglas Intl. Airport
Carolinas Aviation Mus.
Johnson C. Smith Univ.
Bank of America Stadium
Charlotte Nature Mus.
© MQST

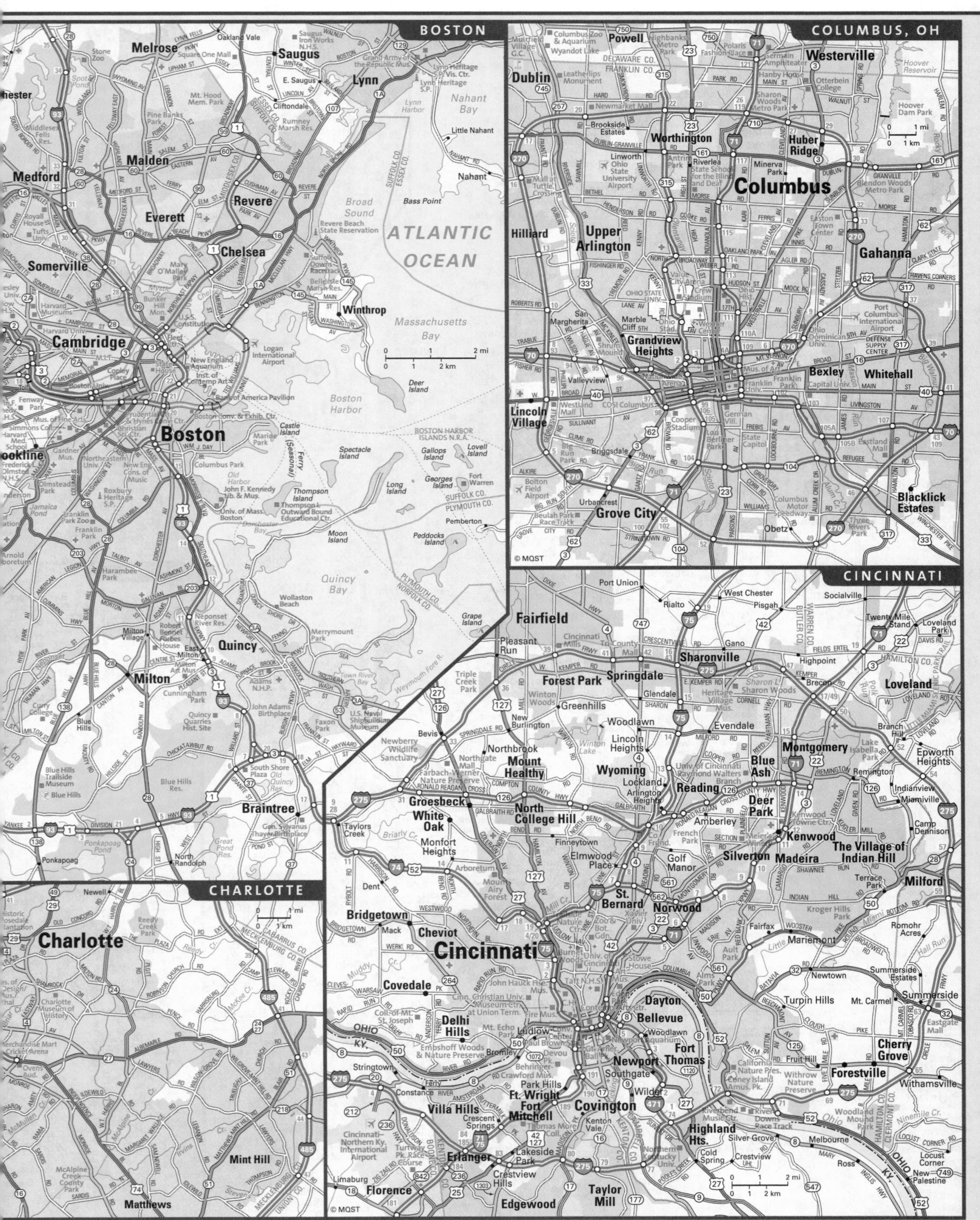
BOSTON
Melrose
Saugus
Lynn
Malden
Medford
Revere
Everett
Chelsea
Somerville
Winthrop
Cambridge
Boston
ATLANTIC OCEAN
Massachusetts Bay
Boston Harbor
Quincy Bay
Quincy
Milton
Braintree
Nahant Bay
Broad Sound
COLUMBUS, OH
Powell
Westerville
Dublin
Worthington
Huber Ridge
Columbus
Hilliard
Upper Arlington
Gahanna
Grandview Heights
Bexley
Whitehall
Lincoln Village
Blacklick Estates
Grove City
Obetz
CINCINNATI
Fairfield
Sharonville
Forest Park
Springdale
Loveland
Montgomery
Mount Healthy
Wyoming
Reading
Blue Ash
Deer Park
Groesbeck
White Oak
North College Hill
Kenwood
Silverton
Madeira
The Village of Indian Hill
Milford
St. Bernard
Norwood
Bridgetown
Cheviot
Cincinnati
Covedale
Delhi Hills
Dayton
Bellevue
Fort Thomas
Newport
Covington
Ft. Wright
Fort Mitchell
Villa Hills
Erlanger
Highland Hts.
Florence
Edgewood
Taylor Mill
Cherry Grove
Forestville
Summerside
Mariemont
CHARLOTTE
Charlotte
Mint Hill
Matthews
© MQST

Denver
Chicago
Detroit
Dallas-Ft. Worth
Charleston

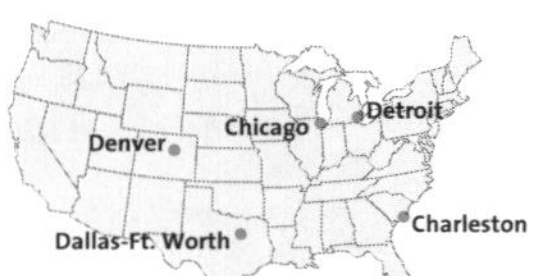

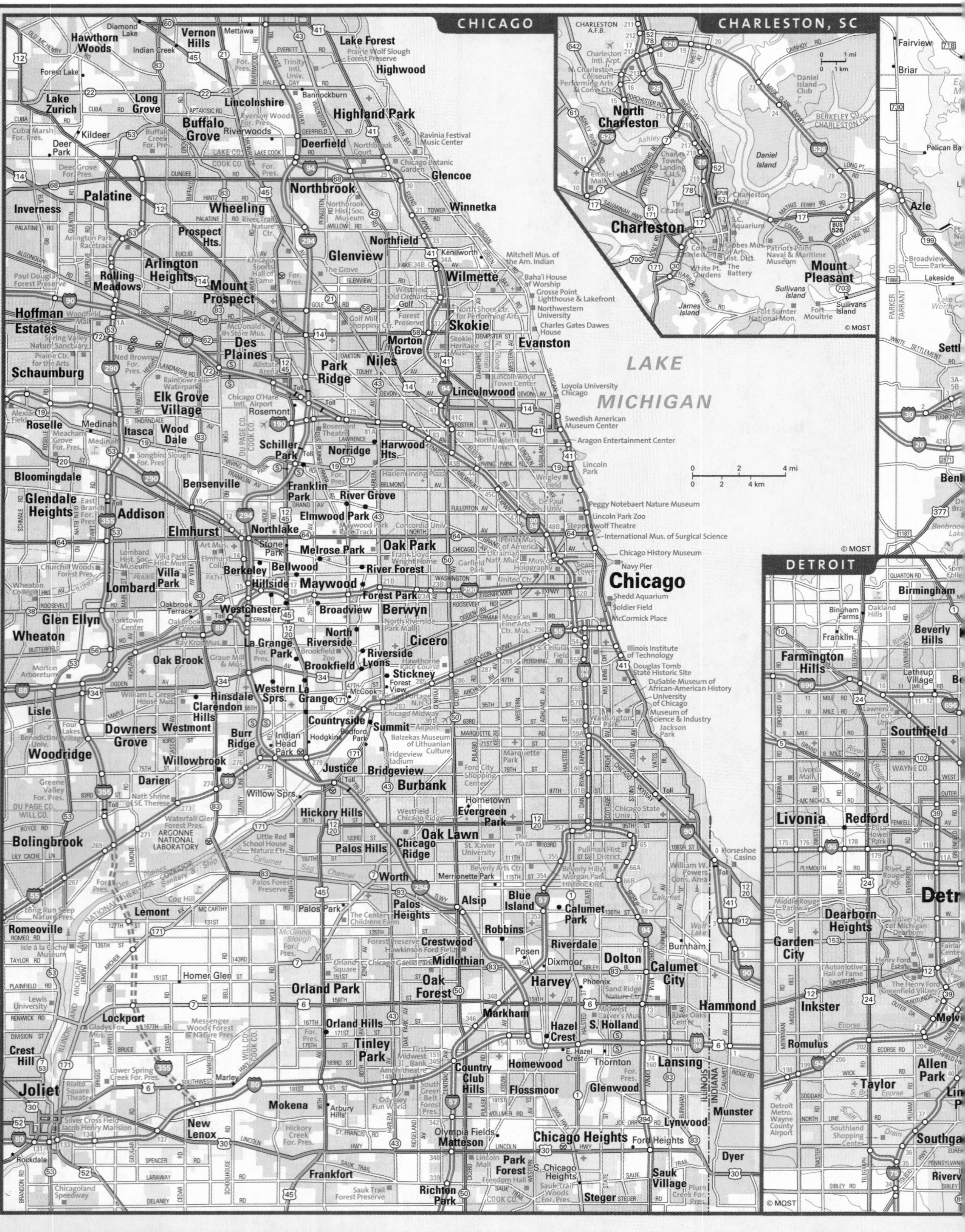
CHICAGO
CHARLESTON, SC
DETROIT
LAKE MICHIGAN
Chicago
Evanston
Skokie
Des Plaines
Schaumburg
Palatine
Northbrook
Highland Park
Oak Park
Cicero
Oak Lawn
Orland Park
Joliet
Harvey
Hammond
Charleston
North Charleston
Mount Pleasant
Livonia
Redford
Southfield
Dearborn Heights
Inkster
Taylor
© MQST

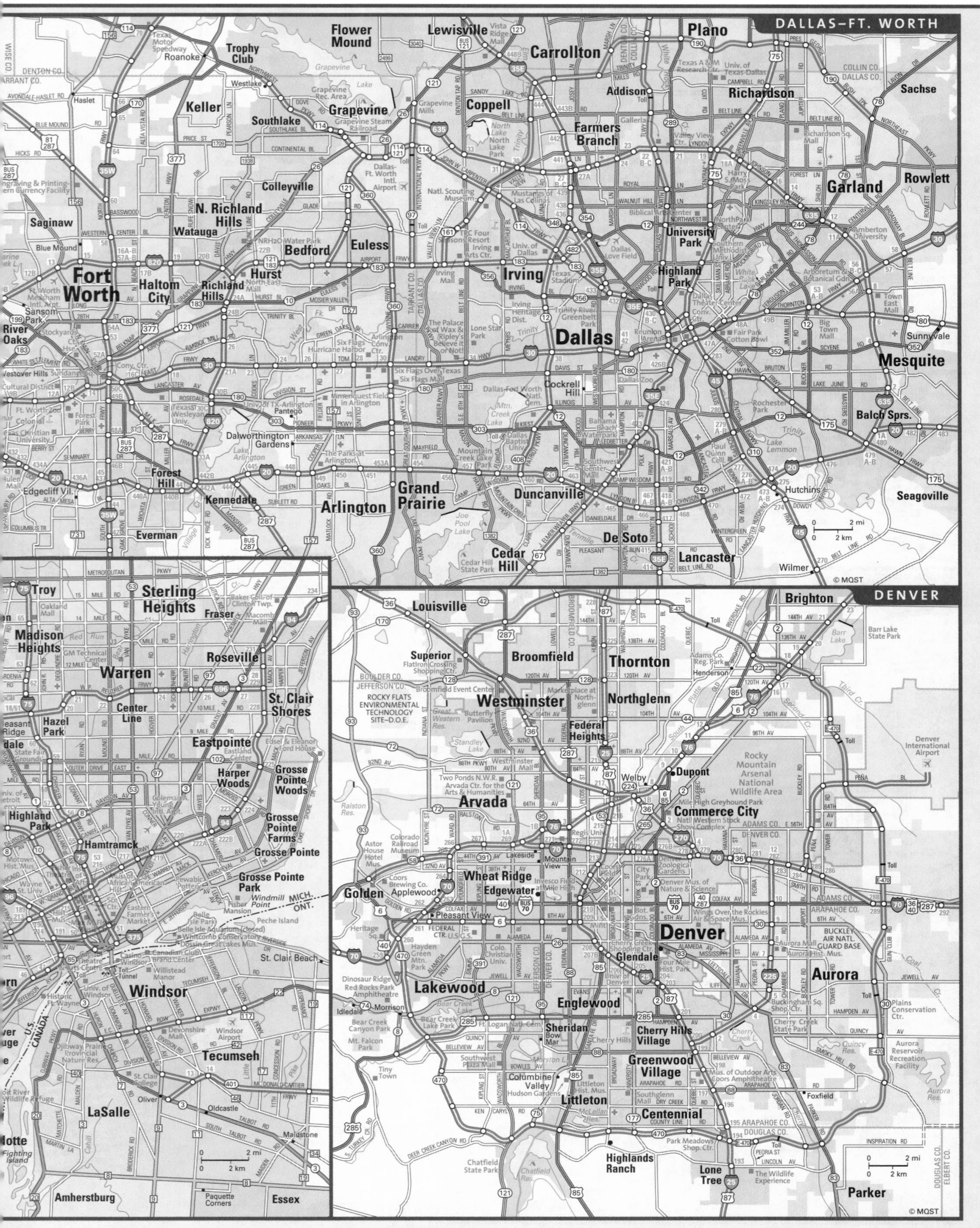
DALLAS–FT. WORTH
Plano
Lewisville
Flower Mound
Carrollton
Trophy Club
Roanoke
Addison
Richardson
Sachse
Coppell
Grapevine
Keller
Southlake
Farmers Branch
Garland
Rowlett
Colleyville
N. Richland Hills
Watauga
Saginaw
Bedford
Euless
University Park
Highland Park
Fort Worth
Haltom City
Richland Hills
Hurst
Irving
Dallas
Mesquite
Sunnyvale
Balch Sprs.
Dalworthington Gardens
Forest Hill
Kennedale
Everman
Arlington
Grand Prairie
Duncanville
De Soto
Cedar Hill
Lancaster
Hutchins
Seagoville
Wilmer
Edgecliff Vil.
Sansom Park
River Oaks
Westover Hills
Cockrell Hill
© MQST
DENVER
Brighton
Louisville
Superior
Broomfield
Thornton
Westminster
Northglenn
Federal Heights
Arvada
Welby
Dupont
Commerce City
Wheat Ridge
Edgewater
Golden
Applewood
Lakewood
Denver
Glendale
Aurora
Englewood
Sheridan
Cherry Hills Village
Greenwood Village
Littleton
Centennial
Highlands Ranch
Lone Tree
Parker
Foxfield
Morrison
Columbine Valley
Bow Mar
Troy
Sterling Heights
Fraser
Madison Heights
Roseville
Warren
Center Line
St. Clair Shores
Hazel Park
Eastpointe
Harper Woods
Grosse Pointe Woods
Highland Park
Hamtramck
Grosse Pointe Farms
Grosse Pointe
Grosse Pointe Park
Windsor
Tecumseh
LaSalle
Amherstburg
Essex
St. Clair Beach
MICH.
ONT.
U.S.
CANADA
© MQST

Hartford
Indianapolis
Kansas City
Louisville
Little Rock
Honolulu
Jacksonville
Houston

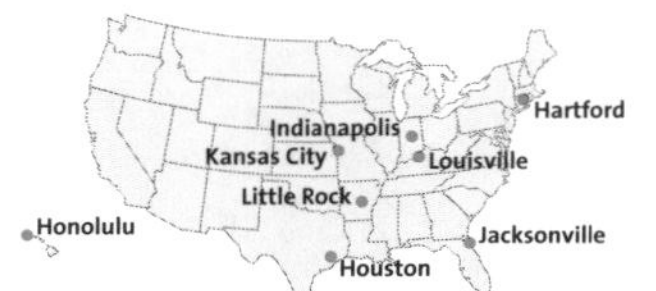

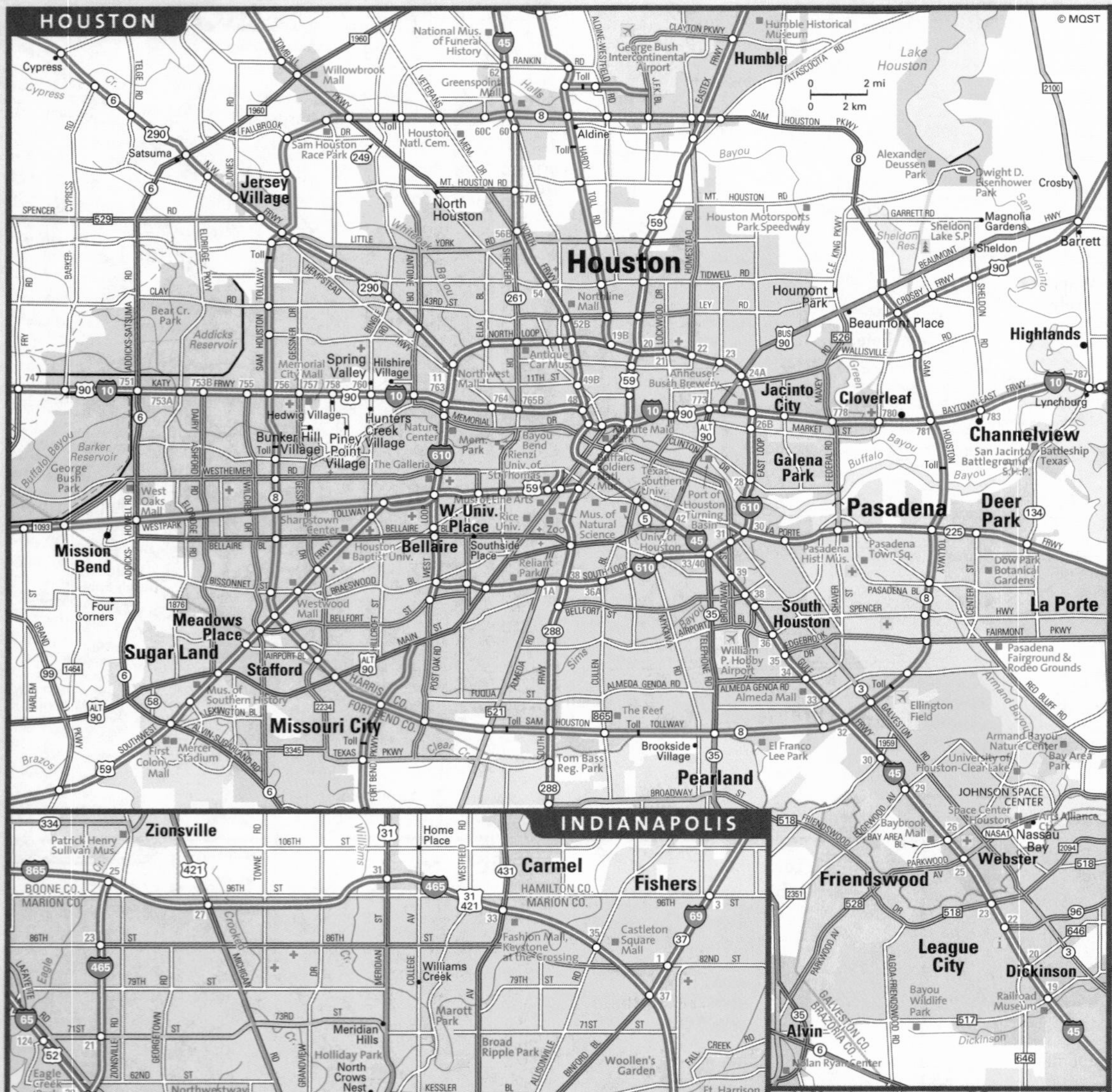
HOUSTON
© MQST
Cypress
Satsuma
Jersey Village
North Houston
Humble
Aldine
Houston
Houmont Park
Beaumont Place
Highlands
Crosby
Barrett
Sheldon
Spring Valley
Hilshire Village
Hedwig Village
Hunters Creek Village
Bunker Hill Village
Piney Point Village
Jacinto City
Cloverleaf
Galena Park
Channelview
Lynchburg
Pasadena
Deer Park
La Porte
Mission Bend
W. Univ. Place
Bellaire
South Houston
Four Corners
Meadows Place
Sugar Land
Stafford
Missouri City
Pearland
Brookside Village
Friendswood
Webster
Nassau Bay
League City
Dickinson
Alvin
George Bush Intercontinental Airport
William P. Hobby Airport
Lake Houston
Addicks Reservoir
Barker Reservoir
Johnson Space Center
Ellington Field

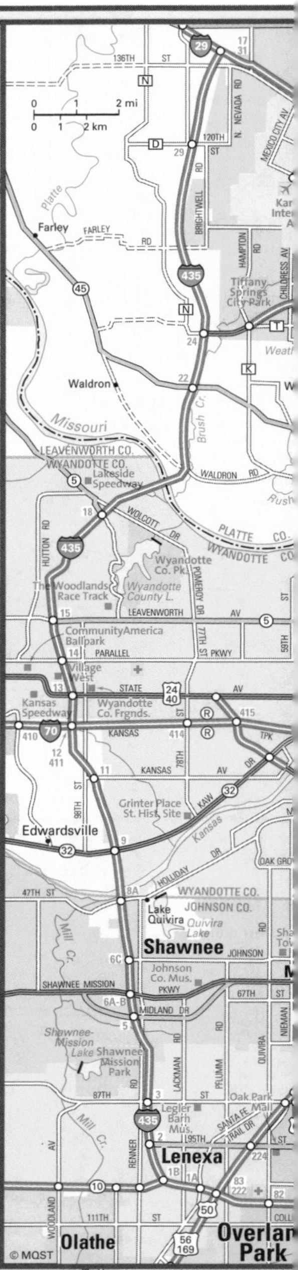
© MQST
Farley
Waldron
Tiffany Springs City Park
Missouri
Leavenworth Co.
Wyandotte Co.
Edwardsville
Shawnee
Lenexa
Olathe
Overland Park
Lake Quivira
Kansas Speedway

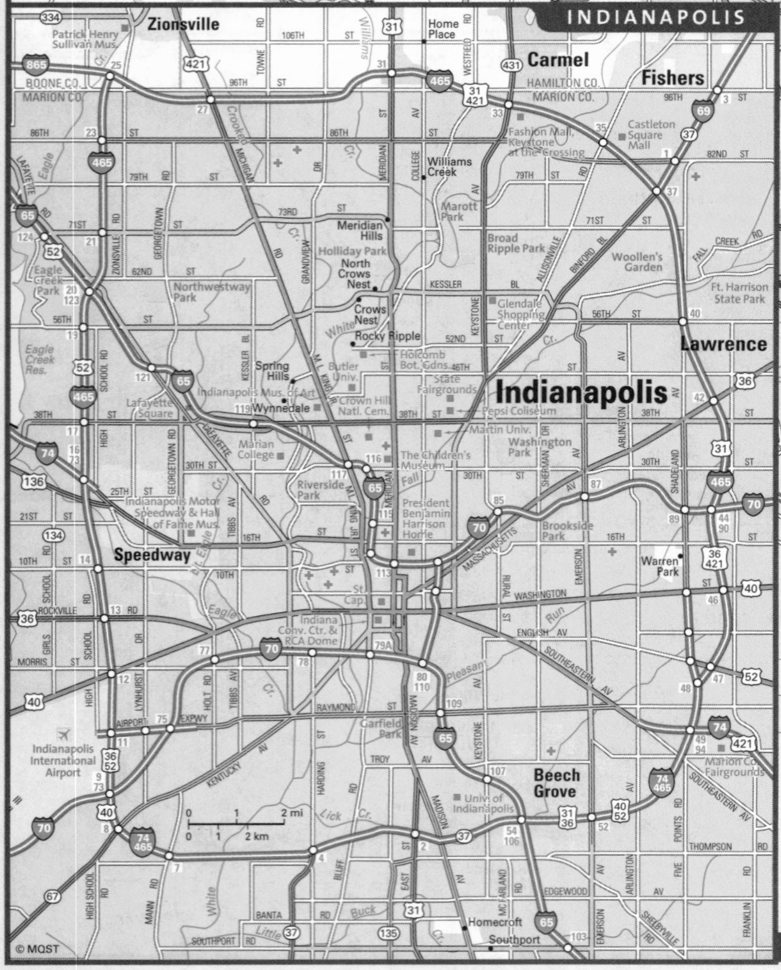
INDIANAPOLIS
Zionsville
Carmel
Fishers
Williams Creek
Meridian Hills
North Crows Nest
Crows Nest
Rocky Ripple
Spring Hills
Wynnedale
Lawrence
Indianapolis
Speedway
Warren Park
Beech Grove
Homecroft
Southport
Indianapolis International Airport
© MQST

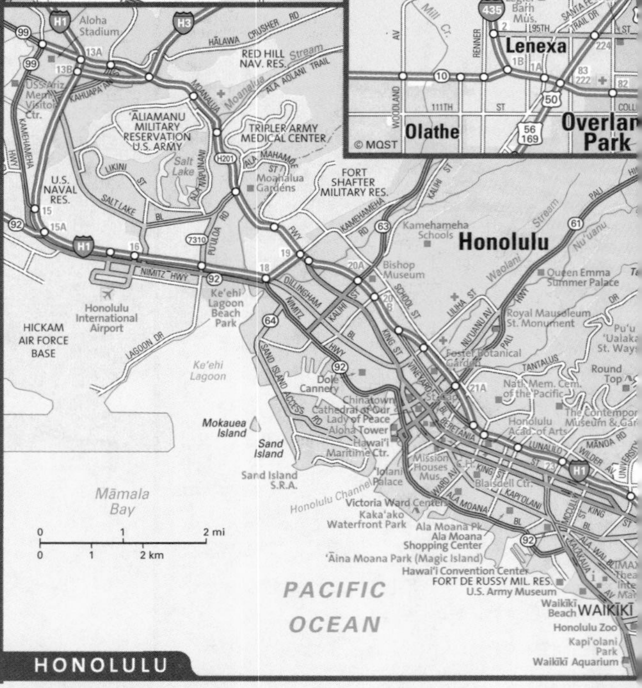
HONOLULU
Aloha Stadium
'Aliamanu Military Reservation U.S. Army
Tripler Army Medical Center
Fort Shafter Military Res.
Moanalua Gardens
U.S. Naval Res.
Honolulu International Airport
Hickam Air Force Base
Ke'ehi Lagoon
Mokauea Island
Sand Island
Māmala Bay
Honolulu
Chinatown
Waikīkī
PACIFIC OCEAN

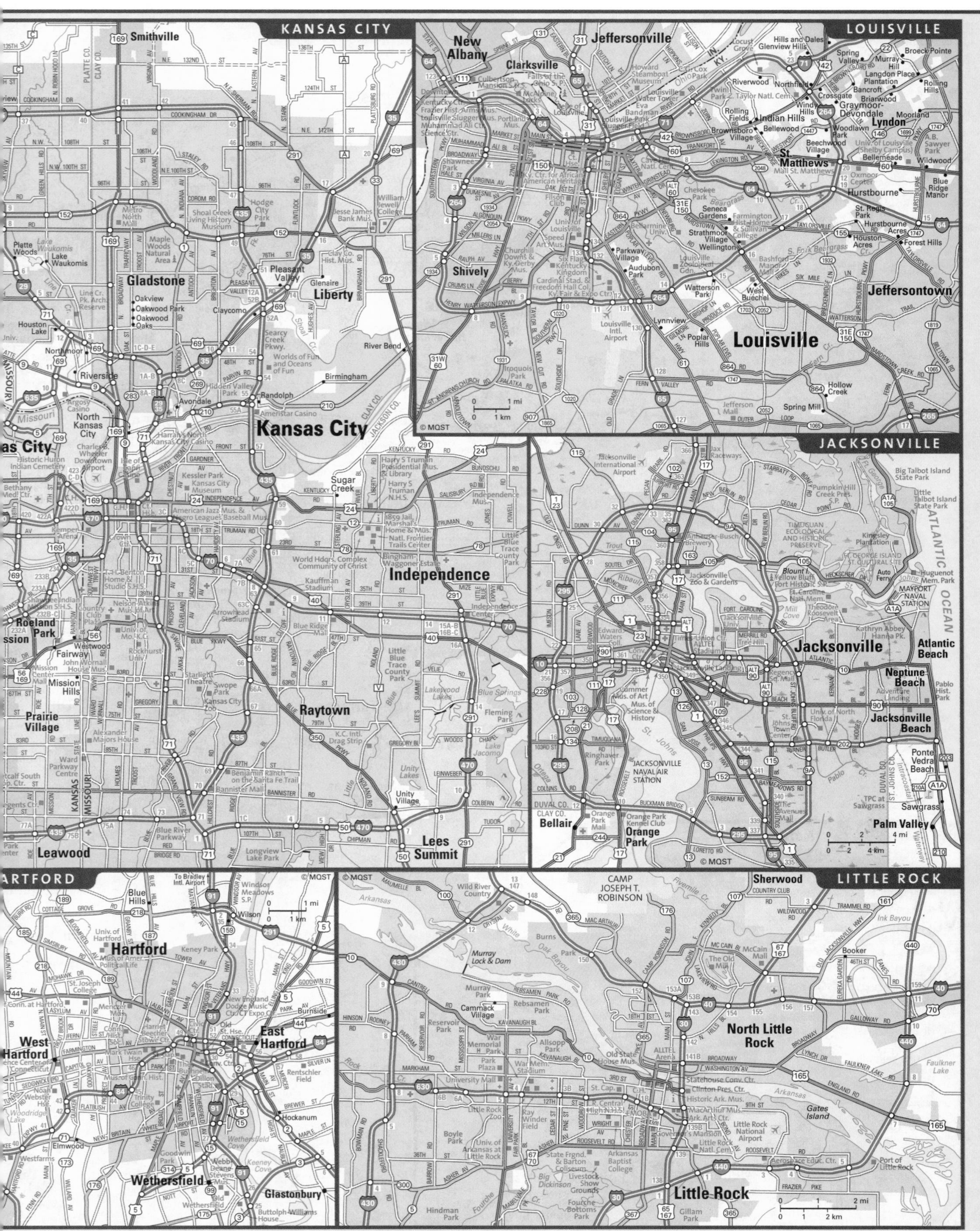
KANSAS CITY
Smithville
Gladstone
Liberty
Pleasant Valley
Claycomo
Kansas City
North Kansas City
Riverside
Randolph
Avondale
Sugar Creek
Independence
Raytown
Roeland Park
Fairway
Mission Hills
Prairie Village
Leawood
Lees Summit
LOUISVILLE
New Albany
Jeffersonville
Clarksville
Shively
Louisville
St. Matthews
Lyndon
Jeffersontown
Hurstbourne
Spring Mill
1 mi
1 km
© MQST
JACKSONVILLE
Jacksonville
Atlantic Beach
Neptune Beach
Jacksonville Beach
Ponte Vedra Beach
Palm Valley
Orange Park
Bellair
ATLANTIC OCEAN
JACKSONVILLE NAVAL AIR STATION
2
4 mi
4 km
© MQST
HARTFORD
Hartford
West Hartford
East Hartford
Wethersfield
Glastonbury
Blue Hills
Wilson
Elmwood
Hockanum
1 mi
1 km
© MQST
LITTLE ROCK
Sherwood
CAMP JOSEPH T. ROBINSON
North Little Rock
Little Rock
Cammack Village
Booker
Gates Island
2 mi
2 km
© MQST

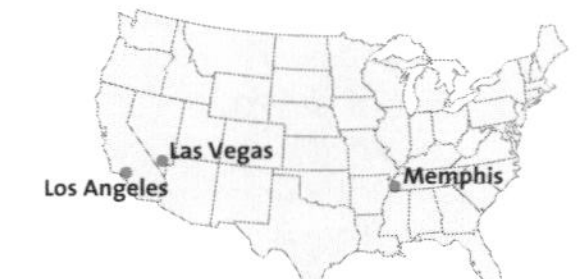

Las Vegas
Los Angeles
Memphis

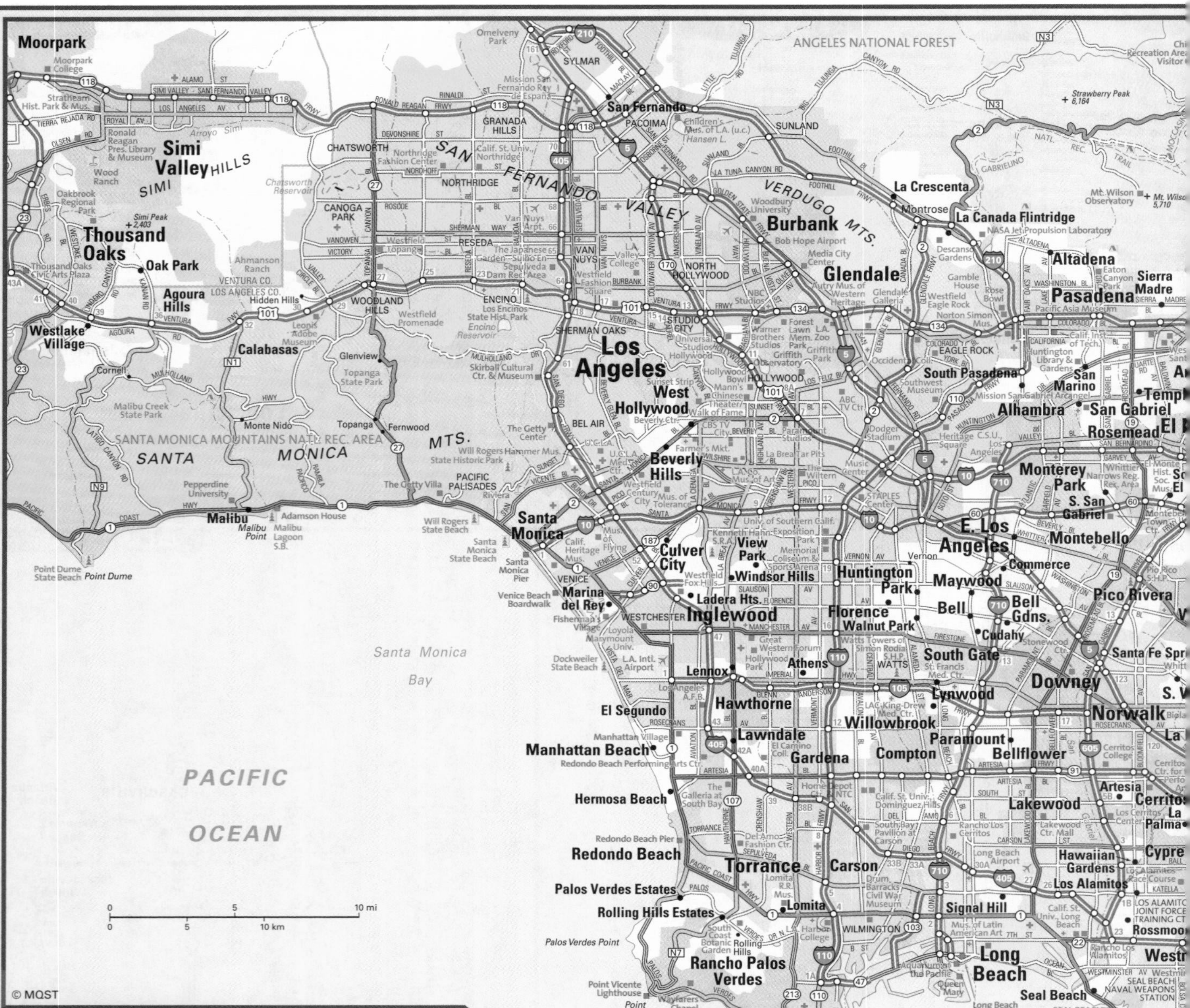
Moorpark
ANGELES NATIONAL FOREST
Simi Valley
SIMI HILLS
Thousand Oaks
Oak Park
Agoura Hills
Westlake Village
Calabasas
CHATSWORTH
SAN FERNANDO VALLEY
San Fernando
SYLMAR
PACOIMA
SUNLAND
GRANADA HILLS
NORTHRIDGE
CANOGA PARK
WOODLAND HILLS
ENCINO
SHERMAN OAKS
VAN NUYS
NORTH HOLLYWOOD
STUDIO CITY
VERDUGO MTS.
La Crescenta
Montrose
La Canada Flintridge
Burbank
Glendale
Altadena
Pasadena
Sierra Madre
Los Angeles
HOLLYWOOD
West Hollywood
Beverly Hills
BEL AIR
EAGLE ROCK
South Pasadena
San Marino
Alhambra
San Gabriel
Rosemead
Monterey Park
SANTA MONICA MOUNTAINS NAT'L. REC. AREA
SANTA MONICA MTS.
Topanga
Fernwood
Malibu
Point Dume
PACIFIC PALISADES
Santa Monica
VENICE
Marina del Rey
Culver City
View Park
Windsor Hills
Ladera Hts.
WESTCHESTER
Inglewood
Huntington Park
Vernon
E. Los Angeles
Commerce
Montebello
Maywood
Bell
Bell Gdns.
Pico Rivera
Cudahy
Florence
Walnut Park
WATTS
South Gate
Downey
Lennox
Athens
Lynwood
Norwalk
El Segundo
Hawthorne
Willowbrook
Manhattan Beach
Lawndale
Gardena
Compton
Paramount
Bellflower
Hermosa Beach
Lakewood
Artesia
Cerritos
Redondo Beach
Torrance
Carson
Hawaiian Gardens
Los Alamitos
Palos Verdes Estates
Rolling Hills Estates
Lomita
Signal Hill
WILMINGTON
Rancho Palos Verdes
Long Beach
Seal Beach
SAN PEDRO
Santa Monica Bay
PACIFIC OCEAN
San Pedro Bay
San Pedro Channel
0 5 10 mi
0 5 10 km
© MQST

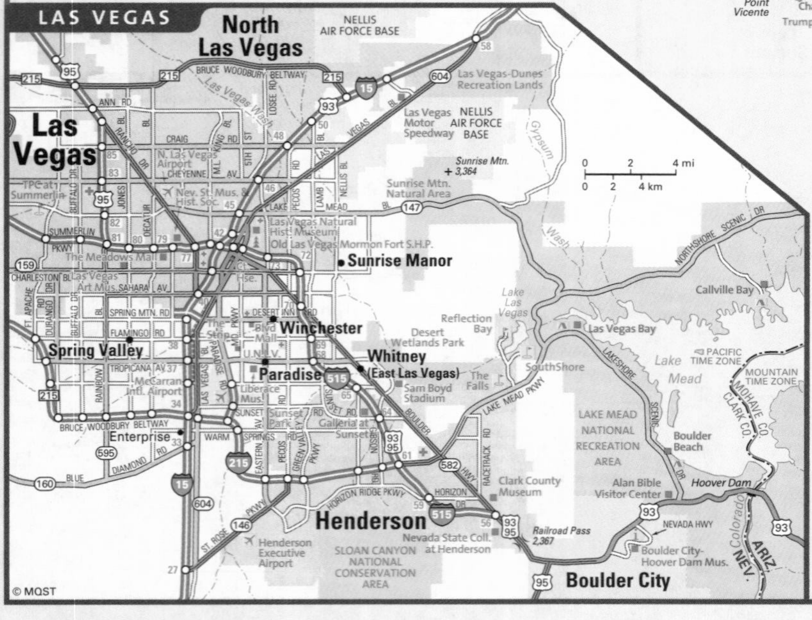
LAS VEGAS
North Las Vegas
NELLIS AIR FORCE BASE
Las Vegas
Sunrise Manor
Winchester
Spring Valley
Paradise
Whitney (East Las Vegas)
Enterprise
Henderson
Boulder City
Lake Mead
LAKE MEAD NATIONAL RECREATION AREA
SLOAN CANYON NATIONAL CONSERVATION AREA
PACIFIC TIME ZONE
MOUNTAIN TIME ZONE
NEV.
ARIZ.
0 2 4 mi
0 2 4 km
© MQST

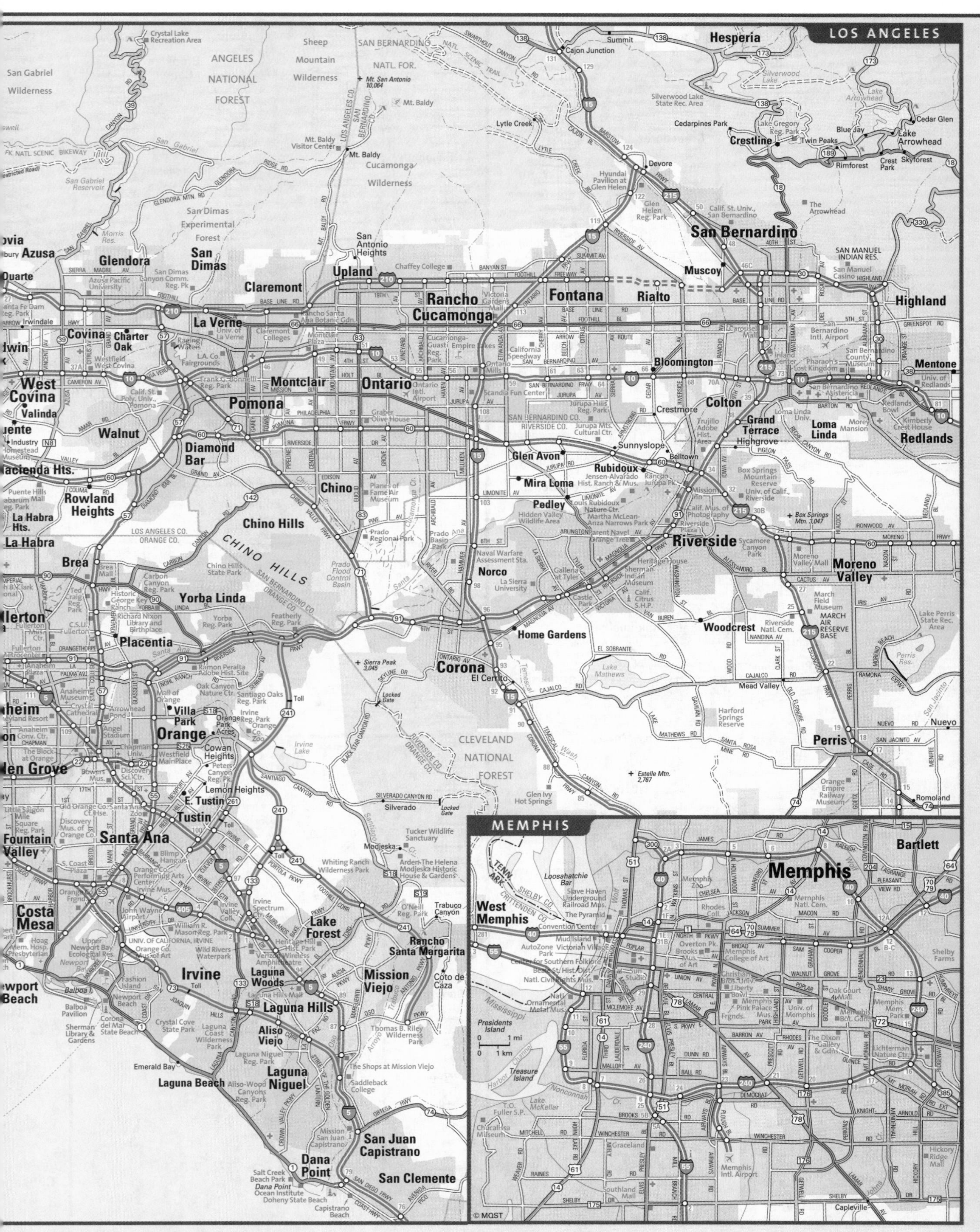
LOS ANGELES
MEMPHIS
ANGELES NATIONAL FOREST
San Gabriel Wilderness
Sheep Mountain Wilderness
Mt. San Antonio 10,064
Mt. Baldy
Cucamonga Wilderness
San Dimas Experimental Forest
Hesperia
Summit
Cajon Junction
Silverwood Lake State Rec. Area
Lytle Creek
Cedarpines Park
Crestline
Lake Gregory Reg. Park
Twin Peaks
Blue Jay
Cedar Glen
Lake Arrowhead
Rimforest
Crest Park
Skyforest
Devore
Hyundai Pavilion at Glen Helen
Glen Helen Reg. Park
Calif. St. Univ., San Bernardino
The Arrowhead
San Bernardino
San Manuel Indian Res.
Azusa
Glendora
San Dimas
San Antonio Heights
Upland
Claremont
Rancho Cucamonga
Fontana
Rialto
Muscoy
Highland
Duarte
Irwindale
Covina
Charter Oak
La Verne
Montclair
Ontario
Bloomington
Colton
Mentone
West Covina
Valinda
Pomona
Walnut
Diamond Bar
Grand Terrace
Highgrove
Loma Linda
Redlands
Industry
Hacienda Hts.
Rowland Heights
Glen Avon
Sunnyslope
Belltown
Rubidoux
Mira Loma
Chino
Pedley
La Habra Hts.
La Habra
Chino Hills
CHINO HILLS
Box Springs Mtn. 3,047
Riverside
Moreno Valley
Brea
Norco
Yorba Linda
Woodcrest
March Air Reserve Base
Lake Perris State Rec. Area
Fullerton
Placentia
Home Gardens
Corona
El Cerrito
Sierra Peak 3,045
Lake Mathews
Mead Valley
Anaheim
Villa Park
Orange
Perris
Nuevo
CLEVELAND NATIONAL FOREST
Garden Grove
Lemon Heights
E. Tustin
Tustin
Santa Ana
Estelle Mtn. 2,767
Romoland
Silverado
Fountain Valley
Modjeska
Costa Mesa
Lake Forest
Rancho Santa Margarita
Trabuco Canyon
Irvine
Mission Viejo
Coto de Caza
Newport Beach
Laguna Woods
Laguna Hills
Aliso Viejo
Emerald Bay
Laguna Beach
Laguna Niguel
San Juan Capistrano
Dana Point
San Clemente
Bartlett
Memphis
West Memphis
Mississippi
Presidents Island
Treasure Island
Memphis Intl. Airport
Capleville
Shelby Farms
© MQST

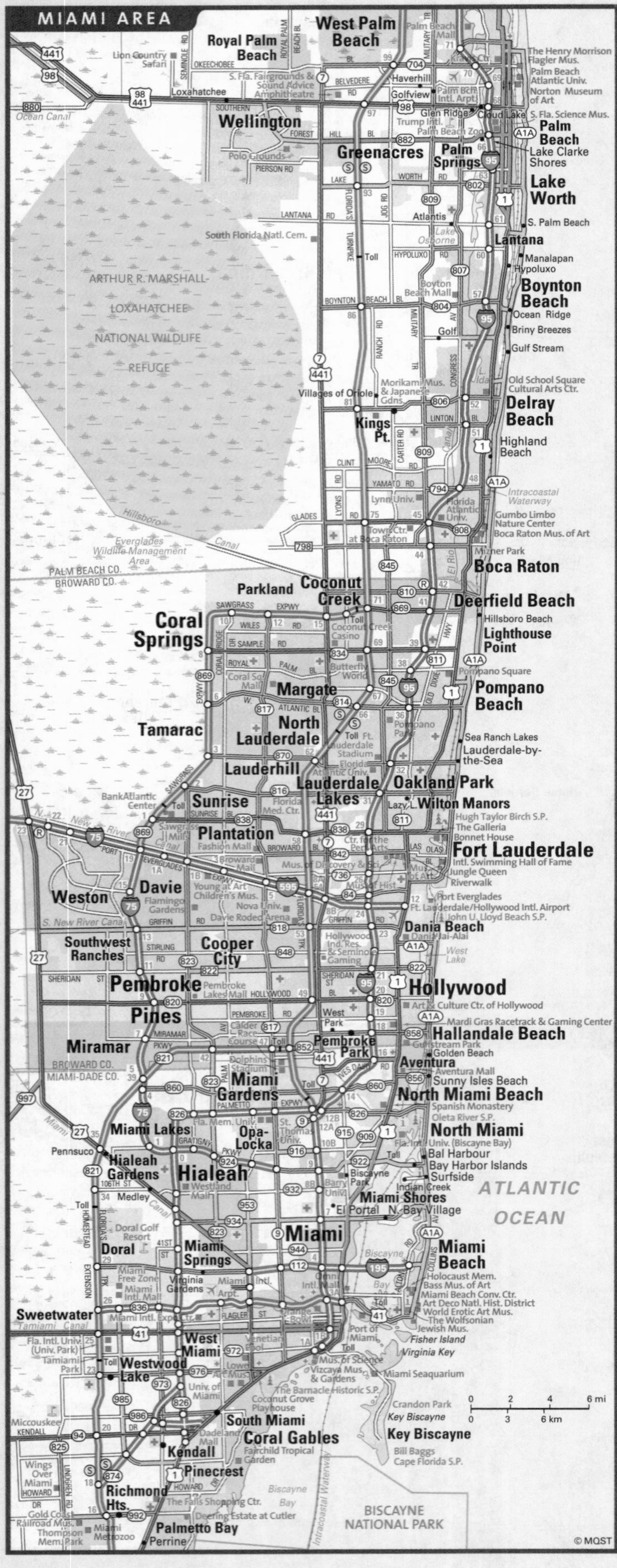

MIAMI AREA

West Palm Beach
Royal Palm Beach
Wellington
Greenacres
Palm Springs
Palm Beach
Lake Clarke Shores
Lake Worth
Atlantis
Lantana
Hypoluxo
Manalapan
Boynton Beach
Ocean Ridge
Briny Breezes
Golf
Gulf Stream
Delray Beach
Highland Beach
Kings Pt.
Boca Raton
ARTHUR R. MARSHALL LOXAHATCHEE NATIONAL WILDLIFE REFUGE
Parkland
Coconut Creek
Deerfield Beach
Hillsboro Beach
Coral Springs
Lighthouse Point
Margate
Pompano Beach
Tamarac
North Lauderdale
Lauderhill
Sea Ranch Lakes
Lauderdale-by-the-Sea
Lauderdale Lakes
Oakland Park
Wilton Manors
Sunrise
Plantation
Fort Lauderdale
Weston
Davie
Dania Beach
Southwest Ranches
Cooper City
Hollywood
Pembroke Pines
Hallandale Beach
Miramar
Pembroke Park
Aventura
Miami Gardens
North Miami Beach
Miami Lakes
Opa-Locka
North Miami
Bal Harbour
Bay Harbor Islands
Surfside
Hialeah Gardens
Hialeah
Miami Shores
El Portal
Biscayne Park
Medley
ATLANTIC OCEAN
Doral
Miami Springs
Miami
Miami Beach
Sweetwater
West Miami
Westwood Lake
Key Biscayne
South Miami
Coral Gables
Kendall
Pinecrest
Richmond Hts.
Palmetto Bay
Perrine
BISCAYNE NATIONAL PARK
0 2 4 6 mi
0 3 6 km
© MQST

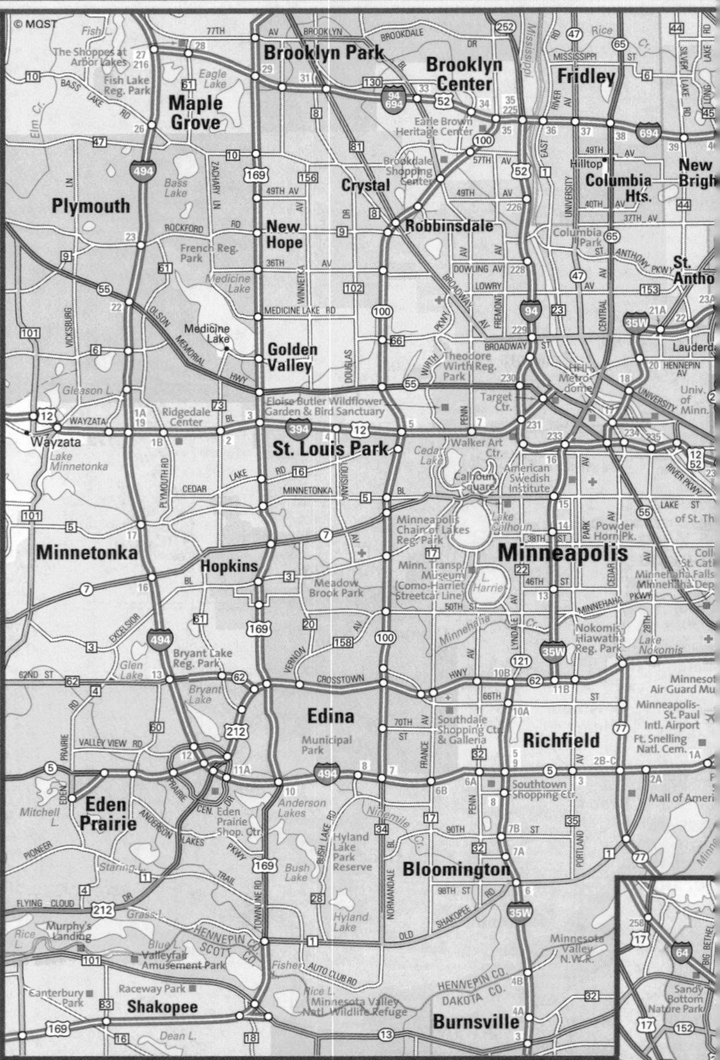

MINNEAPOLIS-ST. PAUL

Brooklyn Park
Brooklyn Center
Fridley
Maple Grove
Plymouth
Crystal
Robbinsdale
New Hope
Columbia Hts.
Golden Valley
Wayzata
St. Louis Park
Minnetonka
Hopkins
Minneapolis
Edina
Richfield
Eden Prairie
Bloomington
Shakopee
Burnsville
© MQST

MILWAUKEE

Brown Deer
Fox Point
River Hills
LAKE MICHIGAN
Menomonee Falls
Glendale
Whitefish Bay
Butler
Shorewood
Brookfield
Milwaukee
Wauwatosa
Elm Grove
West Milwaukee
New Berlin
West Allis
St. Francis
Greenfield
Hales Corners
Greendale
Cudahy
© MQST

NORFOLK-VA. BEACH-NEWPORT NEWS

Newport News
Suffolk
Chesap

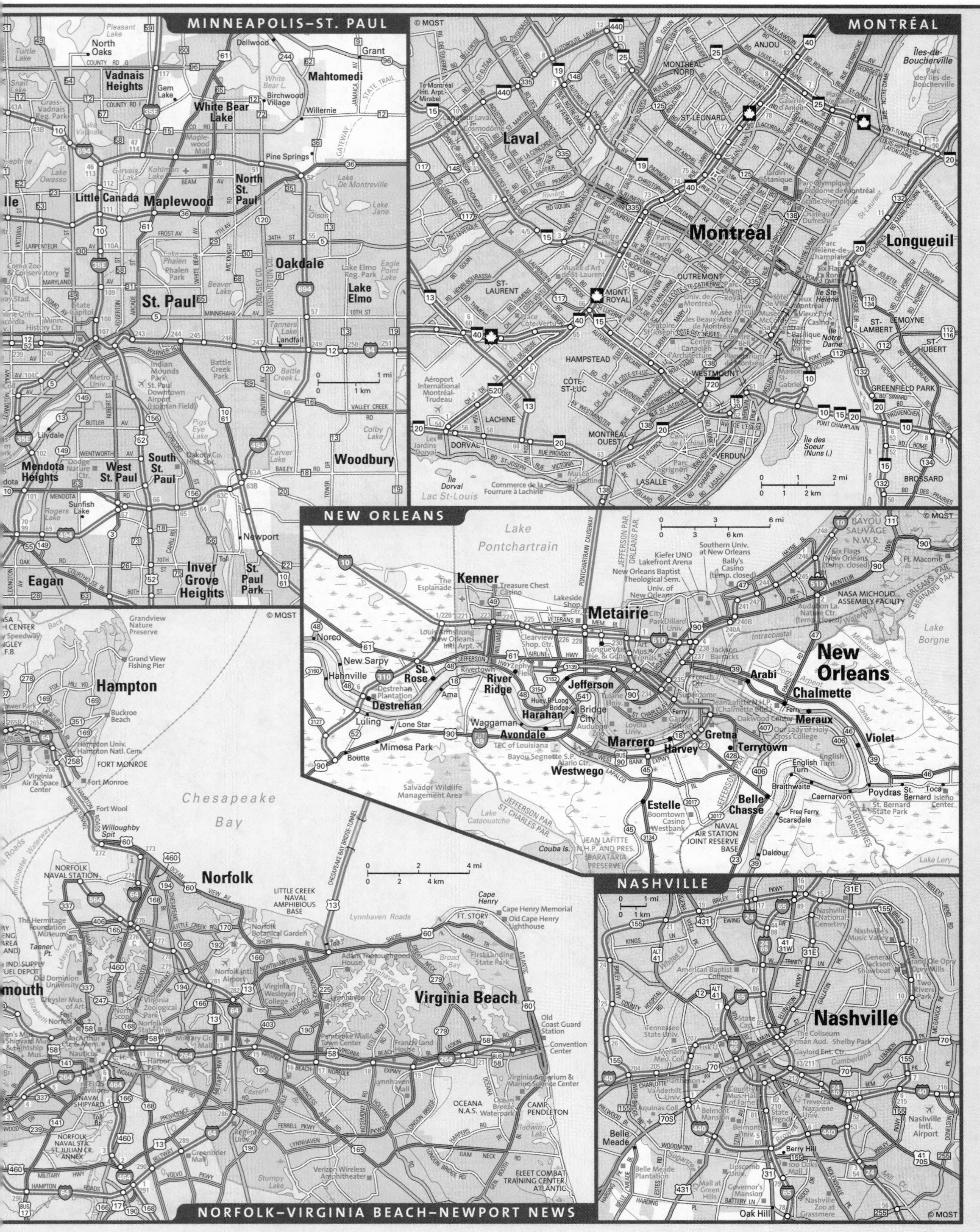
MINNEAPOLIS–ST. PAUL
MONTRÉAL
NEW ORLEANS
NASHVILLE
NORFOLK–VIRGINIA BEACH–NEWPORT NEWS
St. Paul
Maplewood
Oakdale
Woodbury
Montreal
Laval
Longueuil
New Orleans
Metairie
Kenner
Chalmette
Hampton
Norfolk
Virginia Beach
Nashville
© MQST

New York
Pittsburgh
Philadelphia
Oklahoma City

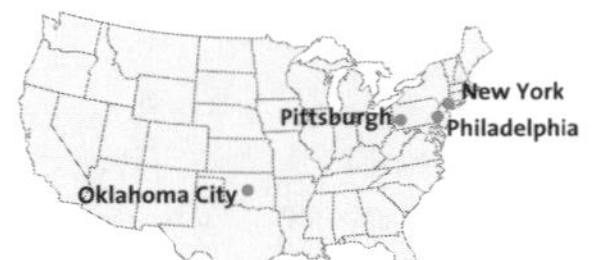

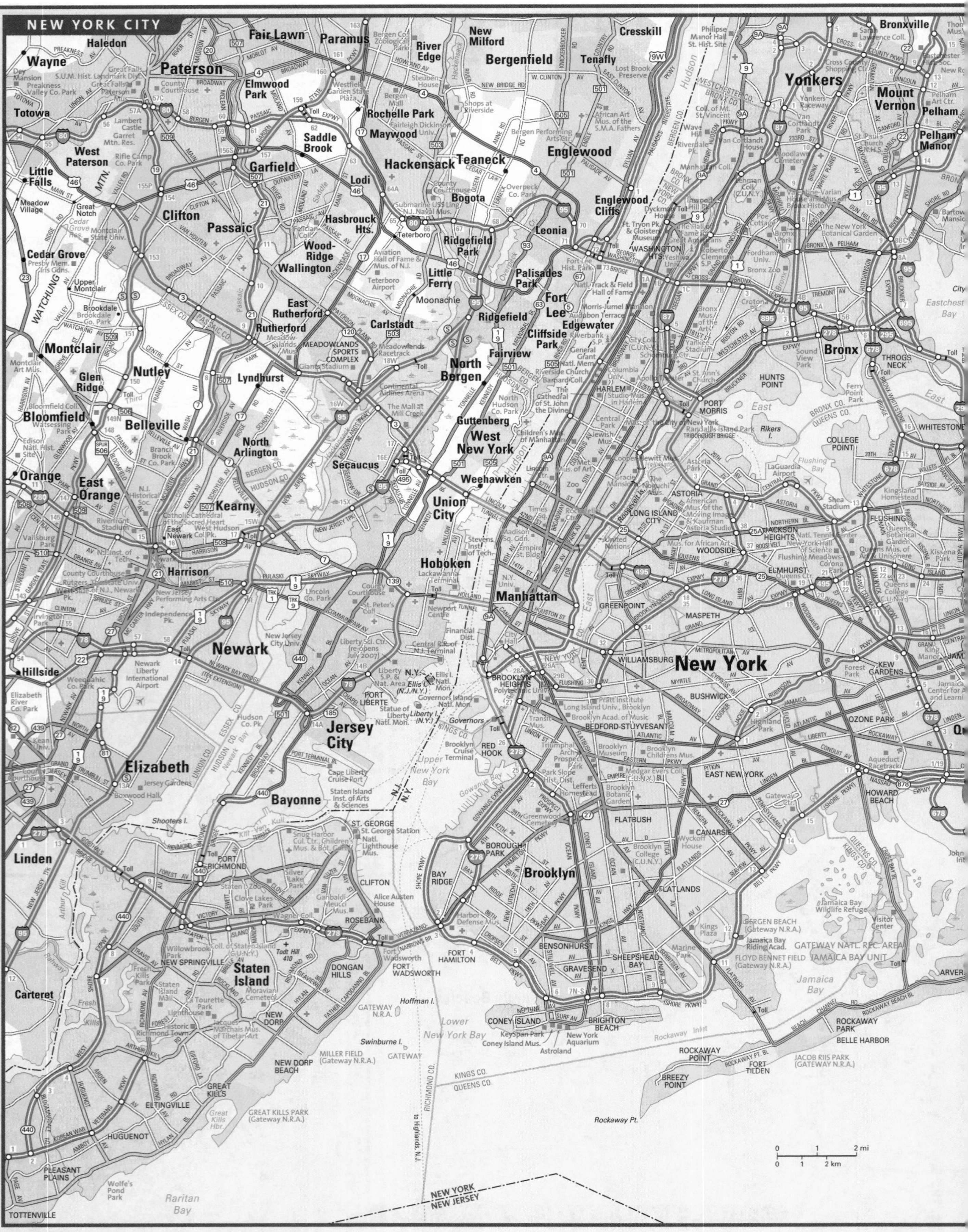
NEW YORK CITY
Haledon
Wayne
Paterson
Fair Lawn
Paramus
River Edge
New Milford
Bergenfield
Tenafly
Cresskill
Bronxville
Yonkers
Mount Vernon
Pelham
Pelham Manor
Totowa
Elmwood Park
Rochelle Park
Saddle Brook
Maywood
Hackensack
Teaneck
Englewood
West Paterson
Little Falls
Garfield
Lodi
Bogota
Englewood Cliffs
Clifton
Passaic
Hasbrouck Hts.
Leonia
Cedar Grove
Wood-Ridge
Wallington
Ridgefield Park
Little Ferry
Palisades Park
Fort Lee
Moonachie
East Rutherford
Rutherford
Carlstadt
Ridgefield
Cliffside Park
Edgewater
Montclair
Nutley
Glen Ridge
Lyndhurst
North Bergen
Fairview
Bronx
Bloomfield
Belleville
North Arlington
Guttenberg
West New York
Secaucus
Orange
East Orange
Kearny
Weehawken
Union City
Harrison
Hoboken
Manhattan
Newark
Hillside
Elizabeth
Jersey City
Bayonne
New York
Brooklyn
Linden
Staten Island
Carteret
Upper New York Bay
Lower New York Bay
Raritan Bay
Jamaica Bay
Rockaway Pt.
Rockaway Inlet
GATEWAY NATL. REC. AREA JAMAICA BAY UNIT
NEW YORK
NEW JERSEY
TOTTENVILLE
0 1 2 mi
0 1 2 km

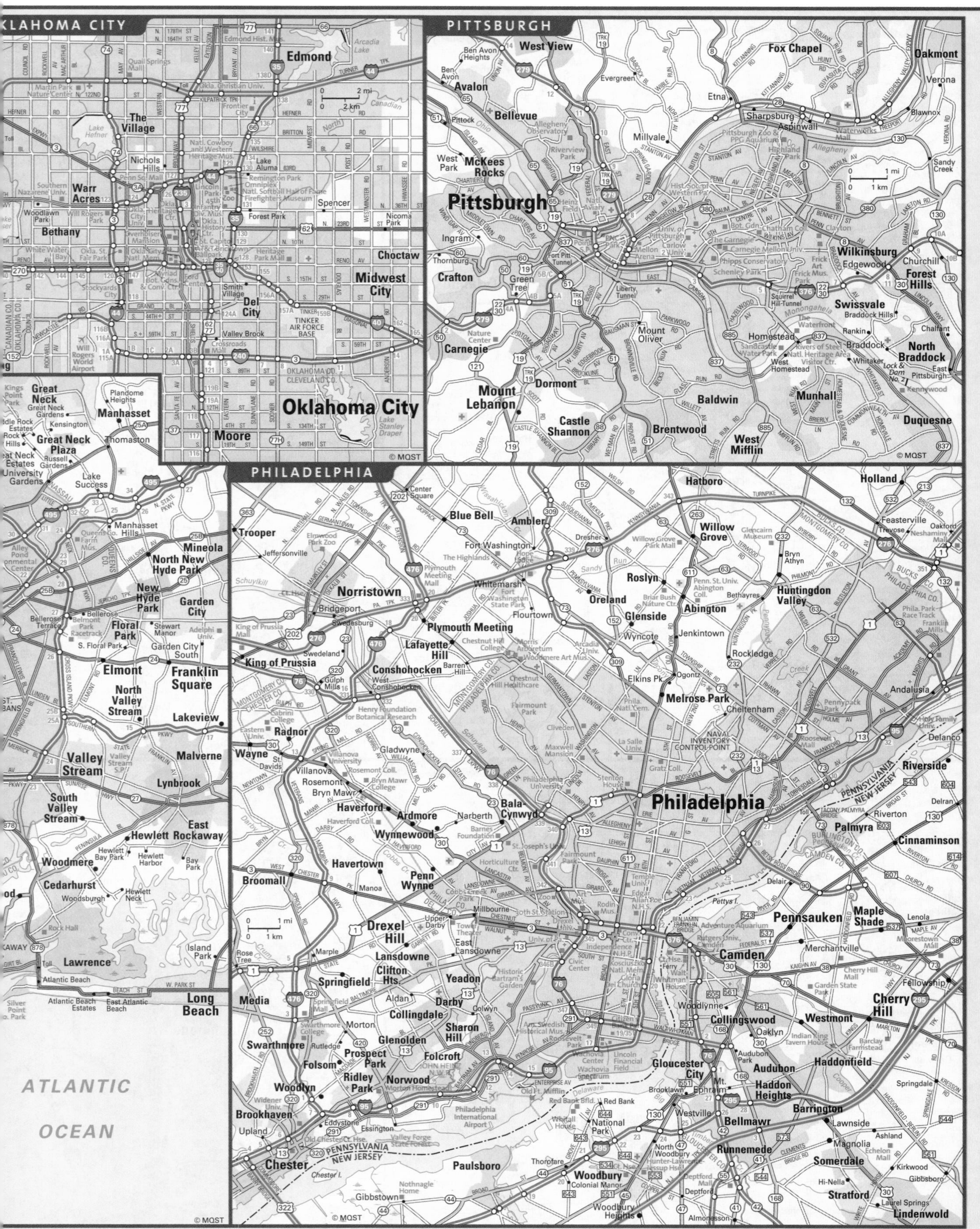
KLAHOMA CITY
Edmond
The Village
Nichols Hills
Warr Acres
Bethany
Spencer
Choctaw
Midwest City
Del City
TINKER AIR FORCE BASE
Valley Brook
Oklahoma City
Moore
PITTSBURGH
West View
Fox Chapel
Oakmont
Avalon
Bellevue
Verona
Millvale
Etna
Sharpsburg
Aspinwall
Blawnox
McKees Rocks
West Park
Pittsburgh
Ingram
Crafton
Carnegie
Wilkinsburg
Edgewood
Churchill
Forest Hills
Swissvale
Mount Oliver
Mount Lebanon
Dormont
Castle Shannon
Baldwin
Brentwood
West Mifflin
Homestead
Munhall
North Braddock
Braddock
Duquesne
Great Neck
Manhasset
Great Neck Plaza
Lake Success
Mineola
North New Hyde Park
New Hyde Park
Garden City
Floral Park
Elmont
Franklin Square
North Valley Stream
Lakeview
Valley Stream
Malverne
Lynbrook
South Valley Stream
East Rockaway
Hewlett
Woodmere
Cedarhurst
Lawrence
Island Park
Long Beach
ATLANTIC
OCEAN
PHILADELPHIA
Hatboro
Holland
Blue Bell
Ambler
Trooper
Willow Grove
Norristown
Roslyn
Oreland
Abington
Huntingdon Valley
Plymouth Meeting
Glenside
Jenkintown
King of Prussia
Conshohocken
Lafayette Hill
Melrose Park
Cheltenham
Radnor
Wayne
Philadelphia
Bala-Cynwyd
Haverford
Ardmore
Narberth
Wynnewood
Havertown
Broomall
Penn Wynne
Drexel Hill
Lansdowne
Clifton Hts.
Yeadon
Springfield
Media
Darby
Collingdale
Sharon Hill
Glenolden
Prospect Park
Folcroft
Swarthmore
Folsom
Ridley Park
Norwood
Woodlyn
Brookhaven
Chester
Paulsboro
Woodbury
Camden
Pennsauken
Maple Shade
Riverside
Palmyra
Cinnaminson
Cherry Hill
Westmont
Collingswood
Oaklyn
Audubon
Haddonfield
Gloucester City
Mt. Ephraim
Haddon Heights
Barrington
Bellmawr
Runnemede
Somerdale
Stratford
Lindenwold
PENNSYLVANIA
NEW JERSEY
© MQST

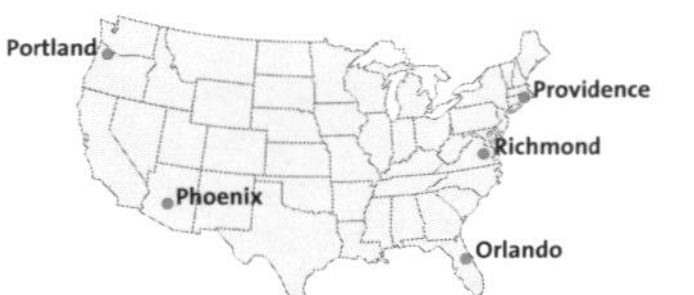

Portland
Providence
Richmond
Phoenix
Orlando

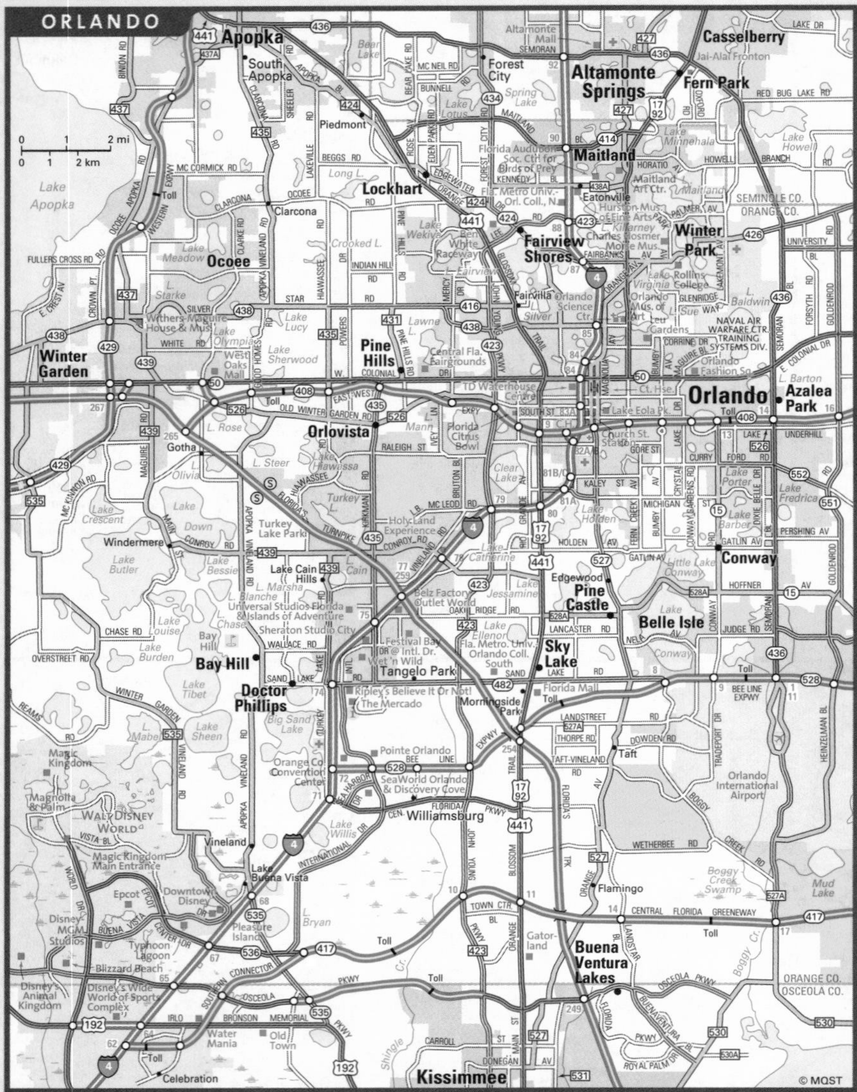
ORLANDO
Apopka
South Apopka
Altamonte Springs
Casselberry
Fern Park
Forest City
Maitland
Lockhart
Winter Park
Fairview Shores
Ocoee
Winter Garden
Pine Hills
Orlando
Azalea Park
Orlovista
Conway
Pine Castle
Belle Isle
Sky Lake
Tangelo Park
Bay Hill
Doctor Phillips
Williamsburg
Buena Ventura Lakes
Kissimmee
Orlando International Airport
© MQST

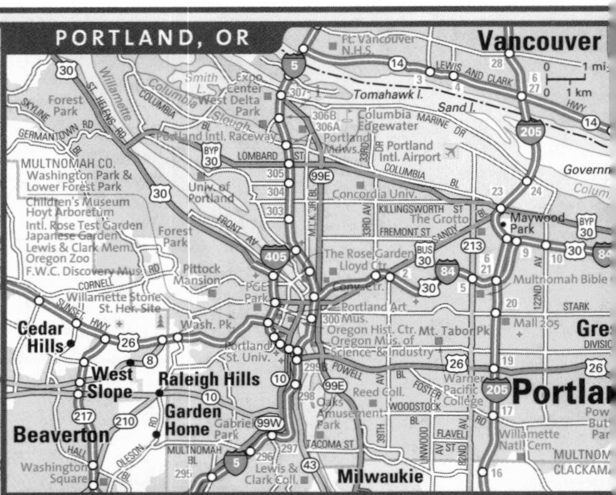
PORTLAND, OR
Vancouver
Cedar Hills
West Slope
Raleigh Hills
Garden Home
Beaverton
Milwaukie
Portland

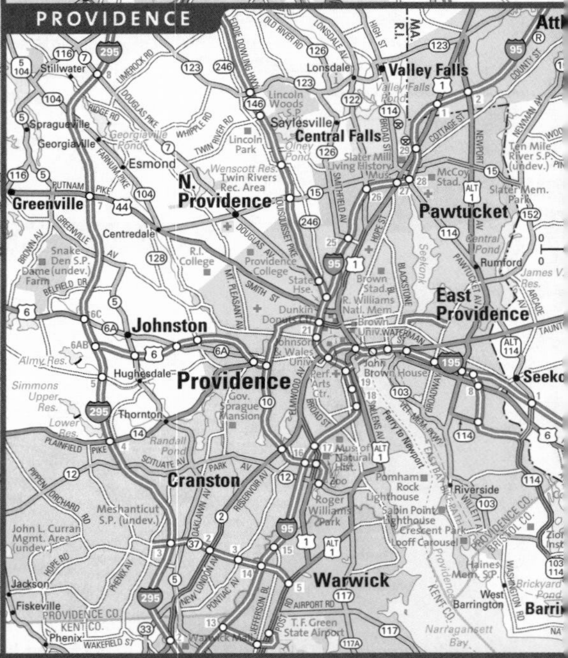
PROVIDENCE
Valley Falls
Central Falls
Pawtucket
N. Providence
Greenville
East Providence
Johnston
Providence
Cranston
Warwick

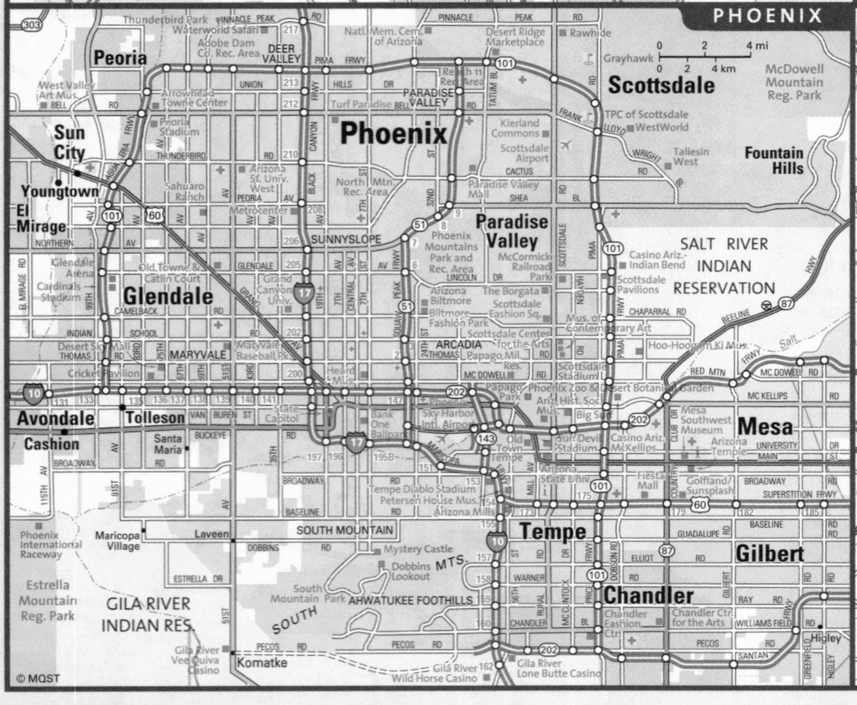
PHOENIX
Peoria
Scottsdale
Sun City
Phoenix
Fountain Hills
Youngtown
El Mirage
Paradise Valley
SALT RIVER INDIAN RESERVATION
Glendale
Avondale
Tolleson
Cashion
Mesa
Tempe
Gilbert
Chandler
GILA RIVER INDIAN RES.
© MQST

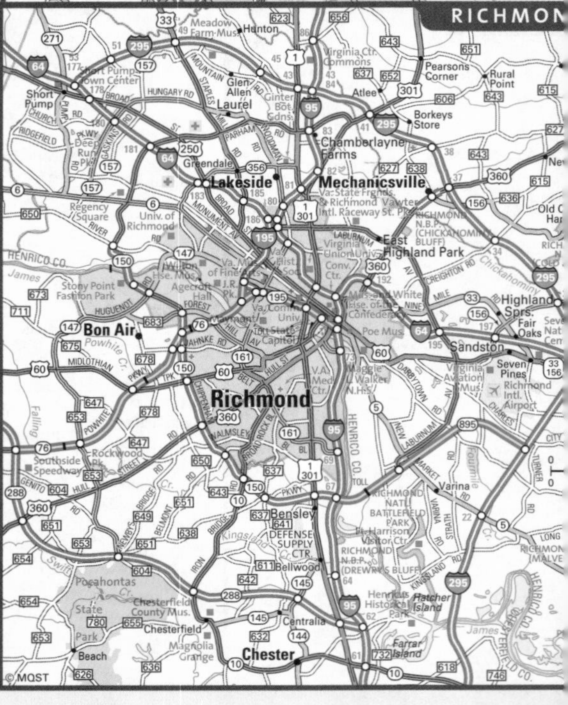
RICHMON
Lakeside
Mechanicsville
Bon Air
Richmond
Chester
© MQST

N FRANCISCO BAY

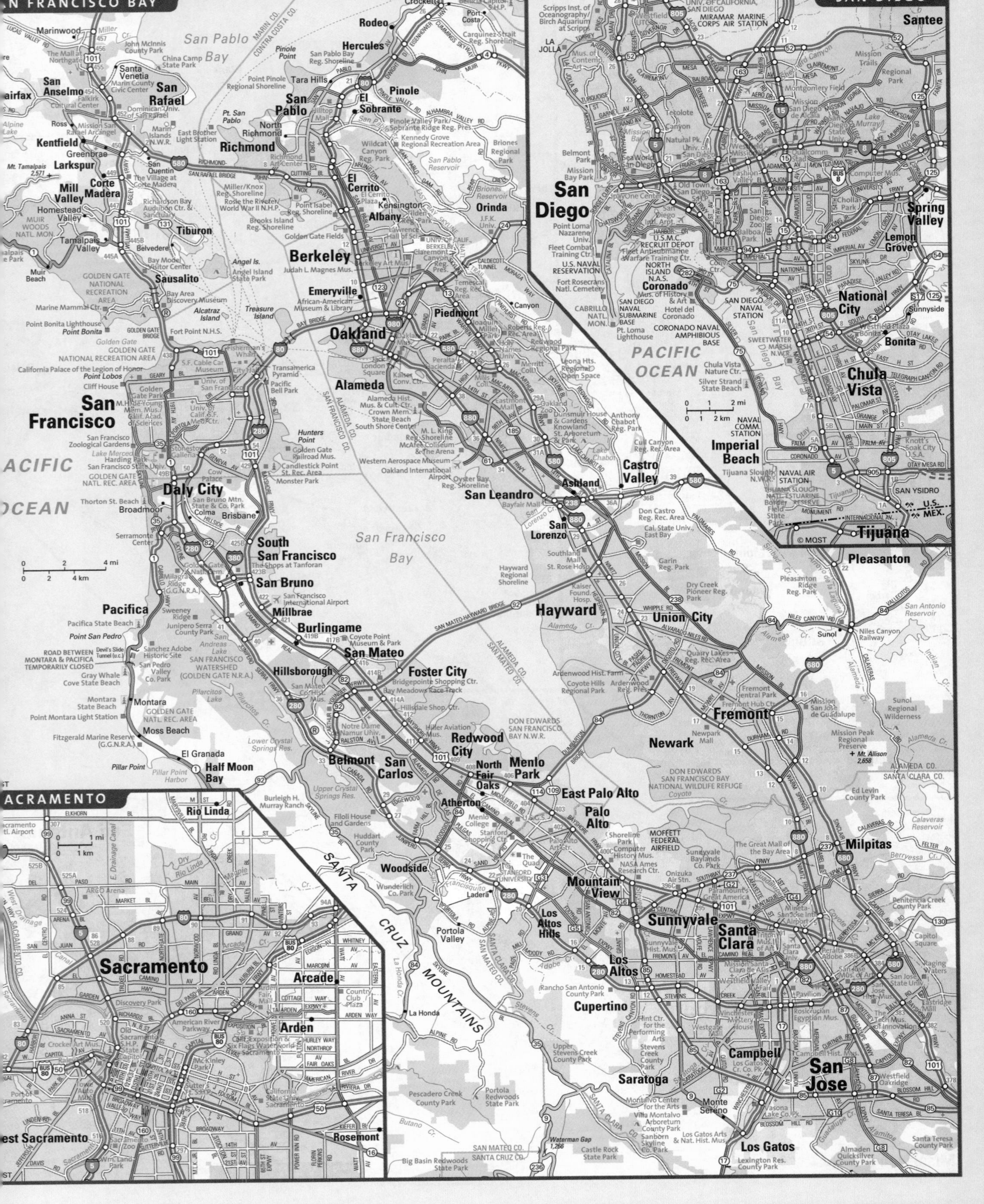

SAN DIEGO

© MOST

ACRAMENTO

SEATTLE–TACOMA

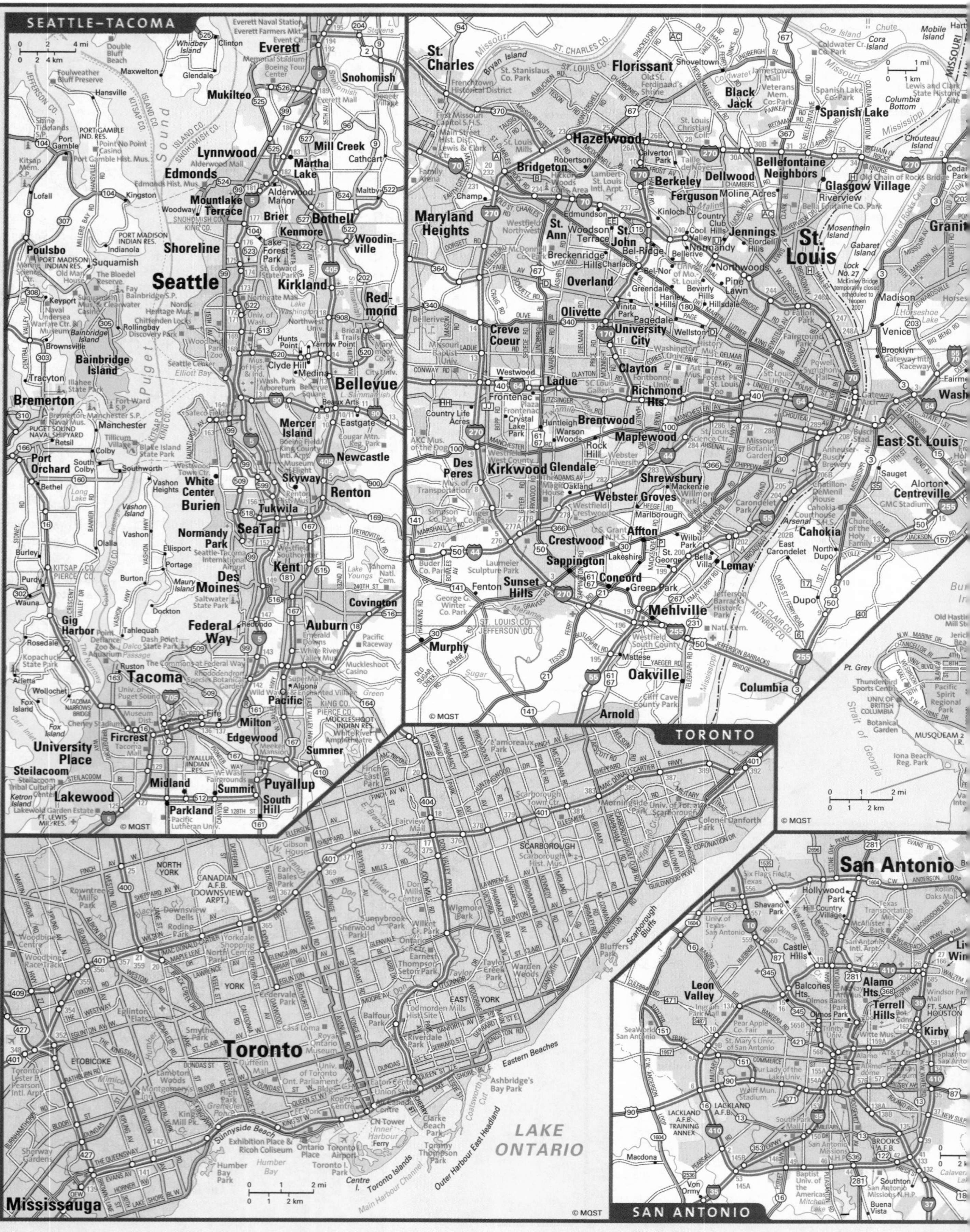

ST. LOUIS

TORONTO

VANCOUVER

SAN ANTONIO

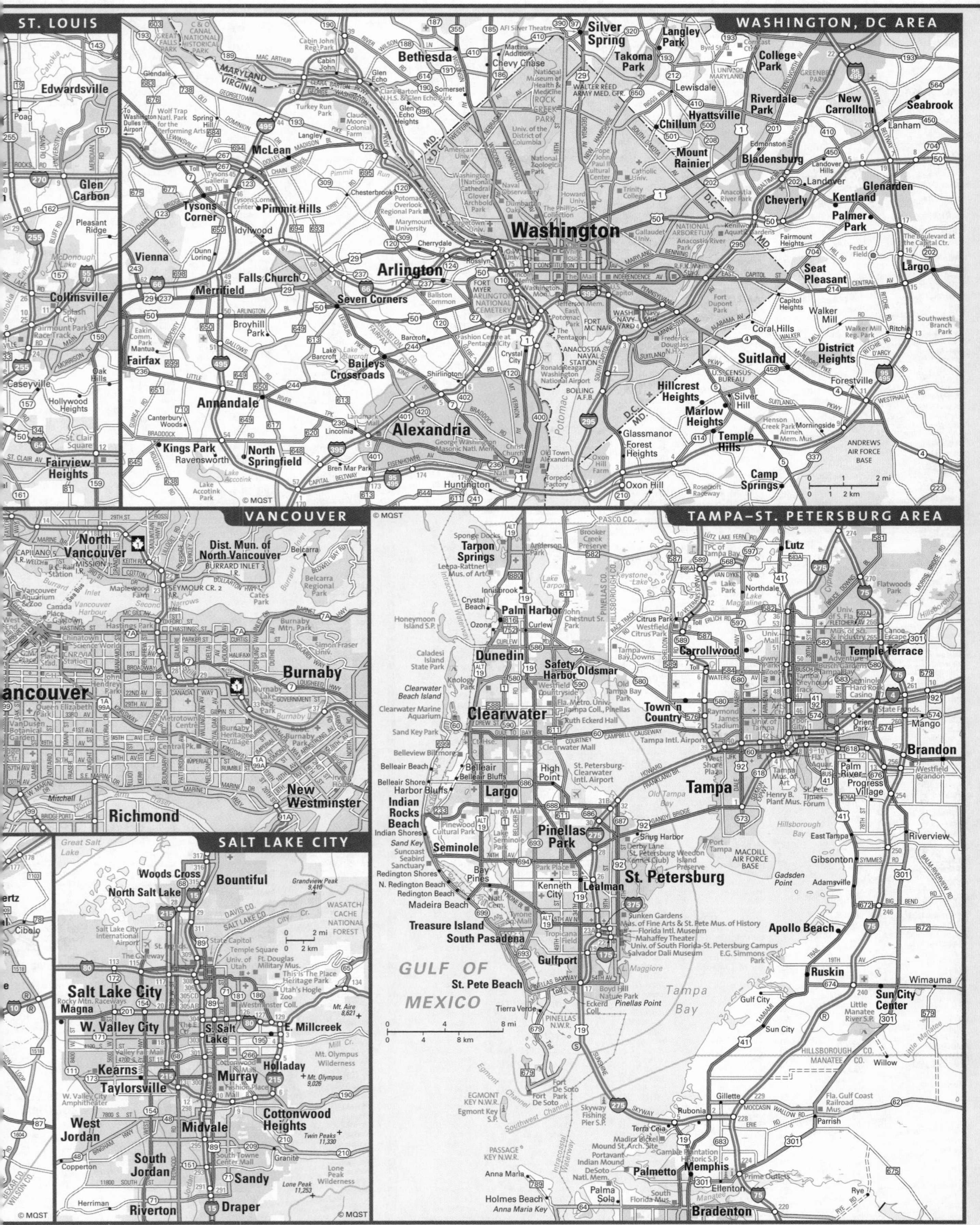
ST. LOUIS
WASHINGTON, DC AREA
VANCOUVER
TAMPA–ST. PETERSBURG AREA
SALT LAKE CITY
Washington
Arlington
Alexandria
Bethesda
Silver Spring
Edwardsville
Collinsville
Burnaby
North Vancouver
Richmond
New Westminster
Clearwater
St. Petersburg
Tampa
Largo
Bradenton
GULF OF MEXICO
Salt Lake City
West Jordan
Sandy
Bountiful
© MQST

Note: Population figures are from the latest census or the most recent available estimates

ORIDA
G. 28
APITAL
lahassee
CKNAME
nshine State
OPULATION
,982,378, rank 4
EA
,664 sq mi, rank 22

GEORGIA
PG. 29
CAPITAL
Atlanta
NICKNAME
Empire State of the South
POPULATION
8,186,453, rank 10
AREA
58,910 sq mi, rank 21

HAWAI'I
PG. 19
CAPITAL
Honolulu
NICKNAME
Aloha State
POPULATION
1,211,537, rank 42
AREA
6,471 sq mi, rank 47

IDAHO
PG. 30
CAPITAL
Boise
NICKNAME
Gem State
POPULATION
1,293,953, rank 39
AREA
83,564 sq mi, rank 13

ILLINOIS
PG. 31
CAPITAL
Springfield
NICKNAME
Land of Lincoln
POPULATION
12,419,293, rank 5
AREA
56,345 sq mi, rank 24

INDIANA
PG. 32
CAPITAL
Indianapolis
NICKNAME
Hoosier State
POPULATION
6,080,485, rank 14
AREA
36,185 sq mi, rank 38

IOWA
PG. 33
CAPITAL
Des Moines
NICKNAME
Hawkeye State
POPULATION
2,926,324, rank 30
AREA
56,275 sq mi, rank 25

KANSAS

PG. 36

CAPITAL
Topeka

NICKNAME
Sunflower State

POPULATION
2,688,418, rank 32

AREA
82,277 sq mi, rank 14

KENTUCKY

PG. 34-35

CAPITAL
Frankfort

NICKNAME
Bluegrass State

POPULATION
4,041,769, rank 25

AREA
40,409 sq mi, rank 37

LOUISIANA

PG. 37

CAPITAL
Baton Rouge

NICKNAME
Pelican State

POPULATION
4,468,976, rank 22

AREA
47,751 sq mi, rank 31

MAINE

PG. 38

CAPITAL
Augusta

NICKNAME
Pine Tree State

POPULATION
1,274,923, rank 40

AREA
33,265 sq mi, rank 39

MARYLAND

PG. 25

CAPITAL
Annapolis

NICKNAME
Old Line State

POPULATION
5,296,486, rank 19

AREA
10,460 sq mi, rank 42

MASSACHUSETTS

PG. 26-27

CAPITAL
Boston

NICKNAME
Bay State

POPULATION
6,349,097, rank 13

AREA
8,284 sq mi, rank 45

MICHIGAN

PG. 40-41

CAPITAL
Lansing

NICKNAME
Great Lakes State

POPULATION
9,938,444, rank 8

AREA
58,527 sq mi, rank 23

W. Milford, 26410 B5
W. Orange, 44943 C5
Westwood, 10999 B6
Whiting, 1800 F5
Wildwood, 5436 K4
Wildwood Crest, 3980 K4
Williamstown, 11812 G3
Willingboro, 36300 F4
Woodbine, 2716 J4
Woodbury, 10307 G3
Woodstown, 3136 G2

NEW MEXICO
PG. 49

CAPITAL
Santa Fe

NICKNAME
Land of Enchantment

POPULATION
1,819,046, rank 36

AREA
121,593 sq mi, rank 5

Alameda, 4200 D3
Alamo, 1183 E3
Alamogordo, 35582 G4
Albuquerque, 448607 D3
Angel Fire, 1048 B5
Anthony, 7904 J3
Artesia, 10692 H6
Aztec, 6378 B2
Bayard, 2534 H2
Belen, 6901 E3
Bernalillo, 6611 D4
Bloomfield, 6417 B2
Bosque Farms, 3931 E3
Capitan, 1443 F5
Carlsbad, 25625 H6
Carrizozo, 1036 F4
Casa Blanca, 669 D3
Chama, 1199 A4
Chaparral, 6117 J4
Chimayo, 2924 C4
Church Rock, 1077 C1
Cimarron, 917 B5
Clayton, 2524 B7
Cloudcroft, 749 G4
Clovis, 32667 E7
Columbus, 1765 J2
Crownpoint, 2630 C2
Cuba, 590 C3
Deming, 14116 H2
Dexter, 1235 G6
Doña Ana, 1379 H3
Dulce, 2623 A3
Edgewood, 1893 D4
Espanola, 9688 C4
Estancia, 1584 E4
Eunice, 2562 H7
Farmington, 37844 B2
Flora Vista, 1383 B2
Ft. Sumner, 1249 E6
Gallup, 20209 D1
Grants, 8806 D2
Hagerman, 1168 G6
Hatch, 1673 H3
Hobbs, 28657 H7
Hurley, 1464 H2
Jal, 1996 J7
Jemez Pueblo, 1953 C3
Kirtland, 6190 B2
La Cienega, 3007 C4
La Luz, 1615 G4
Las Cruces, 74267 H3
Las Vegas, 14565 C5
Logan, 1094 D7
Lordsburg, 3379 H1
Los Alamos, 11909 C4
Los Chavez, 5033 E3
Los Lunas, 10034 E3
Los Padillas, 1800 D3
Loving, 1326 H6
Lovington, 9471 G7
Magdalena, 913 F3
Melrose, 736 E7
Mescalero, 1233 G4
Mesilla, 2180 H3
Mesita, 776 D3
Midway, 700 G6
Milan, 1891 D2
Moriarty, 1765 D4
Mountainair, 1116 E4
Navajo, 2097 C1
Pecos, 1441 C5
Penasco, 572 C4
Pojoaque, 1261 C4
Portales, 11131 E7
Questa, 1864 B5
Radium Sprs., 1518 H3
Ranchos de Taos, 2390 B5
Raton, 7282 A6
Rio Rancho, 51765 D3
Roswell, 45293 G6
Ruidoso, 7698 G5
Salem, 795 H3
San Felipe Pueblo, 2080 D4
Santa Clara, 1944 H2
Santa Fe, 62203 C4
Santa Rosa, 2744 D6
Santo Domingo Pueblo, 2550 D4
Shiprock, 8156 B1
Silver City, 10545 H2
Socorro, 8877 F3
Springer, 1285 B6
Sunland Park, 13309 J4
Taos, 4700 B5
Tatum, 683 G7
Tesuque, 909 C4
Texico, 1065 E7
Thoreau, 1863 D2
Tohatchi, 1037 C1
Truth or Consequences, 7289 G3
Tucumcari, 5989 D7
Tularosa, 2864 G4
University Park, 2732 H3
Vado, 3003 J3
Valencia, 4500 E3
Vaughn, 539 E5
White Rock, 6045 C4
Williamsburg, 527 G3
Yah-Tah-Hey, 580 C1
Zia Pueblo, 646 D3
Zuni Pueblo, 6367 D1

NEW YORK
PG. 50-51

CAPITAL
Albany

NICKNAME
Empire State

POPULATION
18,976,457, rank 3

AREA
49,108 sq mi, rank 30

Adams, 1624 E9
Addison, 1797 K6
Akron, 3085 G4
Albany, 95658 H13
Albion, 7438 F4
Alden, 2666 G4
Alfred, 3954 J5
Allegany, 1883 K4
Altamont, 1737 H13
Amsterdam, 18355 G13
Angola, 2266 H3
Arcade, 2026 H4
Athens, 1695 J13
Attica, 2597 G4
Auburn, 28574 G8
Avon, 2977 G5
Baldwinsville, 7053 G8
Ballston Spa, 5556 G13
Batavia, 16256 G4
Bath, 5641 J6
Bay Shore, 23852 D4
Beacon, 13808 B3
Big Flats, 2482 K7
Binghamton, 47380 K9
Blasdell, 2718 H3
Boonville, 2138 F10
Brentwood, 53917 D4
Brewerton, 3453 F9
Brewster, 2162 B4
Bridgeport, 1665 G9
Brockport, 8103 F5
Buffalo, 292648 G3
Calcium, 3346 D9
Caledonia, 2327 G5
Cambridge, 1925 G14
Camden, 2330 F9
Canajoharie, 2257 G12
Canandaigua, 11264 G6
Canastota, 4425 G9
Canisteo, 2336 J5
Canton, 5882 B11
Carmel, 5650 B3
Carthage, 3721 D10
Castleton-on-Hudson, 1619 H13
Catskill, 4392 J13
Cazenovia, 2614 G9
Central Islip, 31950 D5
Central Square, 1646 F9
Chatham, 1758 J14
Cheektowaga, 79988 G3
Chester, 3445 B2
Chittenango, 4855 G9
Churchville, 1887 G5
Clayton, 1821 C9
Clifton Park, 4600 G13
Clifton Sprs., 2223 G6
Clinton, 1952 G10
Clyde, 2269 G7
Cobleskill, 4533 H12
Cohoes, 15521 H13
Colonie, 7916 H13
Comstock, 1900 F14
Cooperstown, 2032 H11
Corinth, 2474 F13
Corning, 10842 K7
Cornwall-on-Hudson, 3058 B3
Cortland, 18740 H9
Coxsackie, 2895 J13
Croton-on-Hudson, 7606 C3
Cuba, 1633 J4
Dannemora, 4129 B13
Dansville, 4832 H5
Delhi, 2583 J11
Delmar, 8292 H13
Depew, 16629 G3
Deposit, 1699 K10
Dolgeville, 2166 G11
Dover Plains, 1996 A4
Dryden, 1832 J8
Dundee, 1690 J7
Dunkirk, 13131 J2
E. Aurora, 6673 H4
E. Northport, 20845 D4
E. Patchogue, 20824 D5
Eden, 3579 H3
Ellenville, 4130 A2
Elmira, 30940 K7
Elmira Hts., 4170 K7
Endicott, 13038 K9
Endwell, 11706 K9
Fairmount, 10795 G8
Fairport, 5740 G6
Falconer, 2540 K2
Fayetteville, 4190 G9
Fishkill, 1735 B3
Florida, 2571 B2
Ft. Edward, 3141 F14
Ft. Plain, 2288 G12
Frankfort, 2537 G11
Franklinville, 1855 J4
Fredonia, 10706 J2
Freeport, 43783 D4
Frewsburg, 1965 K2
Fulton, 11855 F8
Geneseo, 7579 H5
Geneva, 13617 G7
Glen Cove, 26622 D4
Glens Falls, 14354 F14
Goshen, 5676 B2
Gouverneur, 4263 C10
Gowanda, 2842 J3
Granville, 2644 F14
Great Neck, 9538 D3
Greece, 14614 F5
Greene, 1701 J9
Greenport, 2048 C6
Greenwich, 1902 G14
Greenwood Lake, 3411 C2
Groton, 2470 H8
Hadley, 2240 F13
Hamburg, 10116 H3
Hamilton, 3509 H10
Hampton Bays, 12236 D6
Harriman, 2252 B3
Hempstead, 56554 D4
Henrietta, 6600 G6
Herkimer, 7498 G11
Hicksville, 41260 D4
Highland, 5060 A3
Highland Falls, 3678 B3
Hilton, 5856 F5
Holbrook, 27512 D5
Holley, 1802 F5
Homer, 3368 H9
Honeoye Falls, 2595 G6
Hoosick Falls, 3436 G14
Hornell, 9019 J5
Horseheads, 6452 K7
Houghton, 1748 J4
Hudson, 7524 J13
Hudson Falls, 6927 F14
Huntington Sta., 29910 D4
Hurley, 3561 K13
Hyde Park, 2900 A3
Ilion, 8610 G11
Irondequoit, 52354 F6
Islip, 20575 D5
Ithaca, 29287 J8
Jamestown, 31730 K2
Johnson City, 15535 K9
Johnstown, 8511 G12
Keeseville, 1850 B14
Kenmore, 16426 G3
Kerhonkson, 1732 A2
Kingston, 23456 K13
Lackawanna, 19064 H3
Lake Luzerne, 2240 F13
Lake Placid, 2638 C13
Lakewood, 3258 K2
Lansing, 3417 J8
Le Roy, 4462 G5
Levittown, 53067 D4
Lewiston, 2781 F3
Liberty, 3975 A1
Lima, 2459 G5
Lindenhurst, 27819 D4
Little Falls, 5188 G11
Lockport, 22279 F3
Lowville, 3476 E10
Lyons, 3695 G7
Mahopac, 8478 B3
Malone, 6075 A12
Mamaroneck, 18752 C3
Manlius, 4819 G9
Marlboro, 2339 A3
Massapequa, 22652 D4
Massena, 11209 A11
Mastic, 15436 D5
Mastic Beach, 11543 D5
Mattituck, 4198 C6
Mayville, 1756 J2
Mechanicville, 5019 G13
Medina, 6415 F4
Middleport, 1917 F4
Middletown, 25388 B2
Mineola, 19234 D4
Mineville, 1747 D14
Minoa, 3348 G9
Mohawk, 2660 G11
Monroe, 7780 B2
Montauk, 3851 C7
Montgomery, 3636 B2
Monticello, 6512 A1
Montour Falls, 1797 J7
Morrisonville, 1702 B14
Morrisville, 2148 G10
Mt. Kisco, 9983 C3
Mt. Morris, 3266 H5
Newark, 9682 G7
Newburgh, 28259 B3
New City, 34038 C3
Newfane, 3129 F3
New Hartford, 1886 G10
New Paltz, 6034 A3
New Rochelle, 72182 D3
New York, 8008278 D3
Niagara Falls, 55593 G3
N. Boston, 2680 H3
N. Chili, 4300 G5
N. Syracuse, 6862 G9
N. Tonawanda, 33262 G3
Norwich, 7355 H10
Norwood, 1685 B11
Nyack, 6737 C3
Oakfield, 1805 G4
Oceanside, 32733 D4
Ogdensburg, 12364 B10
Olean, 15347 K4
Oneida, 10987 G10
Oneonta, 13292 J11
Orchard Park, 3294 H3
Ossining, 24010 C3
Oswego, 17954 F8
Owego, 3911 K8
Painted Post, 1842 J7
Palmyra, 3490 G6
Pawling, 2233 B4
Peekskill, 22441 B3
Penn Yan, 5219 H7
Perry, 3945 H5
Phelps, 1969 G7
Phoenix, 2251 F8
Plattsburgh, 18816 B14
Pleasant Valley, 1839 A3
Port Chester, 27867 C4
Port Jefferson, 7837 C5
Port Jervis, 8860 B1
Port Washington, 15215 D4
Potsdam, 9425 B11
Poughkeepsie, 29871 A3
Pulaski, 2398 E9
Ravena, 3369 J13
Red Hook, 1805 K13
Rensselaer, 7761 H13
Rhinebeck, 3077 K13
Riverhead, 10513 C6
Rochester, 219773 G6
Rocky Pt., 10185 C5
Rome, 34950 F10
Rouses Pt., 2277 A14
Sag Harbor, 2313 C6
St. Johnsville, 1685 G12
Salamanca, 6097 K3
Saranac Lake, 5041 C13
Saratoga Sprs., 26186 G13
Saugerties, 4955 K13
Sayville, 16735 D5
Schenectady, 61821 H13
Scotia, 7957 G13
Scottsville, 2128 G5
Seneca Falls, 6861 G7
Sherrill, 3147 G10
Sidney, 4068 J10
Silver Creek, 2896 H2
Skaneateles, 2616 G8
Sodus, 1735 F7
Somers, 2000 B3
Southampton, 3965 D6
S. Fallsburg, 2061 A2
Southold, 5465 C6
Southport, 7396 K7
Spencerport, 3559 F5
Spring Valley, 25464 C3
Springville, 4252 J3
Stillwater, 1644 G14
Stony Brook, 13727 C5
Stony Pt., 11744 C3
Suffern, 11006 C3
Syracuse, 147306 G9
Tarrytown, 11090 C3
Ticonderoga, 2800 D14
Tillson, 1709 A3
Tonawanda, 16136 G3
Troy, 49170 H14
Tupper Lake, 3935 C12
Utica, 60651 G10
Valatie, 1712 J14
Victor, 2433 G6
Voorheesville, 2705 H13
Walden, 6164 B2
Wallkill, 2143 A3
Walton, 3070 K11
Wappingers Falls, 4929 A3
Warrensburg, 3208 E13
Warsaw, 3814 H4
Warwick, 6412 B2
Washingtonville, 5851 B3
Waterloo, 5111 G7
Watertown, 26705 D9
Waterville, 1721 G10
Watkins Glen, 2149 J7
Waverly, 4607 K8
Wayland, 1893 H6
Webster, 5216 F6
Weedsport, 2017 G8
Wellsville, 5171 K5
W. Carthage, 2102 D10
Westfield, 3481 J2
W. Hurley, 2105 K13
W. Seneca, 45943 H3
Whitehall, 2667 E14
White Plains, 53077 C3
Whitesboro, 3943 G10
Williamson, 2100 F6
Wolcott, 1712 F7
Woodbourne, 1600 A2
Woodstock, 2187 K13
Yonkers, 196086 C3
Yorktown Hts., 7972 B3
Youngstown, 1957 F3

NORTH CAROLINA
PG. 52-53

CAPITAL
Raleigh

NICKNAME
Tar Heel State

POPULATION
8,049,313, rank 11

AREA
52,669 sq mi, rank 28

Aberdeen, 3400 D8
Ahoskie, 4523 A12
Albemarle, 15680 C7
Andrews, 1602 D1
Apex, 20212 C9
Archdale, 9014 B7
Asheboro, 21672 C7
Asheville, 68889 C3
Atlantic Beach, 1781 E12
Ayden, 4622 C11
Beaufort, 3771 E12
Belhaven, 1968 C12
Belmont, 8705 D5
Benson, 2923 C9
Bethel, 1681 B11
Biscoe, 1700 C7
Black Mtn., 7511 C3
Bladenboro, 1718 E9
Boiling Spr. Lakes, 2972 F10
Boiling Sprs., 3866 D4
Boone, 13472 B4
Brevard, 6789 D3
Burgaw, 3337 E10
Burlington, 44917 B8
Burnsville, 1623 B3
Butner, 5792 B9
Canton, 4029 C3
Carolina Beach, 4701 F10
Carthage, 1871 C8
Cary, 94536 B9
Chadbourn, 2129 F9
Chapel Hill, 48715 B9
Charlotte, 540828 D6
Cherryville, 5361 C5
China Grove, 3616 C6
Clayton, 6973 C10
Clemmons, 13827 B6
Clinton, 8600 D10
Concord, 55977 C6
Conover, 6604 C5
Cornelius, 11969 C6
Creedmoor, 2232 B9
Cullowhee, 3579 C2
Davidson, 7139 C6
Dunn, 9196 C9
Durham, 187035 B9
Eden, 15908 A7
Edenton, 5394 B12
Elizabeth City, 17188 A13
Elizabethtown, 3698 E9
Elkin, 4109 A6
Emerald Isle, 3488 E12
Enfield, 2347 B11
Erwin, 4537 C9
Fairmont, 2604 E9
Fairview, 2495 C3
Farmville, 4302 C11
Fayetteville, 121015 D9
Flat Rock, 2565 C3
Fletcher, 4185 C3
Forest City, 7549 C4
Franklin, 3490 D2
Franklinton, 1745 B9
Fuquay-Varina, 7898 C9
Gamewell, 3644 B5
Garner, 17757 C9
Gastonia, 66277 D5
Goldsboro, 39043 C10
Graham, 12833 B8
Granite Falls, 4612 B5
Granite Quarry, 2175 C6
Greensboro, 223891 B7
Greenville, 60476 C11
Grifton, 2073 C11
Hamlet, 6018 D8
Harkers Island, 1525 E12
Harrisburg, 4493 C6
Havelock, 22442 D12
Henderson, 16095 A10
Hendersonville, 10420 D3
Hertford, 2070 A12
Hickory, 37222 C5
High Point, 85839 B7
Hillsborough, 5446 B9
Hope Mills, 11237 D9
Hudson, 3078 B5
Jacksonville, 66715 E11
Jonesville, 2259 B6
Kannapolis, 36910 C6
Kenly, 1569 C10
Kernersville, 17126 B7
Kill Devil Hills, 5897 B14
King, 5952 A6
Kings Mountain, 9693 D5
Kinston, 23688 D11
Kitty Hawk, 2991 B14
Kure Beach, 1507 F10
La Grange, 2844 C11
Laurinburg, 15874 E8
Leland, 1938 F10
Lenoir, 16793 B5
Lexington, 19953 B7
Liberty, 2661 B8
Lillington, 2915 C9
Lincolnton, 9965 C5
Locust, 2416 D6
Louisburg, 3111 B10
Lumberton, 20795 E9
Madison, 2262 A7
Maiden, 3282 C5
Marion, 4943 C4
Mars Hill, 1764 B3
Matthews, 22127 D6
Maxton, 2551 E8
Mayodan, 2417 A7
Mebane, 7284 B8
Mint Hill, 14922 D6
Mocksville, 4178 B6
Monroe, 26228 D6
Mooresville, 18823 C6
Morehead City, 7691 E12
Morganton, 17310 C4
Mtn. Home, 2169 C3
Mt. Airy, 8484 A6
Mt. Holly, 9618 D5
Mt. Olive, 4567 D10
Mulberry, 2269 A5
Murfreesboro, 2045 A12
Murphy, 1568 D1
Nags Head, 2700 B14
Nashville, 4309 B10
New Bern, 23128 D12
Newport, 3349 E12
Newton, 12560 C5
N. Wilkesboro, 4116 B5
Norwood, 2216 D7
Oak Island, 6571 F10
Oxford, 8338 A9
Pembroke, 2399 E8
Pinehurst, 9706 D8
Piney Green, 11658 E11
Pittsboro, 2226 C8
Plymouth, 4107 B12
Raeford, 3386 D8
Raleigh, 276093 B9
Ramseur, 1588 C8
Randleman, 3557 B7
Red Sprs., 3493 E8
Reidsville, 14485 A8
River Bend, 2923 D12
Roanoke Rapids, 16957 A11
Rockingham, 9672 D7
Rockwell, 1971 C6
Rocky Mount, 55893 B10
Roxboro, 8696 A9
Rural Hall, 2464 B6
Rutherfordton, 4131 C4
St. Pauls, 2137 E9
Salisbury, 26462 C6
Sanford, 23220 C8
Scotland Neck, 2362 B11
Sharpsburg, 2421 B10
Shelby, 19477 D5
Siler City, 6966 C8
Smithfield, 11510 C10
Sneads Ferry, 2248 E11
Snow Hill, 1514 C11
Southern Pines, 10918 D8
Southern Shores, 2201 B14
Southport, 2351 F10
Sparta, 1817 A5
Spencer, 3355 C6
Spring Lake, 8098 D9
Spruce Pine, 2030 B4
Stanley, 3053 C5
Statesville, 23320 C6
Stokesdale, 3267 B7
Summerfield, 7018 B7
Sunset Beach, 1824 G9
Swannanoa, 4132 C3
Sylva, 2435 C2
Tabor City, 2509 F9
Tarboro, 11138 B11
Taylorsville, 1799 B5
Thomasville, 19788 B7
Trent Woods, 4192 D12
Troutman, 1592 C6
Troy, 3430 C7
Tryon, 1760 D4
Unionville, 4797 D6
Valdese, 4485 C5
Wadesboro, 3552 D7
Wake Forest, 12588 B9
Wallace, 3344 E10
Wanchese, 1527 B14
Warsaw, 3051 D10
Washington, 9583 C12
Waxhaw, 2625 D6
Waynesville, 9232 C2
Weaverville, 2416 C3
Weddington, 6696 D6
Wentworth, 2779 A7
Whiteville, 5148 F9
Wilkesboro, 3159 B5
Williamston, 5843 B12
Wilmington, 75838 F10
Wilson, 44405 C10
Windsor, 2283 B12
Wingate, 2406 D6
Winston-Salem, 185776 B7
Winterville, 4791 C11
Woodfin, 3162 C3
Wrightsville Beach, 2593 F11
Yadkinville, 2818 B6
Yanceyville, 2091 A8
Zebulon, 4046 B10

NORTH DAKOTA
PG. 54

CAPITAL
Bismarck

NICKNAME
Flickertail State

POPULATION
642,200, rank 47

AREA
70,703 sq mi, rank 17

Arthur, 402 E10
Ashley, 882 F7
Beach, 1116 E1
Belcourt, 2440 B6
Belfield, 866 E2
Berthold, 466 C4
Beulah, 3152 D4
Bismarck, 55532 E5
Bottineau, 2336 B5
Bowbells, 406 B3
Bowman, 1600 F1
Burlington, 1096 C4
Cando, 1342 B7
Cannon Ball, 864 F5
Carrington, 2268 D7
Casselton, 1855 E10
Cavalier, 1537 B9
Center, 678 E4
Cooperstown, 1053 D8
Crosby, 1089 B2
Devils Lake, 7222 C7
Dickinson, 16010 E2
Drayton, 913 B9
Dunseith, 739 B6
Edgeley, 637 F8
Elgin, 659 F3
Ellendale, 1559 F8
Emerado, 510 C9
Enderlin, 947 E9
Fairmount, 406 F10
Fargo, 90599 E10
Fessenden, 625 D6
Finley, 515 D9
Forman, 506 F9
Ft. Totten, 952 C7
Garrison, 1318 D4
Glen Ullin, 865 E3
Grafton, 4516 B9
Grand Forks, 49321 C10
Gwinner, 717 F9
Hankinson, 1058 F10
Harvey, 1989 C6
Harwood, 607 E10
Hatton, 707 D9
Hazen, 2457 D4
Hebron, 803 E3
Hettinger, 1307 F2
Hillsboro, 1563 D10
Horace, 915 E10
Jamestown, 15527 E8
Kenmare, 1081 B3
Killdeer, 713 D2
Kindred, 614 E10
Kulm, 422 F7
Lakota, 781 C8
LaMoure, 944 F8
Langdon, 2101 B8
Larimore, 1433 C9
Leeds, 464 C7
Lidgerwood, 738 F10
Lincoln, 1730 E5
Linton, 1321 F6
Lisbon, 2292 F9
Maddock, 498 C6
Mandan, 16718 E5
Mandaree, 558 C2
Mapleton, 606 E10
Mayville, 1953 D9
McClusky, 415 D5
McVille, 470 C8
Milnor, 711 F9
Minot, 36567 C4
Minto, 657 C9
Mohall, 812 B4
Mott, 808 F3
Napoleon, 857 F6
Neche, 437 A9
New England, 555 E2
New Rockford, 1463 D7
New Salem, 938 E4
New Town, 1367 C3
Northwood, 959 C9
Oakes, 1979 F8
Park River, 1535 B9
Parshall, 981 C3
Pembina, 642 A9
Portland, 604 D9
Ray, 534 B2
Richardton, 619 E3
Rolette, 538 B6
Rolla, 1417 B6
Rugby, 2939 B6
St. Thomas, 447 B9
Stanley, 1279 C3
Steele, 761 E6
Strasburg, 549 F6
Surrey, 917 C4
Thompson, 1006 C10
Tioga, 1125 B2
Towner, 574 B5
Turtle Lake, 580 D5
Underwood, 812 D4
Valley City, 6826 E8
Velva, 1049 C5
Wahpeton, 8586 F10
Walhalla, 1057 B9
Washburn, 1389 D5
Watford City, 1435 C2
W. Fargo, 14940 E10
Westhope, 533 B5
Williston, 12512 C1
Wilton, 807 D5
Wishek, 1122 F6
Wyndmere, 533 F10

OHIO
PG. 56-57

CAPITAL
Columbus

NICKNAME
Buckeye State

POPULATION
11,353,140, rank 7

AREA
41,330 sq mi, rank 35

Ada, 5582 F3
Akron, 217074 E8
Alliance, 23253 F9
Amelia, 2752 L2
Arcanum, 2076 H1
Archbold, 4290 D2
Ashland, 21249 F6
Ashtabula, 20962 C10
Athens, 21342 K7
Aurora, 13556 E8
Austintown, 31627 E10
Baltimore, 2881 J6
Barberton, 27899 F8
Barnesville, 4225 J9
Beavercreek, 37984 J2
Bedford, 14214 E8
Bellaire, 4892 H10
Bellefontaine, 13069 G3
Bellevue, 8193 E5
Bellville, 1773 G6
Belpre, 6660 K8
Bethel, 2637 L2
Blanchester, 4220 K2
Bluffton, 3896 F3
Boardman, 37215 E10
Bowling Green, 29636 E3
Bradford, 1859 H1
Brewster, 2324 F8
Brookville, 5289 J2
Brunswick, 33388 E7
Bryan, 8333 D1
Buckeye Lake, 3049 J6
Bucyrus, 13224 F5
Byesville, 2574 J8
Cadiz, 3308 H9
Caldwell, 1956 J8
Cambridge, 11520 H8
Camden, 2302 J1
Canal Fulton, 5061 F8
Canal Winchester, 4478 J5
Canfield, 7374 F10
Canton, 80806 F8
Cardington, 1849 G5
Carey, 3901 F4
Carlisle, 5121 K2
Carrollton, 3190 G9
Cedarville, 3828 J3
Celina, 10303 G1
Centerville, 23024 J2
Champion, 4727 E9
Chardon, 5156 D9
Cheviot, 9015 L1
Chillicothe, 21796 K5
Cincinnati, 331285 L1
Circleville, 13485 K5
Cleveland, 478403 D8
Cleveland Hts., 49958 D8
Clyde, 6064 E5
Coal Grove, 2027 M6
Coldwater, 4482 G1
Columbiana, 5635 F10
Columbus, 711470 H5
Columbus Grove, 2200 F2
Conneaut, 12485 C10
Cortland, 6830 E10
Coshocton, 11682 H7
Covington, 2559 H2
Crestline, 5088 F5
Cridersville, 1817 F2
Crooksville, 2483 J7
Cuyahoga Falls, 49374 E8
Dayton, 166179 J2
Defiance, 16465 E2
Delaware, 25243 H4
Delphos, 6944 F2
Delta, 2930 D3
Dennison, 2992 G8
Deshler, 1831 E3
Devola, 2771 K8
Dover, 12210 G8
Doylestown, 2799 F8
Dublin, 31392 H4
E. Liverpool, 13089 F10
E. Palestine, 4917 F10
Eaton, 8133 J1
Edgerton, 2117 D1
Elida, 1917 F2
Elyria, 55953 E7
Englewood, 12235 J2
Euclid, 52717 D8
Fairborn, 32052 J2
Fairfield, 42097 K1
Fairport Harbor, 3180 D8
Findlay, 38967 E3
Ft. Shawnee, 3855 F2
Fostoria, 13931 E4
Franklin, 11396 K2
Fredericktown, 2428 G6
Fremont, 17375 E4
Gahanna, 32636 H5
Galion, 11341 F5
Gallipolis, 4180 M6
Gambier, 1871 G6
Garrettsville, 2262 E9
Geneva, 6595 C9
Genoa, 2230 D4
Georgetown, 3691 L3
Germantown, 4884 J2
Gibsonburg, 2506 E4
Glouster, 1972 K7
Grafton, 2302 E7
Granville, 3167 H6
Green, 22817 F8
Greenfield, 4906 K4
Greenville, 13294 H1
Grove City, 27075 J4
Hamilton, 60690 K1
Hartville, 2174 F8
Heath, 8527 H6
Hebron, 2034 J6
Hicksville, 3649 E1
Hillsboro, 6368 L3
Hubbard, 8284 E10
Hudson, 22439 E8
Huron, 7958 E6
Ironton, 11211 M5
Jackson, 6184 L5
Jamestown, 1917 J3
Jefferson, 3572 D10
Johnstown, 3440 H5
Kent, 27906 E8
Kenton, 8336 G3
Kettering, 57502 J2
Kirtland, 6670 D8
Lakewood, 56646 D7
Lancaster, 35335 J6
Lebanon, 16962 K2
Leipsic, 2236 E3
Lewisburg, 1798 J1
Lexington, 4165 F6
Lima, 40081 F2
Lisbon, 2788 F10
Lodi, 3061 F7
Logan, 6704 K6
London, 8771 J4
Lorain, 68652 D7
Lordstown, 3633 E9
Loudonville, 2906 G6
Louisville, 8904 F9
Loveland, 11677 K2
Manchester, 2043 M3
Mansfield, 49346 F6
Marietta, 14515 K8
Marion, 35318 G4
Martins Ferry, 7226 H10
Marysville, 15942 H4
Mason, 22016 K2
Massillon, 31325 F8
Maumee, 15237 D3
Mayfield Hts., 19386 D8
McArthur, 1888 K6
Medina, 25139 E7
Mentor, 50278 D8
Mentor-on-the-Lake, 8127 D8
Miamisburg, 19489 J2
Middleport, 2525 L7
Middletown, 51605 K2
Milford, 6284 L2
Millersburg, 3326 G7
Minerva, 3934 F9
Mingo Jct., 3631 G10
Minster, 2794 G2
Monroe, 7133 K2
Montpelier, 4320 D1
Mt. Gilead, 3290 G5
Mt. Orab, 2307 L3
Mt. Sterling, 1865 J4
Mt. Vernon, 14375 G6
Napoleon, 9318 E2
Nelsonville, 5230 K6
Newark, 46279 H6
New Boston, 2340 M5
New Bremen, 2909 G2
New Carlisle, 5735 J2
Newcomerstown, 4008 H8
New Concord, 2651 H8
New Lebanon, 4231 J2
New Lexington, 4689 J6
New London, 2696 E6
New Miami, 2469 K1
New Philadelphia, 17056 G8
New Richmond, 2219 L2
Newton Falls, 5002 E9
Niles, 20932 E10
N. Baltimore, 3361 E3
N. Canton, 16369 F8
N. Kingsville, 2658 C10
N. Olmsted, 34113 E7
Northridge, 6853 H3
Norwalk, 16238 E6
Oak Harbor, 2841 D4
Oberlin, 8195 E6
Oregon, 19355 D4
Orrville, 8551 F7
Ottawa, 4367 F2
Oxford, 21943 K1
Painesville, 17503 D9
Parma, 85655 E8
Pataskala, 10249 H5
Paulding, 3595 E1
Perrysburg, 16945 D3
Pickerington, 9792 J5
Piketon, 1907 L5
Piqua, 20738 H2
Plain City, 2832 H4
Plymouth, 1852 F5
Pomeroy, 1966 L7
Port Clinton, 6391 D5
Portsmouth, 20909 M5
Ravenna, 11771 E9
Reading, 11292 K1
Reynoldsburg, 32069 J5
Richfield, 3286 E8
Richwood, 2156 G4
Rittman, 6314 F7
Roseville, 1936 J7
Rossford, 6406 D3
Sabina, 2780 K3
St. Clairsville, 5057 H9
St. Henry, 2271 G1
St. Marys, 8342 G2
St. Paris, 1998 H3
Salem, 12197 F9
Sandusky, 27844 D5
Seville, 2160 F7
Shadyside, 3675 H10
Shelby, 9821 F5
Sidney, 20211 H2
Solon, 21802 D8
S. Charleston, 1850 J3
S. Point, 3742 N6
S. Zanesville, 1936 J7
Spencerville, 2235 F2
Springboro, 12380 K2
Springfield, 65358 J3
Steubenville, 19015 G10
Strasburg, 2310 G8
Streetsboro, 12311 E8
Strongsville, 43858 E7
Sugarcreek, 2174 G8
Sunbury, 2630 H5
Swanton, 3307 D3
Sylvania, 18670 D3
The Plains, 2931 K7
Tiffin, 18135 E4
Tipp City, 9221 J2
Toledo, 313619 D4
Toronto, 5676 G10
Trenton, 8746 K1
Trotwood, 27420 J2
Troy, 21999 H2
Uhrichsville, 5662 G8
Union City, 1767 H1
Upper Sandusky, 6533 F4
Urbana, 11613 H3
Utica, 2130 H6
Vandalia, 14603 J2
Van Wert, 10690 F1
Vermilion, 10927 E6
Versailles, 2589 H1
Wapakoneta, 9474 G2
Warren, 46832 E9
Washington C.H., 13524 K4
Waterville, 4828 D3
Wauseon, 7091 D2
Waverly, 4433 L5
Waynesville, 2558
Wellington, 4511
Wellston, 6078
Wellsville, 4133
Westerville, 35318
W. Jefferson, 4331
W. Lafayette, 2313
W. Liberty, 1813
W. Milton, 4645
W. Portsmouth, 3458
W. Union, 2903
W. Unity, 1790
Wheelersburg, 6471
Willard, 6806
Williamsburg, 2358
Willowick, 14361
Wilmington, 11921
Wintersville, 4067
Woodsfield, 2598
Woodville, 1977
Wooster, 24811
Xenia, 24164
Yellow Sprs., 3761
Youngstown, 82026
Zanesville, 25586

OKLAHOMA
PG. 58

CAPITAL
Oklahoma City

NICKNAME
Sooner State

POPULATION
3,450,654, rank …

AREA
69,956 sq mi, ran…

Ada, 15691
Altus, 21447
Alva, 5288
Anadarko, 6645
Antlers, 2552
Apache, 1616
Ardmore, 23711
Atoka, 2988
Barnsdall, 1325
Bartlesville, 34748
Beaver, 1570
Beggs, 1364
Bixby, 13336
Blackwell, 7668
Blanchard, 2816
Boise City, 1483
Bristow, 4325
Broken Arrow, 75427
Broken Bow, 4230
Burns Flat, 1782
Cache, 2371
Calera, 1739
Carnegie, 1637
Chandler, 2842
Checotah, 3481
Chelsea, 2136
Cherokee, 1630
Chickasha, 15850
Choctaw, 9377
Chouteau, 1931
Claremore, 15873
Cleveland, 3282
Clinton, 8833
Coalgate, 2005
Collinsville, 4077
Comanche, 1556
Cordell, 2867
Coweta, 7139
Crescent, 1281
Cushing, 8371
Davis, 2610
Dewey, 3179
Drumright, 2905
Duncan, 22505
Durant, 13549
Edmond, 68315
Elk City, 10510
El Reno, 16212
Enid, 47045
Eufaula, 2639
Fairfax, 1555
Fairview, 2733
Ft. Gibson, 4054
Frederick, 4637
Geary, 1258
Glenpool, 8123
Granite, 1844
Grove, 5131
Guthrie, 9925
Guymon, 10472
Hartshorne, 2102
Haskell, 1765
Healdton, 2786
Heavener, 3201
Hennessey, 2058
Henryetta, 6096
Hinton, 2175
Hobart, 3997
Holdenville, 4732
Hollis, 2264
Hominy, 2584
Hooker, 1788
Hugo, 5536
Idabel, 6952
Inola, 1589
Jay, 2482
Kingfisher, 4380
Kingston, 1390
Konawa, 1479
Langston, 1670
Lawton, 92757
Lindsay, 2889
Lone Grove, 4631
Madill, 3410

UTAH

PG. 64

CAPITAL
Salt Lake City

NICKNAME
Beehive State

POPULATION
2,233,169, rank 34

AREA
84,899 sq mi, rank 11

VERMONT

PG. 47

CAPITAL
Montpelier

NICKNAME
Green Mountain State

POPULATION
608,827, rank 49

AREA
9,614 sq mi, rank 43

VIRGINIA

PG. 66–67

CAPITAL
Richmond

NICKNAME
Old Dominion

POPULATION
7,078,515, rank 12

AREA
40,767, rank 36

WASHINGTON

PG. 65

CAPITAL
Olympia

NICKNAME
Evergreen State

POPULATION
5,894,121, rank 15

AREA
68,138 sq mi, rank 20

WEST VIRGINIA

PG. 66–67

CAPITAL
Charleston

NICKNAME
Mountain State

POPULATION
1,808,344, rank 37

AREA
24,231 sq mi, rank 41

WISCONSIN

PG. 68

CAPITAL
Madison

NICKNAME
Badger State

POPULATION
5,363,675, rank 18

AREA
56,153 sq mi, rank 26

WYOMING

PG. 69

CAPITAL
Cheyenne

NICKNAME
Equality State

POPULATION
493,782, rank 50

AREA
97,809 sq mi, ran

Canada

ALBERTA
PG. 73
CAPITAL
Edmonton
POPULATION
2,974,807, rank 4
AREA
255,541 sq mi, rank 6

BRITISH COLUMBIA
PG. 72–73
CAPITAL
Victoria
POPULATION
3,907,738, rank 3
AREA
364,764 sq mi, rank 5

MANITOBA
PG. 75
CAPITAL
Winnipeg
POPULATION
1,119,583, rank 5
AREA
250,116 sq mi, rank 8

NEW BRUNSWICK
PG. 80
CAPITAL
Fredericton
POPULATION
729,498, rank 8
AREA
28,150 sq mi, rank 11

NEWFOUNDLAND & LAB.
PG. 81
CAPITAL
St. John's
POPULATION
512,930, rank 9
AREA
156,453 sq mi, rank 10

NORTHWEST TERRITORIES
PG. 70
CAPITAL
Yellowknife
POPULATION
37,360, rank 11
AREA
519,734 sq mi.
rank 3

NOVA SCOTIA
PG. 80–81
CAPITAL
Halifax
POPULATION
908,007, rank 7
AREA
21,345 sq mi, rank 12

NUNAVUT
PG. 70–71
CAPITAL
Iqaluit
POPULATION
26,745, rank 13
AREA
808,185 sq mi,
rank 1

ONTARIO
PG. 76–77
CAPITAL
Toronto
POPULATION
11,410,046, rank 1
AREA
415,598 sq mi, rank 4

PRINCE EDWARD ISLAND
PG. 80–81
CAPITAL
Charlottetown
POPULATION
135,294, rank 10
AREA
2,185 sq mi, rank 13

QUÉBEC
PG. 78–79
CAPITAL
Québec
POPULATION
7,237,479, rank 2
AREA
595,391 sq mi, rank 2

* City indexed to pg. 80

SASKATCHEWAN
PG. 74–75
CAPITAL
Regina
POPULATION
978,933, rank 6
AREA
251,366 sq mi, rank 7

YUKON TERRITORY
PG. 70
CAPITAL
Whitehorse
POPULATION
28,674, rank 12
AREA
186,272 sq mi, rank 9

Mexico

MEXICO
PG. 82
CAPITAL
Mexico City
POPULATION
95,772,462
AREA
756,066 sq mi

Puerto Rico

PUERTO RICO
PG. 82
CAPITAL
San Juan
POPULATION
3,808,610
AREA
3,435 sq mi

JANUARY

CALIFORNIA

Tournament of Roses Parade, Pasadena.
It's ten times more fun in person than watching it on TV. Most folks come the night before and camp on the sidewalk, waiting for the passing parade of the best floats in the world.
626.449.4100

COLORADO

National Western Stock Show and Rodeo, Denver.
What do ranchers do in the middle of winter? They go to Denver to exhibit–and buy–horses and cattle. Sheep, hogs, llamas, and a vast array of farm machinery are also on display. This is the largest livestock show in the world.
800.336.6977

FLORIDA

Annual Florida Citrus Festival and Polk County Fair, Winter Haven.
An 11-day celebration of the citrus industry is set in a country-fair atmosphere, with livestock exhibits, quilt shows, and entertainment.
863.292.9810

MINNESOTA

St. Paul Winter Carnival, St. Paul.
In North America's oldest and largest winter carnival, the frigid depths of a Twin Cities winter come to life for a week with antique sleigh and cutter parades, fireworks, car races on ice, and ice-carving and snow-sculpting competitions.
651.223.4700, 800.488.4023

NEVADA

National Cowboy Poetry Gathering, Elko.
An institution in its own right, the "granddaddy of all poetry gatherings" is a weeklong celebration of the Old West, complete with dances, workshops on rawhide braiding and the like, guitar-and-fiddle jams into the small hours, and, of course, poetry readings.
775.738.7508

PENNSYLVANIA

Mummers Parade, Philadelphia.
The world-famous New Year's Day parade features 30,000 spectacularly costumed mummers, including string bands and comics.
215.336.3050

UTAH

Sundance Film Festival, Park City.
Hollywood pulls on its snow pants to find the next big thing at Robert Redford's annual showcase of independent film.
801.328.3456

FEBRUARY

CALIFORNIA

Chinese New Year Festival, San Francisco.
Dancing dragons, fireworks, and great food in celebration of the lunar New Year, and the best time to visit San Francisco's famed Chinatown.
415.982.3071

COLORADO

Steamboat Springs Winter Carnival, Steamboat Springs.
Almost like a rodeo on ice, with strange events like snow-shovel racing, broomball, and a parade on skis.
970.879.0880

FLORIDA

Speed Weeks, Daytona.
The world's best road racers and stock-car drivers converge on the Daytona International Speedway for some of motor sport's biggest events from the Rolex 24 through the Daytona 500.
386.254.2700

LOUISIANA

Mardi Gras, New Orleans.
Rollicking, raucous, and ritualistic, Mardi Gras is New Orleans's legendary carnival, featuring freewheeling street celebrations, formal masquerade balls, and the famous parade in which the "Krewes" try to outdo each other's floats and costumes.
504.566.5003, 877.791.8272

MANITOBA

Le Festival du Voyageur, Winnipeg.
Manitoba commemorates its French-Canadian heritage, when fur traders were king, with this ten-day winter carnival that includes period costumes, arts and crafts, and a downtown street party.
204.237.7692

QUÉBEC

Winter Carnival of Québec City.
A citywide celebration of winter for the whole family, with art exhibits, sporting events such as the famed canoe race across the ice-choked St. Lawrence, ice sculptures (and an ice palace), and general bonhomie.
418.626.3716

TEXAS

Charro Days Fiesta, Brownsville.
Starting with the traditional *grito* yell and a blast of mariachi music, this southernmost Texas city celebrates the *charro*–skilled horseman, hero of neighboring Mexico's folklore–with parades, street dances, and carnivals... not to mention great food. Begins last Thursday of the month.
956.542.4245

MARCH

ALASKA

Iditarod Trail Sled Dog Race, Anchorage to Nome.
The world's longest dogsled race heads through the streets of Anchorage, mushes through mountains and ice-locked seas, and ends 9 to 13 days later in Nome.
907.376.5155

ARIZONA

Scottsdale Arts Festival, Scottsdale.
Arts and crafts from across the nation abound at this annual event in an upscale Phoenix suburb that has become a major center for Western, Native American, and contemporary art.
480.994.2787

MAINE

Maine Maple Sunday
The Governor kicks off this statewide event with a proclamation, and several dozen maple-sugar producers open their doors for tours and sampling. Savor the traditional snack of sugar on snow" (that's syrup poured on shaved ice, for out-of-towners) with plain doughnuts.
207.287.3491

NEBRASKA

Sandhill Crane Spring Migration, Platte.
One of the most magnificent sights anywhere in the Great Plains is watching half a million sandhill cranes swoop over the Platte River as they return to the adjoining wetlands in spring. Special sunrise and sunset crane tours are organized by a volunteer group, Wings Over the Platte.
800.658.3178

NEW YORK

St. Patrick's Day, New York City.
New Yorkers have their own unique ways of celebrating St. Patrick's Day. More than 150,000 marchers, representing the various Irish societies of the city, participate in the parade up 5th Avenue from 44th to 86th Streets.

SOUTH CAROLINA

Festival of Houses and Gardens, Charleston.
The historic neighborhoods and private gardens of one of America's most beautiful cities reveal themselves to visitors during this monthlong event.
843.722.3405

APRIL

DISTRICT OF COLUMBIA

National Cherry Blossom Festival, Washington, D.C.
Washingtonians celebrate the blossoming of more than 6,000 Japanese cherry trees with festivities that include the crowning of the Cherry Blossom Festival Queen and a parade.
202.547.1500

HAWAII

Merrie Monarch Festival, Hilo, Big Island
The premier hula competition and event of the year, this festival draws a multitude of hula *halau* (schools) to Hilo, where performers dance ancient and modern hula, perform traditional chanting, and play ancient Hawaiian instruments.
808.935.9168

KENTUCKY

American Quilter's Society National Show and Contest, Paducah.
Quilters from around the country gather for one of the nation's largest shows of its kind.
502.898.7903

MASSACHUSETTS

Boston Marathon, Boston.
The Patriot's Day 26.2-mile course starts in Hopkinton, winds through eight cities and towns, and finishes near Copley Square.
617.236.1652

ONTARIO

The Shaw Festival, Niagara-on-the-Lake.
From April through October the works of George Bernard Shaw and his contemporaries come alive on three stages in the heart of Ontario's wine country.
800.511.7429

TEXAS

Fiesta San Antonio, San Antonio.
The city's Hispanic roots come out in full force during this boisterous, exuberant, citywide party that includes parades, costume balls with revelers in historical outfits, and great Tex-Mex food.
210.227.5191

WASHINGTON

Washington State Apple Blossom Festival, Wenatchee.
Here in the fruit basket of the Northwest, a vast array of produce thrives–but the apple is still king. Wenatchee becomes a wonderland of blossoms in late April and early May, and dozens of events celebrate the flowering of commercial orchards.
509.662.3616

MAY

DELAWARE

Winterthur Point-to-Point Races, Winterthur.
Exciting amateur competitions include steeplechase and flat races. The day includes a parade of antique horse-drawn carriages, canine demonstrations, and pony races, as well as a tailgate-picnic competition.
800.448.3883

KENTUCKY

Kentucky Derby and Derby Festival, Louisville.
Festivities leading up to the legendary horse race, which is held each year on the first Saturday in May, begin two weeks before the event.
800.928.3378

INDIANA

500 Festival, Indianapolis.
Before the racers start their engines and embark on 3 plus hours of counter-clockwise spectacle, visitors can drive their own cars on the fabled oval and glimpse drivers and celebrities in the Festival Parade.
800.638.4296

NORTH CAROLINA

Ole Time Fiddler's & Bluegrass Festival, Union Grove.
The oldest festival of its kind in North America, this down-home, family-oriented get-together highlights traditional American music through fiddle contests, informal jam sessions, and workshops.
828.478.3735

SOUTH CAROLINA

Spoleto Festival U.S.A., Charleston.
Originally founded by composer Gian Carlo Menotti, this 17-day festival fills Charleston's historic churches and theaters with more than 120 performances of opera, dance, theater, jazz and classical music.
843.722.2764

TENNESSEE

Beale Street Music Festival. Memphis
American blues, as irresistible as the neighboring Mississippi River, and blues-inspired music streams from the celebrated Beale Street clubs and temporary stages, performed by "legends" and newcomers.
901.525.4611

WASHINGTON

Northwest Folklife Festival, Seattle.
Billed as the largest festival of its kind in the U. S., Folklife is an ethnic extravaganza celebrating traditional arts, with participatory dancing (square, swing), jam sessions, craft demonstrations, and music workshops.
206.684.7300

JUNE

ALASKA

Midnight Sun Festival, Fairbanks.
What do you do on the summer solstice with more than 22 hours of direct sunlight? Celebrate with sportin events, a parade, lots of stree activities, and baseball playe under the midnight sun.
907.452.8671

MASSACHUSETTS

Jacob's Pillow, Becket.
From late June through earl August, the United States' oldest dance festival attract dancers and troupes from around the world.
413.243.0745

Scooper Bowl, Boston.
The nation's largest all-you-can eat ice cream festival unofficially kicks off summe in Boston to help the Jimmy Fund's fight against cancer.
617.632.4215

MICHIGAN

The Frankenmuth Bavarian Festival, Frankenmuth.
Michigan's "Little Bavaria" rolls out the *willkommen* m for its annual multiday heritage celebration, hostin some of the nation's best polka bands and serving up locally brewed ale, home-made bratwurst, and pretze
800.386.3378

OKLAHOMA

Red Earth Festival, Oklahoma City.
Representatives from a hundred tribes in Oklahoma and throughout the U. S. an Canada gather for competitions, displays of traditional crafts and fine ar and dancing contests.
405.427.5228

OREGON

Portland Rose Festival, Portland.
The Grand Floral Parade is th second largest in the country Eighty events in 25 days, including parties, music, and celebration, with a special welcome mat laid out for th Navy crews docked downtown.
503.227.2681

Oregon Shakespeare Festiva Ashland.
It's definitely worth the trip t this eclectic town of Victoria homes and galleries to catch its Tony Award-winning festival of the Bard's best. Productions run February through October, but the Elizabethan outdoor stage opens in June.
541.482.4331

ULY

BERTA

lgary Exhibition and ampede, Calgary.
is wild celebration of the est has been held since 1912. ghlights include the uck-wagon race at ampede Park and one of the ggest rodeos in Canada.
0.661.1260

LIFORNIA

roy Garlic Festival, Gilroy.
rlic ice cream, garlic eesecake, even chocolate-vered garlic. This harvest tival celebrates 101 uses for pungent herb.
8.842.1625

STRICT OF COLUMBIA

lependence Day lebration, ashington, D.C.
tivities include colonial litary maneuvers, a parade wn Constitution Avenue, free tertainment, and a concert by National Symphony chestra followed by fireworks er the Washington onument.
2.619.7222

ICHIGAN

tional Cherry Festival, averse City.
the Grand Traverse region, own for the world's greatest ncentration of tart cherries, s summer resort town hosts multiday celebration that ludes parades, fireworks, -name entertainers, and ty cherry pies.
.947.4230, 0.968.3380

ISSOURI

m Sawyer Days, Hannibal.
e childhood home of Mark ain–known then as Samuel emens–celebrates with a ghty frog-jumping contest d a just-for-fun fence-inting championship. Take ook at the author's yhood home while you're ere.
6.263.4825

ISCONSIN

A AirVenture, hkosh.
nual gathering of some 000 homebuilt, antique d aerobatic planes, as well military and general ation aircraft.
0.564.6322
0.843.3612

YOMING

eyenne Frontier Days, eyenne.
hefty prize purse–the gest for any outdoor rodeo the world–draws the best this celebration, which also ludes country-western tertainment and parades.
0.227.6336

AUGUST

BRITISH COLUMBIA

Peach Festival, Penticton.
The Okanagan Valley celebrates its biggest agriculture crop with a festival that is 50 years old. The week-long event includes music, sporting events, and lots of peaches.
250.493.4055
800.663.5052

IDAHO

Idaho International Dance & Music Festival, Rexburg.
Lectures and workshops supplement the dancing, colorfully exhibited by more than 300 participants from a host of countries
208.356.5700

MAINE

Maine Lobster Festival, Rockland.
This five-day event, held at Harbor Park overlooking Penobscot Bay, features all sorts of waterfront recreation, parades, marine exhibits, boat and helicopter rides – and, of course, steamed lobsters.
800.562.2529

NEVADA

Burning Man, Black Rock Desert.
Erupting from life on a stark desert playa in northwestern Nevada, Burning Man rejoices in unconventionality, drawing more than 25,000 people eager to forge a temporary, experimental community where residents will discover self-reliance and will explore radical self-expression.
415.863.5263

PENNSYLVANIA

Musikfest, Bethlehem.
More than 650 free concerts by over 250 national, local and regional groups, ranging from salsa to swing, classical to conga, and folk to funk.
610.332.1300

RHODE ISLAND

Newport JVC Jazz Festival, Newport.
One of the most prestigious jazz events in the U. S., showcasing legendary performers and rising stars.
401.847.3700

SOUTH CAROLINA

Jubilee: Festival of Heritage, Columbia.
This celebration of African-American culture emphasizes traditional art forms, such as basketry, drumming, and story-telling.
803.252.7742 (ext. 25)

VIRGINIA

Old Fiddlers' Convention, Galax.
Musicians from around the world gather to jam and compete in the largest musical convention of its kind in the country.
276.236.8541

SEPTEMBER

BRITISH COLUMBIA

The Fringe–Vancouver's Theatre Festival, Vancouver.
Vancouver hosts an eclectic group of theater, dance, and musical groups from around the world for this 11-day festival modeled after the popular event in Edinburgh, Scotland.
604.257.0350

LOUISIANA

The Original Southwest Louisiana Zydeco Music Festival, Opelousas.
Performers play authentic Creole and Zydeco music in the rural setting where it was born.
337.232.7672

MISSISSIPPI

Mississippi Delta Blues and Heritage Festival, Greenville.
Nationally and internationally known artists perform at one of the South's largest music festivals, dedicated to the plaintive native sound of the Delta.
800.467.3582

NORTH CAROLINA

Mayberry Days, Mount Airy.
For three days each fall, residents of Andy Griffith's real-life hometown celebrate Mayberry, his TV hometown on *The Andy Griffith Show*. Thousands of fans march in the Mayberry Days parade and wait on block-long lines to order pork-chop sandwiches at the Snappy Lunch cafe.
800.286.6193

ONTARIO

Toronto International Film Festival, Toronto.
Established directors and little-known independents alike present their latest dramas, comedies, documentaries, and animated films at one of the world's top-rated film festivals.
416.968.3456

VERMONT

Northeast Kingdom Fall Foliage Festival, Marshfield, Walden, Cabot, Plainfield, Peacham, Barnet, Groton, St. Johnsbury.
Towns throughout Vermont honor the fall foliage with village tours, bazaars, exhibits, and sumptuous church suppers.
800.639.6379

WASHINGTON

Bumbershoot, Seattle.
An old English term for umbrella, this Bumbershoot is a mammoth annual music festival that draws big names of all genres. In spite of its name, sunny skies often bless the festival over Labor Day weekend. Food, crafts, film screenings, and dance performances round out the offerings.
206.281.7788

OCTOBER

ALABAMA

National Shrimp Festival, Gulf Shores.
Four days of beachfront festivities include a parade, music, arts and crafts, and a sumptuous abundance of seafood.
251.968.6904

ARKANSAS

Arkansas Blues & Heritage Festival, Helena.
Some say this Mississippi River town is the birthplace of the blues. They make a strong case by hosting one of the largest blues festivals in the nation every year.
870.338.8798

FLORIDA

Fantasy Fest, Key West.
The Southernmost City pulls out all the stops with Caribbean carnival revelry, Halloween parades, and a touch of wrong-time-of-the-year Mardi Gras.
305.296.1817

GEORGIA

Stone Mountain Highland Games and Scottish Festival, Stone Mountain.
The clans gather for this world-famous festival of all things Scottish–including such traditional Scottish athletic competitions as Tossing the Caber (best described as heaving a telephone pole), Celtic music and dancing, and hearty Highland food.
770.521.0228

NEW MEXICO

Kodak Albuquerque International Balloon Fiesta, Albuquerque.
Over 850 participants gather for the greatest spectacle of its kind in the world. Uniquely shaped balloons and massed sunrise ascensions are featured.
505.842.9918

NOVA SCOTIA

Celtic Colours International Festival, Cape Breton Island.
An international Celtic festival featuring the sounds of local artists together with the burgeoning talents of the global Celtic community. Concerts, dancing, theater, and Celtic-language events make this an exciting ten days.
877.285.2321

OHIO

Pumpkin Show, Circleville.
The state's oldest festival displays more than 100,000 pounds of pumpkin-related products and features three stages of entertainment, contests, and rides.
740.474.7000

NOVEMBER

ALASKA

Alaska Bald Eagle Festival, Haines.
This month the winter population of American bald eagles reaches its peak as some 3,000 eagles congregate around the banks of the Chilkat River, feeding on late-running salmon. This three-day event includes nature tours and educational seminars about the great birds.
907.766.3094

ARKANSAS

World's Championship Duck Calling Contest and Wings Over the Prairie Festival, Stuttgart.
Festivities for the world and state duck calling championships include a duck gumbo cook-off and the Queen Mallard pageant.
870.673.1602

FLORIDA

Florida Pirate Festival, Clearwater
Grab your eye patches and cutlasses, perhaps even your mascara and eyeliner, and practice your "ahrrrs" – then set sail for this family-friendly buccaneer bacchanalia. And remember not to scratch with a hook-hand.
727.518.5341

ILLINOIS

Magnificent Mile Lights Festival, Chicago.
Occurring each year on the Saturday before Thanksgiving, this holiday-season festival of ice-carving demonstrations, strolling carolers, traditional holiday foods, and the unveiling of commercial window displays culminates in a parade on Michigan Avenue and fireworks on the lake. Displays stay up through January.
312.642.3570

MARYLAND

Waterfowl Festival, Easton.
Some 500 artisans exhibit and sell original wildfowl art, carvings, antique decoys and guns, duck stamps and gifts. Also a special sculpture exhibit, seminars, and goose- and duck-calling contests.
410.822.4567

TEXAS

International Chili Championship, Terlingua.
How do you like your chili? Beans or no beans, hotter than a pistol or mildly seasoned? Find out at the granddaddy of chili cook-offs.
888.227.4468

DECEMBER

ARIZONA

Annual Indian Market, Phoenix.
Some 600 Native American artisans from more than 50 tribes demonstrate and sell their works. Activities include music, singing, and dancing.
602.495.0901

BRITISH COLUMBIA

British Columbia Whistler Film Festival, Whistler
Independent international and Canadian films, orbited by media and "industry" glitterati, are a stylishly cool complement to the superb winter sports at this famous resort.
604.935.8035

DISTRICT OF COLUMBIA

National Christmas Tree Lighting/Pageant of Peace, Washington, D.C.
Each year the President lights the the National Christmas Tree on the South Lawn of the White House.
202.619.7222

GEORGIA

Festival of Trees, Atlanta.
Decorated trees and holiday tableaus created by Atlanta's premier artists and designers are the centerpieces of the festival, joined by extravagant gingerbread houses, children's activities, and live entertainment.
404.785.8815

HAWAII

Rip Curl Pipeline Masters, Ehukai Beach Park, Oahu
Held at the North Shore's famous Banzai Pipeline break, this annual showdown of the world's top surfers is the longest running pro surf competition in the U. S.
808.638.7700

NEW MEXICO

Old Town Luminaria Festival, Albuquerque.
An old New Mexican holiday tradition is to set lit candles in paper bags along walkways and rooflines. The illuminated neighborhoods can be admired on foot or from specially provided buses.
800.284.2282

ONTARIO

Winter Festival of Lights, Niagara Falls.
The festival, which begins in late November and runs through early January, includes illumination of Horseshoe Falls and a spectacular fireworks show on New Year's Eve.
800.563.2557

TOURISM INFORMATION

Alabama
Alabama Bureau of Tourism & Travel
401 Adams Ave., P.O. Box 4927
Montgomery, AL 36103
800.252.2262, 334.242.4169
www.800alabama.com

Alaska
Alaska Travel Industry Association
2600 Cordova St., Suite 201
Anchorage, AK 99503-2745
800.862.5275
www.travelalaska.com

Arizona
Arizona Office of Tourism
1110 W. Washington, Suite 155
Phoenix, AZ 85007
866.275.5816, 602.374.3700
www.arizonaguide.com

Arkansas
Arkansas Dept. of Parks & Tourism
One Capitol Mall, Department 7701
Little Rock, AR 72201
800.628.8725, 501.682.7777
www.arkansasstateparks.com

California
California Division of Tourism
980 9th St., Suite 480
Sacramento, CA 95814
800.862.2543, 916.444.4429
www.visitcalifornia.com

Colorado
Colorado Tourism Office
1625 Broadway, Suite 2700
Denver, CO 80202
800.265.6723, 303.892.3885
www.colorado.com

Connecticut
Connecticut Office of Tourism
1 Financial Plaza
755 Main St
Hartford, CT 06103
888.288.4748, 860.256.2800
www.ctvisit.com

Delaware
Delaware Tourism Office
99 Kings Hwy
Dover, DE 19901
866.284.7483, 302.739.4271
www.visitdelaware.com

Florida
Visit Florida
661 E. Jefferson St., Suite 300
Tallahassee, FL 32301
850.488.5607, 888.735.2872
www.visitflorida.com

Georgia
Georgia Department of Industry, Trade & Tourism
75 Fifth St. NW, Suite 1200
Atlanta, GA 30308
800.847.4842
www.georgia.org/travel

Hawaii
Hawaii Visitors & Conv. Bureau
2270 Kalakaua Ave., 8th Floor
Honolulu, HI 96815
800.464.2924, 808.923.1811
www.gohawaii.com

Idaho
Idaho Department of Commerce
700 W. State St.
P.O. Box 83720
Boise, ID 83720-0093
800.635.7820, 208.334.2470
www.visitid.org

Illinois
Illinois Bureau of Tourism
100 W. Randolph St., Suite 3-400
Chicago, IL 60601
800.406.6418
www.enjoyillinois.com

Indiana
Indiana Tourism
1 N. Capitol Ave., Suite 700
Indianapolis, IN 46204
800.759.9191, 317.232.8860
www.enjoyindiana.com

Iowa
Iowa Division of Tourism
200 E. Grand Ave.
Des Moines, IA 50309
888.472.6035, 515.242.4705
www.traveliowa.com

Kansas
Kansas Travel & Tourism
1000 S.W. Jackson St., Suite 100
Topeka, KS 66612-1354
800.252.6727, 785.296.2009
www.travelks.com

Kentucky
Department of Tourism
Capital Plaza Tower
500 Mero St., Suite 2200
Frankfort, KY 40601
800.225.8747, 502.564.4930
www.kentuckytourism.com

Louisiana
Louisiana Office of Tourism
1051 N. 3rd St.
Baton Rouge, LA 70802
225.342.8119
www.louisianatravel.com

Maine
Maine Office of Tourism & Film
59 State House Station
Augusta, ME 04333-0059
888.624.6345, 207.624.7843
www.visitmaine.com

Maryland
Maryland Office of Tourism Develop.
217 E. Redwood St., 9th Floor
Baltimore, MD 21202
877.333.4455
www.visitmaryland.org

Massachusetts
Massachusetts Office of Travel & Tourism
10 Park Plaza, Suite 4510
Boston, MA 02116
800.227.6277, 617.973.8500
www.massvacation.com

Michigan
Travel Michigan
300 N. Washington Square, 2nd Floor
Lansing, MI 48913
888.784.7328, 517.373.0670
www.michigan.org

Minnesota
Minnesota Tourism
100 Metro Square
121 Seventh Place East
St. Paul, MN 55101
888.868.7476, 651.296.5029
www.exploreminnesota.com

Mississippi
Mississippi Development Authority/Tourism
PO Box 849
Jackson, MS 39205
866.733.6477, 601.359.3297
www.visitmississippi.org

Missouri
Missouri Division of Tourism
PO Box 1055
Jefferson City, MO 65102
800.519.2100, 573.751.4133
www.visitmo.com

Montana
Travel Montana
301 South Park
PO Box 200533
Helena, MT 59620
800.847.4868, 406.841.2870
www.visitmt.com

Nebraska
Nebraska Travel & Tourism
PO Box 98907
Lincoln, NE 68509-8907
877.632.7275, 402.471.3796
www.visitnebraska.org

Nevada
Nevada Commission on Tourism
401 N. Carson St.
Carson City, NV 89701
800.638.2328, 775.687.4322
www.travelnevada.com

New Hampshire
New Hampshire Division of Travel & Tourism Development
172 Pembroke Rd., PO Box 1856
Concord, NH 03302
800.386.4664, 603.271.2665
www.visitnh.gov

New Jersey
New Jersey Office of Travel & Tourism
PO Box 820
Trenton, NJ 08625-0820
800.847.4865, 609.777.0885
www.visitnj.org

New Mexico
New Mexico Department of Tourism
491 Old Santa Fe Trail
Santa Fe, NM 87503
800.545.2070, 505.827.7400
www.newmexico.org

New York
New York State Division of Tourism
PO Box 2603
Albany, NY 12220-0603
800.225.5697, 518.474.4116
www.iloveny.com

North Carolina
North Carolina Division of Tourism, Film & Sports Development
301 N. Wilmington St.
Raleigh, NC 27601
800.847.4862, 919.733.4171
www.visitnc.com

North Dakota
North Dakota Tourism
1600 E. Century Ave., Suite 2
P.O. Box 2057
Bismarck, ND 58503
800.435.5663, 701.328.2525
www.ndtourism.com

Ohio
Ohio Division of Travel & Tourism
77 S. High St., 29th Floor
Columbus, OH 43215
800.282.5393, 614-466-8844
www.discoverohio.com

Oklahoma
Oklahoma Department of Tourism & Recreation
120 N. Robinson Ave., Suite 600
P.O. Box 52002
Oklahoma City, OK 73152-2002
800.652.6552, 405.230.8420
www.travelok.com

Oregon
Oregon Tourism Commission, d.b.a. Travel Oregon
670 Hawthorne Ave. SE, Suite 240
Salem, OR 97301
800.547.7842, 503.378.8850
www.traveloregon.com

Pennsylvania
Pennsylvania Tourism Office
Commonwealth Keystone Building
400 North St., 4th Floor
Harrisburg, PA 17120
800.847.4872
www.visitpa.com

Puerto Rico
Puerto Rico Tourism Company
P.O. Box 902-3960
#2 Paseo La Princesa
San Juan, PR 00902-3960
800.866.7827, 787.721.2400
www.gotopuertorico.com

Rhode Island
Rhode Island Tourism Division
1 W. Exchange St.
Providence, RI 02903
800.556.2484, 401.222.2601
www.visitrhodeisland.com

South Carolina
South Carolina Department of Parks, Recreation & Tourism
1205 Pendleton St., Room 505
Columbia, SC 29201
888.727.6453, 803.734.1700
www.discoversouthcarolina.com

South Dakota
South Dakota Department of Tourism
711 E. Wells Ave.
Pierre, SD 57501-3369
800.732.5682, 605.773.3301
www.travelsd.com

Tennessee
Tennessee Department of Tourist Development
312 8th Ave. N, 25th Floor
Nashville, TN 37243
800.462.8366, 615.741.2159
www.tnvacation.com

Texas
Texas Department of Economic Development, Tourism Division
PO Box 12728
Austin, TX 78711-2728
800.888.8839
www.traveltex.com

Utah
Utah Office of Tourism
300 N. State St.
Salt Lake City, UT 84114
800.200.1160, 801.538.1030
www.utah.com

Vermont
Vermont Department of Tourism & Marketing
National Life Building, Drawer 20
Montpelier, VT 05620-1501
800.837.6668, 802.828.3237
www.vermontvacation.com

Virginia
Virginia Tourism Corporation
901 E. Byrd St.
Richmond, VA 23219
800.847.4882, 804.786.4485
www.virginia.org

Virgin Islands
United States Virgin Islands Department of Tourism
PO Box 6400
St. Thomas, VI 00804
800.372.8784, 340.774.8784
www.usvitourism.vi

Washington
Dept. of Community Trade & Economic Development
Washington State Tourism Div.
PO Box 42525
Olympia, WA 98504-2525
800.544.1800
www.experiencewashington.com

Washington, DC
DC Convention and Tourism Corp.
901 7th St. NW, 4th Floor
Washington, DC 20001-3719
800.422.8644, 202.789.7000 or 7030
www.washington.org

West Virginia
West Virginia Division of Tourism
90 MacCorkle Ave. SW
South Charleston, WV 25303
800.225.5982, 304.558.2200
www.wvtourism.com

Wisconsin
Wisconsin Department of Tourism
201 W. Washington Ave.
Madison, WI 53703
800.432.8747, 608.266.2161
www.travelwisconsin.com

Wyoming
Wyoming Division of Tourism
I-25 at College Dr.
Cheyenne, WY 82002
800.225.5996, 307.777.7777
www.wyomingtourism.org

Alberta
Travel Alberta Canada
PO Box 2500
Edmonton, AB, Canada T5J 2Z4
800.252.3782, 780.427.4321
www.travelalberta.com

British Columbia
Tourism British Columbia
Box 9830
Stn. Prov. Govt.
Victoria, BC, Canada V8W 9W5
800.663.6000, 250.356.6363
www.hellobc.com

Manitoba
Travel Manitoba
155 Carlton St., Seventh Floor
Winnipeg, MB, Canada R3C 3H8
800.665.0040
www.travelmanitoba.com

New Brunswick
Tourism Communication Center
26 Roseberry St.
Campbellton, NB, Canada E3N 2G4
800.561.0123, 506.444.5205
www.tourismnewbrunswick.ca

Newfoundland & Labrador
Newfoundland & Labrador Tourism
PO Box 8730
St. John's, NL, Canada A1B 4K2
800.563.6353, 709.729.2830
www.gov.nl.ca/tourism

Nova Scotia
Tourism Nova Scotia
PO Box 456
Halifax, NS, Canada B3J 2R5
800.565.0000, 902.425.5781
www.novascotia.com

Ontario
Ontario Tourism
10th Floor, Hearst Block
900 Bay St.
Toronto, ON, Canada M7A 2E1
800.668.2746, 905.282.1721
www.ontariotravel.net

Prince Edward Island
PEI Tourism
53 Watts Ave., P.O. Box 940
Charlottetown, PE, Canada C1A 7M5
800.734.7529, 902.368.4444
www.gentleisland.com

Québec
Tourisme Québec
1255 Peel Street, 4th Floor, Room 400
PO Box 979
Montréal, QC, Canada H3B 4V4
877.266.5687, 514.873.2015
www.bonjourquebec.com

Saskatchewan
Tourism Saskatchewan
1922 Park St.
Regina, SK, Canada S4N 7M4
877.237.2273, 306.787.9600
www.sasktourism.com

Mexico
Mexico Ministry of Tourism
Ave. Presidente Masaryk 172
Col. Chapultepec Morales
11587 México, D.F. Mexico
800.446.3942
www.visitmexico.com

INTERNET LINKS

nerican Association of Botanical
rdens & Arboreta
vw.aabga.org
formation and links to member
rdens.

nerican Zoo & Aquarium
sociation
vw.aza.org
formation and links to member
os and aquariums.

ntrak
vw.amtrak.com
formation on fares and schedules.

)L Box Office
vw.aolboxoffice.com
nd event information and buy
:kets to concerts, sports events, the
ts and theater, family attractions,
d other local entertainment
oices.

t Museum Network
vw.amn.org
nks to museums and exhibition
lendars.

sociation of Science-Technology
enters
vw.astc.org
formation and links to science
enters in the United States and
anada.

NN
vw.cnn.com
he latest top news stories from the
.S. and around the world; including
olitical, financial, sports, health,
echnology and entertainment news.

igital City
vww.digitalcity.com
our local city resource, with
formation on dining, entertainment
nd other helpful subjects.

ederal Aviation Administration
vww.faa.gov
irport security information, trip
reparation tips and links to airports
nd airlines worldwide.

olf
vww.golfcourse.com
rom the publishers of *Golf Magazine*,
his site provides useful information
bout golf courses throughout the
Jnited States and Canada; including
ee times, course ratings, dress codes,
ocations, and fees.

Government of Canada
www.canada.gc.ca
The official website of the Canadian
government; it includes information
on travelling to Canada.

Major League Baseball
www.mlb.com
Team and schedule information.

Major League Soccer
www.mlsnet.com
Team and schedule information.

MapQuest.com
www.mapquest.com
The one-stop portal for all travel
needs; providing anytime, anywhere
mapping, directions, and destination
information.

Meteorological Service of Canada
www.weatheroffice.ec.gc.ca
Find weather forecasts for cities and
communities throughout Canada.

NASCAR
www.nascar.com
Information on drivers, tracks, and
races for each NASCAR series.

National Basketball Association
www.nba.com
Team and schedule information.

National Football League
www.nfl.com
Team and schedule information.

National Hockey League
www.nhl.com
Team and schedule information.

National Register of Historic Places
www.nationalregisterofhistoricplaces.com
Official list of cultural resources worthy of preservation.

National Ski Areas Association
www.nsaa.org
Links to ski areas in the United States.

National Thoroughbred Racing Association
www.ntra.com
Links to race tracks in the United States, along with the latest news on the Breeders Cup and Triple Crown.

Parks Canada/Parcs Canada
www.parkscanada.gc.ca
Information about Canada's national parks, historic sites and heritage areas.

Scenic Highways
www.byways.org
Descriptions and maps of All-American Roads and National Scenic Byways.

Ski & Snowboard Canada
www.skicanada.org
Links to ski areas in Canada.

Theme Parks
www.themeparksonline.org
Information and links.

U.S. Department of State
www.state.gov
Information on passports, visas and travel abroad.

U.S. Department of Transportation
www.dot.gov
Information on road construction and conditions.

U.S. Fish & Wildlife Service
www.fws.gov
Links to National Wildlife Refuges.

U.S. Forest Service
www.fs.fed.us
Information and links to the national forests and grasslands nationwide.

U.S. National Park Service
www.nps.gov
Links to individual parks as well as campground and tour reservations

U.S. National Weather Service
www.nws.noaa.gov
National, regional and local weather information for the United States.

U.S. Postal Service
www.usps.com
Do you need to find a post office while on vacation or don't remember a zip code? This site will answer all of your U.S. Postal Service questions.

VIA Rail Canada
www.viarail.ca
Information on Canada's passenger rail system.

Virtual Museum Canada
www.virtualmuseum.ca
Information on museums and events in Canada.

BORDER CROSSING

Travel Advisory

As of December 31, 2006, all travelers to or from Canada, Mexico, Central and South America, and the Caribbean utilizing air or sea will be absolutely required to carry a passport. On December 31, 2007, this requirement will be extended to all land border crossings.

Canada

U.S. citizens entering Canada from the U.S. are required to present passports or proof of U.S. citizenship accompanied by photo identification. U.S. citizens entering from a third country must have a valid passport. Visas are not required for U.S. citizens entering from the U.S. for stays of up to 180 days. Naturalized citizens should travel with their naturalization certificates. Alien permanent residents of the U.S. must present their Alien Registration Cards. Individuals under the age of 18 and traveling alone should carry a letter from a parent or legal guardian authorizing their travel in Canada.

U.S. driver's licenses are valid in Canada, and U.S. citizens do not need to obtain an international driver's license. Proof of auto insurance, however, is required.

United States (from Canada)

Canadian citizens entering the U.S. are required to demonstrate proof of their citizenship, normally with a photo identification accompanied by a valid birth certificate or citizenship card. Passports or visas are not required for visits lasting less than six months; for visits exceeding six months, they are mandatory. Individuals under the age of 18 and traveling alone should carry notarized documentation, signed by both parents, authorizing their travel.

Canadian driver's licenses are valid in the U.S. for one year, and automobiles may enter free of payment or duty fees. Drivers need only provide customs officials with proof of vehicle registration, ownership, and insurance.

Mexico

U.S. citizens entering Mexico are required to present passports or proof of U.S. citizenship accompanied by photo identification. Passports are strongly recommended. Visas are not required for stays of up to 180 days. Naturalized citizens should travel with their naturalization certificates, and alien permanent residents must present their Alien Registration Cards. Individuals under the age of 18 traveling alone, with one parent, or with other adults must carry notarized parental authorization or valid custodial documents. All U.S. citizens visiting for up to 180 days must also procure a tourist card, obtainable from Mexican consulates, tourism offices, border crossing points, and airlines serving Mexico. However, tourist cards are not needed for visits shorter than 72 hours to areas within the Border Zone (extending approximately 25 km into Mexico)

U.S. driver's licenses are valid in Mexico.

Visitors who wish to drive beyond the Baja California Peninsula or the Border Zone must obtain a temporary import permit for their vehicles. To acquire a permit, one must submit evidence of citizenship and of the vehicle's title and registration, as well as a valid driver's license. A processing fee must be paid. Permits are available at any Mexican Army Bank (Banjercito) located at border crossings or selected Mexican consulates. Mexican law also requires the posting of a refundable bond, via credit card or cash, at the Banjercito to guarantee the departure of the vehicle. Do not deal with any individual operating outside of official channels.

All visitors driving in Mexico should be aware that U.S. auto insurance policies are not valid and that buying short-term tourist insurance is mandatory. Many U.S. insurance companies sell Mexican auto insurance. American Automobile Association (for members only) and Sanborn's Mexico Insurance (800.638.9423) are popular companies with offices at most U.S. border crossings.

Published by MapQuest, Inc.

Printed in Canada

ISBN 1-57262-716-6
ISBN 978-1-57262-716-1

Comments or suggestions should be directed to:
Managing Editor
MapQuest Road Atlas & Travel Planner
MapQuest, Inc.
P.O. Box 601
Mountville, PA 17554-0601
email at roadatlas@mapquest.com

National Parks Photography:
pp. 10–13:
Acadia, Great Smoky Mountains, Shenandoah, and Rocky Mountain: National Park Service; Everglades, Glacier, and Yellowstone NPs, and Sasquatch sign: U.S. Landmarks and Travel/Getty Images; Grand Teton, Grand Canyon, Olympic, Yosemite, and Zion: U.S. Landmarks and Travel 2/Getty Images; Soaring eagle: Nature, Wildlife and the Environment/Getty Images; Black bear, Mountain lion: Lions, Tigers and Bears/Getty Images; Howling wolf: Getty Images

Mileage Chart

Distances in chart are in miles. To convert miles to kilometers, multiply the distance in miles by 1.609

Example:
New York, NY to Boston, MA = 215 miles or 346 kilometers (215 x 1.609)

	ALBUQUERQUE, NM	ATLANTA, GA	BALTIMORE, MD	BILLINGS, MT	BIRMINGHAM, AL	BISMARCK, ND	BOISE, ID	BOSTON, MA	BUFFALO, NY	BURLINGTON, VT	CHARLESTON, SC	CHARLESTON, WV	CHARLOTTE, NC	CHEYENNE, WY	CHICAGO, IL	CINCINNATI, OH	CLEVELAND, OH	DALLAS, TX	DENVER, CO	DES MOINES, IA	DETROIT, MI	EL PASO, TX	HOUSTON, TX	INDIANAPOLIS, IN	JACKSON, MS	KANSAS CITY, MO	LAS VEGAS, NV	LITTLE ROCK, AR	LOS ANGELES, CA	LOUISVILLE, KY
ALBUQUERQUE, NM		1490	1902	991	1274	1333	966	2240	1808	2178	1793	1568	1649	538	1352	1409	1619	754	438	1091	1608	263	994	1298	1157	894	578	900	806	1320
ATLANTA, GA	1490		679	1889	150	1559	2218	1100	910	1158	317	503	238	1482	717	476	726	792	1403	967	735	1437	800	531	386	801	2067	528	2237	419
BALTIMORE, MD	1902	679		1959	795	1551	2401	422	370	481	583	352	441	1665	708	521	377	1399	1690	1031	532	2045	1470	600	1032	1087	2445	1072	2705	602
BILLINGS, MT	991	1889	1959		1839	413	626	2254	1796	2181	2157	1755	2012	455	1246	1552	1597	1433	554	1007	1534	1255	1673	1432	1836	1088	965	1530	1239	1547
BIRMINGHAM, AL	1274	150	795	1839		1509	2170	1215	909	1241	466	578	389	1434	667	475	725	647	1356	919	734	1292	678	481	241	753	1852	381	2092	369
BISMARCK, ND	1333	1559	1551	413	1509		1039	1846	1388	1773	1749	1347	1604	594	838	1144	1189	1342	693	675	1126	1597	1582	1024	1548	801	1378	1183	1702	1139
BOISE, ID	966	2218	2401	626	2170	1039		2697	2239	2624	2520	2182	2375	737	1708	1969	2040	1711	833	1369	1977	1206	1952	1852	2115	1376	760	1808	1033	1933
BOSTON, MA	2240	1100	422	2254	1215	1846	2697		462	214	1003	741	861	1961	1003	862	654	1819	2004	1326	741	2465	1890	940	1453	1427	2757	1493	3046	964
BUFFALO, NY	1808	910	370	1796	909	1388	2239	462		375	899	431	695	1502	545	442	197	1393	1546	868	277	2039	1513	508	1134	995	2299	1066	2572	545
BURLINGTON, VT	2178	1158	481	2181	1241	1773	2624	214	375		1061	782	919	1887	930	817	567	1763	1931	1253	652	2409	1916	878	1479	1366	2684	1437	2957	915
CHARLESTON, SC	1793	317	583	2157	466	1749	2520	1003	899	1061		468	204	1783	907	622	724	1109	1705	1204	879	1754	1110	721	703	1102	2371	900	2554	610
CHARLESTON, WV	1568	503	352	1755	578	1347	2182	741	431	782	468		265	1445	506	209	255	1072	1367	802	410	1718	1192	320	816	764	2122	745	2374	251
CHARLOTTE, NC	1649	238	441	2012	389	1604	2375	861	695	919	204	265		1637	761	476	520	1031	1559	1057	675	1677	1041	575	625	956	2225	754	2453	464
CHEYENNE, WY	538	1482	1665	455	1434	594	737	1961	1502	1887	1783	1445	1637		972	1233	1304	979	100	633	1241	801	1220	1115	1382	640	843	1076	1116	1197
CHICAGO, IL	1352	717	708	1246	667	838	1708	1003	545	930	907	506	761	972		302	346	936	1015	337	283	1543	1108	184	750	532	1768	662	2042	299
CINCINNATI, OH	1409	476	521	1552	475	1144	1969	862	442	817	622	209	476	1233	302		253	958	1200	599	261	1605	1079	116	700	597	1955	632	2215	106
CLEVELAND, OH	1619	726	377	1597	725	1189	2040	654	197	567	724	255	520	1304	346	253		1208	1347	669	171	1854	1328	319	950	806	2100	882	2374	356
DALLAS, TX	754	792	1399	1433	647	1342	1711	1819	1393	1763	1109	1072	1031	979	936	958	1208		887	752	1218	647	241	913	406	554	1331	327	1446	852
DENVER, CO	438	1403	1690	554	1356	693	833	2004	1546	1931	1705	1367	1559	100	1015	1200	1347	887		676	1284	701	1127	1088	1290	603	756	984	1029	1118
DES MOINES, IA	1091	967	1031	1007	919	675	1369	1326	868	1253	1204	802	1057	633	337	599	669	752	676		606	1283	992	481	931	194	1429	567	1703	595
DETROIT, MI	1608	735	532	1534	734	1126	1977	741	277	652	879	410	675	1241	283	261	171	1218	1284	606		1799	1338	318	960	795	2037	891	2310	366
EL PASO, TX	263	1437	2045	1255	1292	1597	1206	2465	2039	2409	1754	1718	1677	801	1543	1605	1854	647	701	1283	1799		758	1489	1051	1085	717	974	801	1499
HOUSTON, TX	994	800	1470	1673	678	1582	1952	1890	1513	1916	1110	1192	1041	1220	1108	1079	1328	241	1127	992	1338	758		1033	445	795	1474	447	1558	972
INDIANAPOLIS, IN	1298	531	600	1432	481	1024	1852	940	508	878	721	320	575	1115	184	116	319	913	1088	481	318	1489	1033		675	485	1843	587	2104	112
JACKSON, MS	1157	386	1032	1836	241	1548	2115	1453	1134	1479	703	816	625	1382	750	700	950	406	1290	931	960	1051	445	675		747	1735	269	1851	594
KANSAS CITY, MO	894	801	1087	1088	753	801	1376	1427	995	1366	1102	764	956	640	532	597	806	554	603	194	795	1085	795	485	747		1358	382	1632	516
LAS VEGAS, NV	578	2067	2445	965	1852	1378	760	2757	2299	2684	2371	2122	2225	843	1768	1955	2100	1331	756	1429	2037	717	1474	1843	1735	1358		1478	274	1874
LITTLE ROCK, AR	900	528	1072	1530	381	1183	1808	1493	1066	1437	900	745	754	1076	662	632	882	327	984	567	891	974	447	587	269	382	1478		1706	526
LOS ANGELES, CA	806	2237	2705	1239	2092	1702	1033	3046	2572	2957	2554	2374	2453	1116	2042	2215	2374	1446	1029	1703	2310	801	1558	2104	1851	1632	274	1706		2126
LOUISVILLE, KY	1320	419	602	1547	369	1139	1933	964	545	915	610	251	464	1197	299	106	356	852	1118	595	366	1499	972	112	594	516	1874	526	2126	
MEMPHIS, TN	1033	389	933	1625	241	1337	1954	1353	927	1297	760	606	614	1217	539	493	742	466	1116	720	752	1112	586	464	211	536	1611	140	1839	386
MIAMI, FL	2155	661	1109	2554	812	2224	2883	1529	1425	1587	583	994	730	2147	1382	1141	1250	1367	2069	1632	1401	1959	1201	1196	915	1466	2733	1190	2759	1084
MILWAUKEE, WI	1426	813	805	1175	763	767	1748	1100	642	1027	1003	601	857	1012	89	398	443	1010	1055	378	380	1617	1193	279	835	573	1808	747	2082	394
MINNEAPOLIS, MN	1339	1129	1121	839	1079	431	1465	1417	958	1343	1319	918	1173	881	409	714	760	999	924	246	697	1530	1240	596	1151	441	1677	814	1951	711
MONTRÉAL, QC	2172	1241	564	2093	1289	1685	2535	313	397	92	1145	822	1003	1799	841	815	588	1772	1843	1165	564	2363	1892	872	1514	1359	2596	1446	2869	920
NASHVILLE, TN	1248	242	716	1648	194	1315	1976	1136	716	1086	543	395	397	1240	474	281	531	681	1162	725	541	1328	801	287	423	559	1826	355	2054	175
NEW ORLEANS, LA	1276	473	1142	1955	351	1734	2234	1563	1254	1588	783	926	713	1502	935	820	1070	525	1409	1117	1079	1118	360	826	185	932	1854	455	1917	714
NEW YORK, NY	2015	869	192	2049	985	1641	2491	215	400	299	773	515	631	1755	797	636	466	1589	1799	1121	622	2235	1660	715	1223	1202	2552	1262	2820	739
OKLAHOMA CITY, OK	546	944	1354	1227	729	1136	1506	1694	1262	1632	1248	1022	1102	773	807	863	1073	209	681	546	1062	737	449	752	612	348	1124	355	1352	774
OMAHA, NE	973	989	1168	904	941	616	1234	1463	1005	1390	1290	952	1144	497	474	736	806	669	541	136	743	1236	910	618	935	188	1294	570	1567	704
ORLANDO, FL	1934	440	904	2333	591	2003	2662	1324	1221	1383	379	790	525	1926	1161	920	1045	1146	1847	1411	1180	1738	980	975	694	1245	2512	969	2538	863
PHILADELPHIA, PA	1954	782	104	2019	897	1611	2462	321	414	371	685	454	543	1725	768	576	437	1501	1744	1091	592	2147	1572	655	1135	1141	2500	1175	2760	678
PHOENIX, AZ	466	1868	2366	1199	1723	1662	993	2706	2274	2644	2184	2035	2107	1004	1819	1876	2085	1077	904	1558	2074	432	1188	1764	1482	1360	285	1367	369	1786
PITTSBURGH, PA	1670	676	246	1719	763	1311	2161	592	217	587	642	217	438	1425	467	292	136	1246	1460	791	292	1893	1366	370	988	857	2215	920	2476	394
PORTLAND, ME	2338	1197	520	2352	1313	1944	2795	107	560	233	1101	839	959	2059	1101	960	751	1917	2102	1424	838	2563	1988	1038	1550	1525	2855	1590	3144	1062
PORTLAND, OR	1395	2647	2830	889	2599	1301	432	3126	2667	3052	2948	2610	2802	1166	2137	2398	2469	2140	1261	1798	2405	1767	2381	2280	2544	1805	1188	2237	971	2362
RAPID CITY, SD	841	1511	1626	379	1463	320	930	1921	1463	1848	1824	1422	1678	305	913	1219	1264	1077	404	629	1201	1105	1318	1101	1458	710	1035	1093	1309	1215
RENO, NV	1020	2440	2623	960	2392	1372	430	2919	2460	2845	2741	2403	2595	959	1930	2191	2262	1933	1054	1591	2198	1315	2072	2073	2337	1598	442	2030	519	2155
RICHMOND, VA	1876	527	152	2053	678	1645	2496	572	485	630	428	322	289	1760	802	530	471	1309	1688	1126	627	1955	1330	641	914	1085	2444	983	2682	572
ST. LOUIS, MO	1051	549	841	1341	501	1053	1628	1181	749	1119	850	512	704	892	294	350	560	635	855	436	549	1242	863	239	505	252	1610	416	1856	264
SALT LAKE CITY, UT	624	1916	2100	548	1868	960	342	2395	1936	2322	2218	1880	2072	436	1406	1667	1738	1410	531	1067	1675	864	1650	1549	1813	1074	417	1507	691	1631
SAN ANTONIO, TX	818	1000	1671	1500	878	1599	1761	2092	1665	2036	1310	1344	1241	1046	1270	1231	1481	271	946	1009	1490	556	200	1186	644	812	1272	600	1356	1125
SAN DIEGO, CA	825	2166	2724	1302	2021	1765	1096	3065	2632	3020	2483	2393	2405	1179	2105	2234	2437	1375	1092	1766	2373	730	1487	2122	1780	1695	337	1703	124	2144
SAN FRANCISCO, CA	1111	2618	2840	1176	2472	1749	646	3135	2677	3062	2934	2620	2759	1176	2146	2407	2478	1827	1271	1807	2415	1181	1938	2290	2232	1814	575	2012	385	2372
SEATTLE, WA	1463	2705	2775	816	2657	1229	500	3070	2612	2997	2973	2571	2827	1234	2062	2368	2413	2208	1329	1822	2350	1944	2449	2249	2612	1872	1256	2305	1148	2364
TAMPA, FL	1949	455	960	2348	606	2018	2677	1380	1276	1438	434	845	581	1941	1176	935	1101	1161	1862	1426	1194	1753	995	990	709	1259	2526	984	2553	878
TORONTO, ON	1841	958	565	1762	958	1354	2204	570	106	419	1006	537	802	1468	510	484	303	1441	1512	834	233	2032	1561	541	1183	1028	2265	1115	2538	589
VANCOUVER, BC	1597	2838	2908	949	2791	1362	633	3204	2745	3130	3106	2705	2960	1368	2196	2501	2547	2342	1463	1956	2483	2087	2583	2383	2746	2007	1390	2439	1291	2497
WASHINGTON, DC	1896	636	38	1953	758	1545	2395	458	384	517	539	346	397	1659	701	517	370	1362	1686	1025	526	2008	1433	596	996	1083	2441	1036	2702	596
WICHITA, KS	707	989	1276	1067	838	934	1346	1616	1184	1554	1291	953	1145	613	728	785	995	367	521	390	984	898	608	674	771	192	1276	464	1513	705

	MEMPHIS, TN	MIAMI, FL	MILWAUKEE, WI	MINNEAPOLIS, MN	MONTRÉAL, QC	NASHVILLE, TN	NEW ORLEANS, LA	NEW YORK, NY	OKLAHOMA CITY, OK	OMAHA, NE	ORLANDO, FL	PHILADELPHIA, PA	PHOENIX, AZ	PITTSBURGH, PA	PORTLAND, ME	PORTLAND, OR	RAPID CITY, SD	RENO, NV	RICHMOND, VA	ST. LOUIS, MO	SALT LAKE CITY, UT	SAN ANTONIO, TX	SAN DIEGO, CA	SAN FRANCISCO, CA	SEATTLE, WA	TAMPA, FL	TORONTO, ON	VANCOUVER, BC	WASHINGTON, DC	WICHITA, KS
ALBUQUERQUE, NM	1033	2155	1426	1339	2172	1248	1276	2015	546	973	1934	1954	466	1670	2338	1395	841	1020	1876	1051	624	818	825	1111	1463	1949	1841	1597	1896	707
ATLANTA, GA	389	661	813	1129	1241	242	473	869	944	989	440	782	1868	676	1197	2647	1511	2440	527	549	1916	1000	2166	2618	2705	455	958	2838	636	989
BALTIMORE, MD	933	1109	805	1121	564	716	1142	192	1354	1168	904	104	2366	246	520	2830	1626	2623	152	841	2100	1671	2724	2840	2775	960	565	2908	38	1276
BILLINGS, MT	1625	2554	1175	839	2093	1648	1955	2049	1227	904	2333	2019	1199	1719	2352	889	379	960	2053	1341	548	1500	1302	1176	816	2348	1762	949	1953	1067
BIRMINGHAM, AL	241	812	763	1079	1289	194	351	985	729	941	591	897	1723	763	1313	2599	1463	2392	678	501	1868	878	2021	2472	2657	606	958	2791	758	838
BISMARCK, ND	1337	2224	767	431	1685	1315	1734	1641	1136	616	2003	1611	1662	1311	1944	1301	320	1372	1645	1053	960	1599	1765	1749	1229	2018	1354	1362	1545	934
BOISE, ID	1954	2883	1748	1465	2535	1976	2234	2491	1506	1234	2662	2462	993	2161	2795	432	930	430	2496	1628	342	1761	1096	646	500	2677	2204	633	2395	1346
BOSTON, MA	1353	1529	1100	1417	313	1136	1563	215	1694	1463	1324	321	2706	592	107	3126	1921	2919	572	1181	2395	2092	3065	3135	3070	1380	570	3204	458	1616
BUFFALO, NY	927	1425	642	958	397	716	1254	400	1262	1005	1221	414	2274	217	560	2667	1463	2460	485	749	1936	1665	2632	2677	2612	1276	106	2745	384	1184
BURLINGTON, VT	1297	1587	1027	1343	92	1086	1588	299	1632	1390	1383	371	2644	587	233	3052	1848	2845	630	1119	2322	2036	3020	3062	2997	1438	419	3130	517	1554
CHARLESTON, SC	760	583	1003	1319	1145	543	783	773	1248	1290	379	685	2184	642	1101	2948	1824	2741	428	850	2218	1310	2483	2934	2973	434	1006	3106	539	1291
CHARLESTON, WV	606	994	601	918	822	395	926	515	1022	952	790	454	2035	217	839	2610	1422	2403	322	512	1880	1344	2393	2620	2571	845	537	2705	346	953
CHARLOTTE, NC	614	730	857	1173	1003	397	713	631	1102	1144	525	543	2107	438	959	2802	1678	2595	289	704	2072	1241	2405	2759	2827	581	802	2960	397	1145
CHEYENNE, WY	1217	2147	1012	881	1799	1240	1502	1755	773	497	1926	1725	1004	1425	2059	1166	305	959	1760	892	436	1046	1179	1176	1234	1941	1468	1368	1659	613
CHICAGO, IL	539	1382	89	409	841	474	935	797	807	474	1161	768	1819	467	1101	2137	913	1930	802	294	1406	1270	2105	2146	2062	1176	510	2196	701	728
CINCINNATI, OH	493	1141	398	714	815	281	820	636	863	736	920	576	1876	292	960	2398	1219	2191	530	350	1667	1231	2234	2407	2368	935	484	2501	517	785
CLEVELAND, OH	742	1250	443	760	588	531	1070	466	1073	806	1045	437	2085	136	751	2469	1264	2262	471	560	1738	1481	2437	2478	2413	1101	303	2547	370	995
DALLAS, TX	466	1367	1010	999	1772	681	525	1589	209	669	1146	1501	1077	1246	1917	2140	1077	1933	1309	635	1410	271	1375	1827	2208	1161	1441	2342	1362	367
DENVER, CO	1116	2069	1055	924	1843	1162	1409	1799	681	541	1847	1744	904	1460	2102	1261	404	1054	1688	855	531	946	1092	1271	1329	1862	1512	1463	1686	521
DES MOINES, IA	720	1632	378	246	1165	725	1117	1121	546	136	1411	1091	1558	791	1424	1798	629	1591	1126	436	1067	1009	1766	1807	1822	1426	834	1956	1025	390
DETROIT, MI	752	1401	380	697	564	541	1079	622	1062	743	1180	592	2074	292	838	2405	1201	2198	627	549	1675	1490	2373	2415	2350	1194	233	2483	526	984
EL PASO, TX	1112	1959	1617	1530	2363	1328	1118	2235	737	1236	1738	2147	432	1893	2563	1767	1105	1315	1955	1242	864	556	730	1181	1944	1753	2032	2087	2008	898
HOUSTON, TX	586	1201	1193	1240	1892	801	360	1660	449	910	980	1572	1188	1366	1988	2381	1318	2072	1330	863	1650	200	1487	1938	2449	995	1561	2583	1433	608
INDIANAPOLIS, IN	464	1196	279	596	872	287	826	715	752	618	975	655	1764	370	1038	2280	1101	2073	641	239	1549	1186	2122	2290	2249	990	541	2383	596	674
JACKSON, MS	211	915	835	1151	1514	423	185	1223	612	935	694	1135	1482	988	1550	2544	1458	2337	914	505	1813	644	1780	2232	2612	709	1183	2746	996	771
KANSAS CITY, MO	536	1466	573	441	1359	559	932	1202	348	188	1245	1141	1360	857	1525	1805	710	1598	1085	252	1074	812	1695	1814	1872	1259	1028	2007	1083	192
LAS VEGAS, NV	1611	2733	1808	1677	2596	1826	1854	2552	1124	1294	2512	2500	285	2215	2855	1188	1035	442	2444	1610	417	1272	337	575	1256	2526	2265	1390	2441	1276
LITTLE ROCK, AR	140	1190	747	814	1446	355	455	1262	355	570	969	1175	1367	920	1590	2237	1093	2030	983	416	1507	600	1703	2012	2305	984	1115	2439	1036	464
LOS ANGELES, CA	1839	2759	2082	1951	2869	2054	1917	2820	1352	1567	2538	2760	369	2476	3144	971	1309	519	2682	1856	691	1356	124	385	1148	2553	2538	1291	2702	1513
LOUISVILLE, KY	386	1084	394	711	920	175	714	739	774	704	863	678	1786	394	1062	2362	1215	2155	572	264	1631	1125	2144	2372	2364	878	589	2497	596	705
MEMPHIS, TN		1051	624	940	1306	215	396	1123	487	724	830	1035	1500	780	1451	2382	1247	2175	843	294	1652	739	1841	2144	2440	845	975	2574	896	597
MIAMI, FL	1051		1478	1794	1671	907	874	1299	1609	1654	232	1211	2390	1167	1627	3312	2176	3105	954	1214	2581	1401	2688	3140	3370	274	1532	3504	1065	1655
MILWAUKEE, WI	624	1478		337	939	569	1020	894	880	514	1257	865	1892	564	1198	2063	842	1970	899	367	1446	1343	2145	2186	1991	1272	607	2124	799	769
MINNEAPOLIS, MN	940	1794	337		1255	886	1337	1211	793	383	1573	1181	1805	881	1515	1727	606	1839	1216	621	1315	1257	2014	2055	1654	1588	924	1788	1115	637
MONTRÉAL, QC	1306	1671	939	1255		1094	1632	383	1625	1300	1466	454	2637	607	282	2963	1758	2756	714	1112	2232	2043	2931	2972	2907	1522	330	3041	600	1547
NASHVILLE, TN	215	907	569	886	1094		539	906	703	747	686	818	1715	569	1234	2405	1269	2198	626	307	1675	954	2056	2360	2463	701	764	2597	679	748
NEW ORLEANS, LA	396	874	1020	1337	1632	539		1332	731	1121	653	1245	1548	1108	1660	2663	1643	2431	1002	690	1932	560	1846	2298	2731	668	1302	2865	1106	890
NEW YORK, NY	1123	1299	894	1211	383	906	1332		1469	1258	1094	91	2481	367	313	2920	1716	2713	342	956	2189	1861	2839	2929	2864	1150	507	2998	228	1391
OKLAHOMA CITY, OK	487	1609	880	793	1625	703	731	1469		463	1388	1408	1012	1124	1792	1934	871	1727	1331	505	1204	466	1370	1657	2002	1403	1295	2136	1350	161
OMAHA, NE	724	1654	514	383	1300	747	1121	1258	463		1433	1228	1440	928	1561	1662	525	1455	1263	440	932	927	1630	1672	1719	1448	971	1853	1162	307
ORLANDO, FL	830	232	1257	1573	1466	686	653	1094	1388	1433		1006	2169	963	1422	3091	1955	2884	750	993	2360	1180	2467	2918	3149	82	1327	3283	860	1434
PHILADELPHIA, PA	1035	1211	865	1181	454	818	1245	91	1408	1228	1006		2420	306	419	2890	1686	2683	254	895	2160	1774	2779	2900	2835	1062	522	2968	140	1330
PHOENIX, AZ	1500	2390	1892	1805	2637	1715	1548	2481	1012	1440	2169	2420		2136	2804	1335	1308	883	2343	1517	651	987	358	750	1513	2184	2307	1655	2362	1173
PITTSBURGH, PA	780	1167	564	881	607	569	1108	367	1124	928	963	306	2136		690	2590	1386	2383	341	611	1859	1519	2494	2599	2534	1019	321	2668	240	1046
PORTLAND, ME	1451	1627	1198	1515	282	1234	1660	313	1792	1561	1422	419	2804	690		3223	2019	3016	670	1279	2493	2189	3162	3233	3168	1478	668	3301	556	1714
PORTLAND, OR	2382	3312	2063	1727	2963	2405	2663	2920	1934	1662	3091	2890	1335	2590	3223		1268	578	2925	2057	771	2322	1093	638	170	3106	2633	313	2824	1775
RAPID CITY, SD	1247	2176	842	606	1758	1269	1643	1716	871	525	1955	1686	1308	1386	2019	1268		1151	1720	963	628	1335	1372	1368	1195	1970	1429	1328	1620	712
RENO, NV	2175	3105	1970	1839	2756	2198	2431	2713	1727	1455	2884	2683	883	2383	3016	578	1151		2718	1850	524	1870	642	217	755	2899	2426	898	2617	1568
RICHMOND, VA	843	954	899	1216	714	626	1002	342	1331	1263	750	254	2343	341	670	2925	1720	2718		834	2194	1530	2684	2934	2869	805	660	3003	108	1274
ST. LOUIS, MO	294	1214	367	621	1112	307	690	956	505	440	993	895	1517	611	1279	2057	963	1850	834		1326	968	1875	2066	2125	1008	782	2259	837	441
SALT LAKE CITY, UT	1652	2581	1446	1315	2232	1675	1932	2189	1204	932	2360	2160	651	1859	2493	771	628	524	2194	1326		1419	754	740	839	2375	1902	973	2094	1044
SAN ANTONIO, TX	739	1401	1343	1257	2043	954	560	1861	466	927	1180	1774	987	1519	2189	2322	1335	1870	1530	968	1419		1285	1737	2275	1195	1714	2410	1635	624
SAN DIEGO, CA	1841	2688	2145	2014	2931	2056	1846	2839	1370	1630	2467	2779	358	2494	3162	1093	1372	642	2684	1875	754	1285		508	1271	2481	2601	1414	2720	1531
SAN FRANCISCO, CA	2144	3140	2186	2055	2972	2360	2298	2929	1657	1672	2918	2900	750	2599	3233	638	1368	217	2934	2066	740	1737	508		816	2933	2643	958	2834	1784
SEATTLE, WA	2440	3370	1991	1654	2907	2463	2731	2864	2002	1719	3149	2835	1513	2534	3168	170	1195	755	2869	2125	839	2275	1271	816		3164	2577	140	2769	1843
TAMPA, FL	845	274	1272	1588	1522	701	668	1150	1403	1448	82	1062	2184	1019	1478	3106	1970	2899	805	1008	2375	1195	2481	2933	3164		1383	3297	916	1448
TORONTO, ON	975	1532	607	924	330	764	1302	507	1295	971	1327	522	2307	321	668	2633	1429	2426	660	782	1902	1714	2601	2643	2577	1383		2711	563	1217
VANCOUVER, BC	2574	3504	2124	1788	3041	2597	2865	2998	2136	1853	3283	2968	1655	2668	3301	313	1328	898	3003	2259	973	2410	1414	958	140	3297	2711		2902	1977
WASHINGTON, DC	896	1065	799	1115	600	679	1106	228	1350	1162	860	140	2362	240	556	2824	1620	2617	108	837	2094	1635	2720	2834	2769	916	563	2902		1272
WICHITA, KS	597	1655	769	637	1547	748	890	1391	161	307	1434	1330	1173	1046	1714	1775	712	1568	1274	441	1044	624	1531	1784	1843	1448	1217	1977	1272	